Lecture Notes in Computer Science 16329

Founding Editors

Gerhard Goos
Juris Hartmanis

Editorial Board Members

Elisa Bertino, *Purdue University, West Lafayette, IN, USA*
Wen Gao, *Peking University, Beijing, China*
Bernhard Steffen, *TU Dortmund University, Dortmund, Germany*
Moti Yung, *Columbia University, New York, NY, USA*

Pari Delir Haghighi · Gabriele Kotsis ·
Toshiyuki Amagasa · Akiyo Nadamoto ·
Ismail Khalil

Editors

Advances in Mobile Computing and Multimedia Intelligence

23rd International Conference, MoMM 2025
Matsue, Japan, December 8–10, 2025
Proceedings

 Springer

Editors
Pari Delir Haghighi
Monash University
Clayton, VIC, Australia

Gabriele Kotsis
Johannes Kepler University Linz
Linz, Austria

Toshiyuki Amagasa
University of Tsukuba
Tsukuba, Japan

Akiyo Nadamoto
Konan University
Kobe, Japan

Ismail Khalil
Johannes Kepler University Linz
Linz, Austria

ISSN 0302-9743   ISSN 1611-3349 (electronic)
Lecture Notes in Computer Science
ISBN 978-3-032-11767-0   ISBN 978-3-032-11768-7 (eBook)
https://doi.org/10.1007/978-3-032-11768-7

This Springer imprint is published by the registered company Springer Nature Switzerland AG
The registered company address is: Gewerbestrasse 11, 6330 Cham, Switzerland

If disposing of this product, please recycle the paper.

Preface

It is our great pleasure to introduce the proceedings of the 23rd International Conference on Advances in Mobile Computing & Multimedia Intelligence (MoMM2025), held jointly with the 27th International Conference on Information Integration and Web Intelligence (iiWAS) in Matsue, Japan, from 8 to 10 December 2025.

This year's conference highlighted research across core areas in wearable computing, mobile security, virtual and augmented reality, mobile multimedia, and AI-driven applications, presenting innovative solutions to real-world challenges in authentication and access control, immersive user experiences, activity and physiological sensing, multimedia content analysis, and context-aware applied computing.

MoMM 2025 received a total of 31 paper submissions from ten different countries, covering a broad spectrum of research in mobile computing and multimedia intelligence. Each paper was thoroughly reviewed by three experts for originality, contribution, and relevance; reviews were single blind. Of these submissions, ten full papers were accepted, with an overall acceptance rate of 32%. In addition, six short papers were selected to present early-stage work, novel concepts, and preliminary results, offering a venue for innovative projects across diverse disciplines and encouraging discussion and future collaboration.

The proceedings are organized into five topics, reflecting current advances in mobile computing, multimedia intelligence, and human-centred applications:

- Mobile Multimedia Processing and Interaction: This topic covers intelligent multimedia processing and adaptive interfaces, emphasising motion prediction, context-aware recommendations, and long-video analysis to support richer human–computer interaction.
- Wearable and Sensor-Based Systems for Human Performance: Contributions explore the use of wearable sensors to enhance human performance and learning, including applications in sports, music, and activity recognition. Collectively, these studies demonstrate how wearable sensors can extend human ability, learning, and interaction.
- Authentication and Security in Mobile Systems: This topic introduces mobile-assisted PC authentication using smartphones and smartwatches, examines methods to analyse and mitigate electromagnetic signal injection attacks on image sensors, and presents silent speech recognition through hearables. Together, these contributions highlight both usability gains and security challenges.
- Virtual and Augmented Reality for Cognitive and Task Support: Papers examine immersive technologies for supporting cognitive tasks, stress reduction, and user focus. Together, these works illustrate the expanding role of VR and AR in enhancing concentration, relaxation, and everyday usability.
- Participatory and Applied Computing in Real-World Contexts: This topic highlights inclusive, domain-focused applications of computing, showcasing participatory

design and human-in-the-loop approaches in diverse real-world domains, including agriculture, insurance, and music recommendation.

We wish to express our profound gratitude to our keynote speakers, Ichiro Ide from Nagoya University, Japan, and Takako Hashimoto from Chiba University of Commerce and University of Tokyo, Japan. Their presentations were highly engaging and insightful, offering valuable perspectives that inspired and informed our participants, and were among the highlights of the event.

The success of the conference is built upon the consistent support and devoted efforts of its participants. We extend our sincere thanks to the dedicated authors, esteemed program committee members, expert session chairs, organizing and steering committee members, and student volunteers, whose continuous support and commitment were instrumental in making this event a success.

We hope these proceedings are both informative and inspiring, and we look forward to the continued growth of the MoMM conference as a premier international forum for exchanging innovative research in mobile computing and multimedia.

December 2025

Pari Delir Haghighi
Gabriele Kotsis
Toshiyuki Amagasa
Akiyo Nadamoto
Ismail Khalil

Organization

Steering Committee

Gabriele Kotsis	Johannes Kepler University Linz, Austria
Ismail Khalil	Johannes Kepler University Linz, Austria
Akiyo Nadamoto	Konan University, Japan
Toshiyuki Amagasa	University of Tsukuba, Japan
Syopiansyah Jaya Putra	Institut Teknologi Indonesia, Indonesia

Publicity Chairs

Yusuke Gotoh	Okayama University, Japan
Naoko Kosugi	Senshu University, Japan

Organization Chairs

Akimitsu Kanzaki	Shimane University, Japan
Takahiro Komamizu	Nagoya University, Japan
Yoshiyuki Shoji	Shizuoka University, Japan

Program Committee Chair

Pari Delir Haghighi	Monash University, Australia

Program Committee Members

Andreas Schrader	University of Lübeck, Germany
Antonio Liotta	Free University of Bozen-Bolzano, Italy
Ayumi Ohnishi	Kobe University, Japan
Benjamine Tag	University of New South Wales, Australia
Carlos Calafate	Universitat Politècnica de València, Spain
Chang Wu Yu	Chung Hua University, Taiwan
Clemens Holzmann	University of Applied Sciences Upper Austria, Austria

Dana Kusumo	Telkom University, Indonesia
Dmytro Chumachenko	National Aerospace University, Ukraine
Eugene Yujun Fu	Education University of Hong Kong, China
Hong Va Leon	Hong Kong Polytechnic University, China
Ivan Zyrianoff	University of Bologna, Italy
Jabed Chowdhury	La Trobe University, Australia
Joe Liu	Monash University, Australia
Kadek Satriadi	Monash University, Australia
Luca Davoli	University of Parma, Italy
Panagiotis Fouliras	University of Macedonia, Greece
Paolo Bellavista	University of Bologna, Italy
Sami Habib	Kuwait University, Kuwait
Sara Comai	Politecnico di Milano, Italy
Solomiia Fedushko	Lviv Polytechnic National University, Ukraine
Sultan Alamri	Saudi Electronic University, Saudi Arabia
Svetlana Boudko	Norsk Regnesentral, Norway
Tetiana Klynina	University of Texas at Austin, USA
Tommi Mikkonen	University of Helsinki, Finland
Tsutomu Terada	Kobe University, Japan
Tzung-Pei Hong	National University of Kaohsiung, Taiwan
Tzung-Shi Chen	National University of Tainan, Taiwan
Vitaliy Yakovyna	University of Warmia and Mazury in Olsztyn, Poland
Wolfgang Schreiner	Johannes Kepler University Linz, Austria
You-Chiun Wang	National Sun Yat-sen University, Taiwan
Yuriy Syerov	Lviv Polytechnic National University, Ukraine
Yusuke Gotoh	Okayama University, Japan

Organizers

Web Applications Society
@iWAS
www.iiwas.org

JMU
Institute for
Telecooperation

KONAN
Digital Twin

DBSJ
THE DATABASE SOCIETY
OF JAPAN

Abstract of Keynote Talks

Quantifying Visual Impressions of Words Based on Real-World Data Analysis

Ichiro Ide

Nagoya University, Japan

Abstract. Attempts to quantify impressions of linguistic information have been made in both Psycholinguistics and Computer Science fields. In Psycholinguistics, various metrics have been proposed to quantify word impressions, and corresponding dictionaries were created based on large-scale subjective evaluations. In contrast, recently, in Computer Science, attempts have been made to estimate Psycholinguistic metrics using real-world data without conducting large-scale subjective evaluations. This talk will introduce our work specifically aimed at quantifying visual impressions of words from real-world data ranging from Web images to Large Language Model (LLM) and Large Vision-Language Model (LVLM).

The Future Opened by Survival Informatics: Data Connecting Human and Social Well-Being

Takako Hashimoto

Chiba University of Commerce and University of Tokyo, Japan

Abstract. Survival Informatics is an emerging interdisciplinary approach, currently being discussed within the Science Council of Japan, that explores how data-driven methods can contribute to sustaining human life and enhancing social well-being in an increasingly complex world. By combining perspectives from information science, artificial intelligence, and the social sciences, Survival Informatics aims to establish reliable ways of understanding and addressing global challenges such as disasters, health crises, climate change, and social inequalities. This talk highlights the role of data as a bridge that connects individuals, communities, and institutions, enabling evidence-based decision-making and fostering resilience in both physical and cyber spaces. Through case studies and recent research, we demonstrate how Survival Informatics not only advances scientific insight but also provides practical solutions that enhance human and societal well-being.

Contents

Mobile and Wearable Systems

Security and Trust in Mobile Environments

Immersive and Context-Aware Computing

Mobile and Wearable Systems

Diffusion-TS: A Hybrid Model for Human Skeleton Prediction

Yuren Zhang⬤, Atsuya Watanabe, Zhongnan Pu⬤, and Lei Jing$^{(\boxtimes)}$⬤

The Graduate School of Computer Science and Engineering, University of Aizu,
Aizuwakamatsu, Japan
`leijing@u-aizu.ac.jp`

Abstract. Human skeleton data plays a crucial role in healthcare, rehabilitation, and human-computer interaction. However, traditional motion capture methods are often expensive and highly dependent on controlled environments. To address these limitations, we propose a novel framework based on Diffusion and Transformer models that reconstructs full-body skeleton sequences from foot pressure data collected via smart insoles.

Keywords: Human motion analysis · Skeleton Reconstruction · Smart Insoles · Deep Learning · Diffusion Model · Transformer

1 Introduction

Human skeleton data is crucial for healthcare, rehabilitation, and human-computer interaction, but traditional motion capture systems are expensive and constrained by environmental requirements. Smart insoles provide a low-cost, non-intrusive alternative by indirectly capturing human motion structure through plantar pressure data. Early methods were limited by model capacity, but recent deep learning approaches—such as CNNs, RNNs, and Transformers—have been applied to map insole data to skeletal poses. Transformers, in particular, excel at modeling temporal dependencies and have shown strong performance in motion generation tasks [6].

In recent years, generative models like VAEs and GANs have been used for motion prediction, but each has its limitations. Diffusion models stand out due to their stability and high-quality outputs. Given the sequential nature of motion data, we also introduce multi-step prediction and temporal reset strategies to address the issue of error accumulation over time, enabling more stable long-term prediction without requiring ground-truth supervision.

Therefore, we propose Diffusion-TS, a hybrid model that combines the generative power of diffusion models with the temporal modeling capability of Transformers. We further design a joint loss function based on joint position and

L. Jing—This work was supported by NEDO Intensive Support for Young Promising Researchers Number 21502121-0, Collaborative Research with Toyota Motor Corporation, and JKA and its promotion funds from KEIRIN RACE.

P. Delir Haghighi et al. (Eds.): MoMM 2025, LNCS 16329, pp. 3–9, 2026.
https://doi.org/10.1007/978-3-032-11768-7_1

angular consistency to achieve more accurate and stable skeleton reconstruction.

2   Diffusion-TS Model

The overall Model architecture is shown in the Fig 1 below. The architecture of the model follows a standard Diffusion framework [2,4], consisting of a forward diffusion process and a reverse denoising process. The Transformer model serves as a core module within this Diffusion framework, responsible for performing the denoising operation.

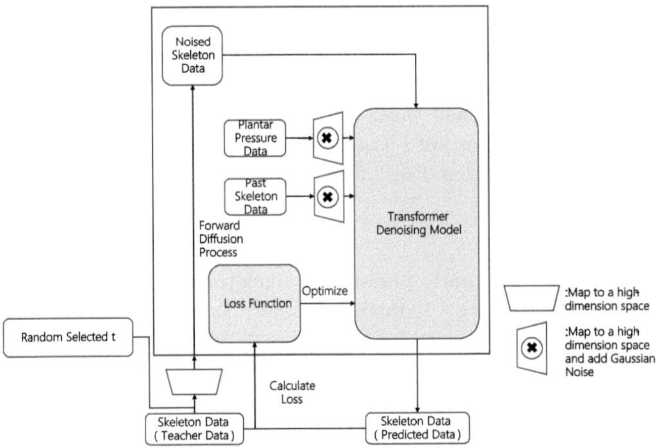

Fig. 1. Diffusion Structure

2.1   Diffusion Structure

The forward diffusion process is same as traditional diffusion models, where noise is gradually added to the input data until it is completely corrupted. This process is used to train the subsequent denoising model.

Forward Diffusion Process. The forward process gradually adds Gaussian noise to skeleton data $x \in \mathbb{R}^{n \times \text{skeleton\_keypoint}}$ over T steps via:

$$\mathbf{x}_t = \sqrt{1 - \beta_t}\,\mathbf{x}_{t-1} + \sqrt{\beta_t} \cdot \boldsymbol{\epsilon}, \quad \boldsymbol{\epsilon} \sim \mathcal{N}(0, \mathbf{I}), \quad t \in [1, T] \tag{1}$$

β_t is a set of predefined hyperparameters used to adjust the ratio between real data and noise. However, during the actual execution, for efficiency, the noise can be sampled directly at step t from the original data x_0 by:

$$x_t = \sqrt{\bar{\alpha}_t}x_0 + \sqrt{1 - \bar{\alpha}_t}\epsilon, \quad \epsilon \sim \mathcal{N}(0, \mathbf{I}), \quad \bar{\alpha}_t = \prod_{s=1}^{t}(1 - \beta_s). \tag{2}$$

Reverse Denoising Process. Instead of predicting noise, our Transformer-based denoising network directly predicts clean skeleton data $\hat{x}_{t-1}$ given noisy input x_t, step t, foot pressure, and past skeleton data:

$$\hat{x}_{t-1} = f_\theta(x_t, t) + \sigma_t \epsilon, \quad \epsilon \sim \mathcal{N}(0, I). \tag{3}$$

Predicting the original data enhances interpretability, facilitates anatomical constraints, and leverages the relatively low dimensionality of skeleton data.

2.2 Transformer Module

In traditional Diffusion models, UNet is commonly used for denoising due to its skip connections, which effectively combine semantic and spatial features—ideal for image tasks. However, UNet performs poorly on sequential data. To address this, we replace UNet with a Transformer, leveraging its ability to model temporal dependencies. Each Transformer block follows the encoder-decoder structure shown in Fig. 2 [5].

- Encoder: The encoder needs to receive three types of input data: foot pressure, noise-level time embedding, and skeleton data from the past seq_length time steps. These three types of data are concatenated along the second dimension, resulting in an input tensor of the following shape:

$$\mathbb{R}^{n \times (2 + seq\_length) \times input\_dim}$$

- Decoder: The decoder input and the output at non-final time steps have the same shape(In fact, there is only one Transformer that continuously processes inputs and outputs), which is:

$$\mathbb{R}^{n \times 1 \times input\_dim}$$

The decoder input is the noisy skeleton data from the previous time step, and the output is the denoised data for the current time step. But in the final time step Transformer, for the purpose of multi-step skeleton prediction (which will be detailed in Sect. 2.4), the decoder output is passed through the output layer and converted into the following format:

$$\mathbb{R}^{n \times window\_size \times input\_dim}$$

window_size refers to the number of future time steps of skeleton poses predicted, which helps alleviate error accumulation and makes the predicted motion more fluent.

2.3 Loss Function

The total loss function combines a weighted reconstruction loss and an angular constraint loss to enforce anatomical plausibility.

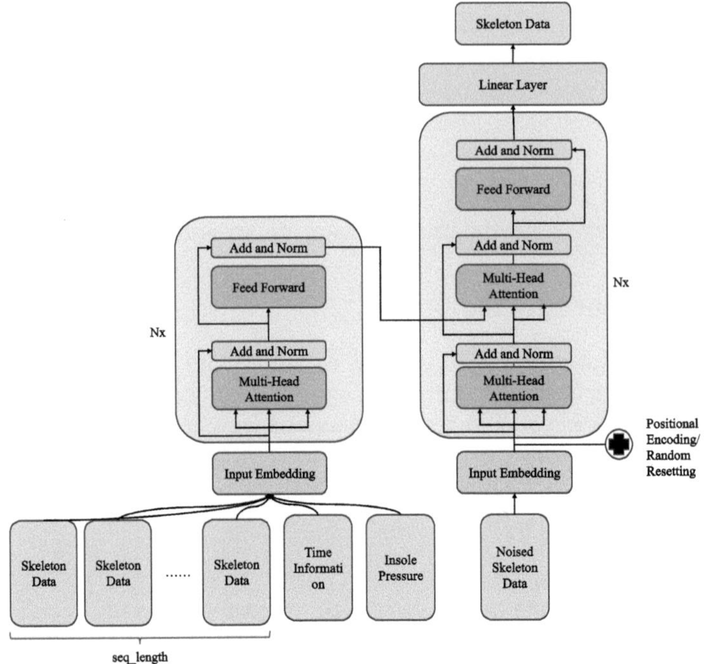

Fig. 2. Transformer Model Structure

Weighted Reconstruction Loss

$$\mathcal{L}_{\text{recon}} = \frac{1}{BWJ} \sum_{b,t,j} w_j \|\hat{p}_{b,t,j} - p_{b,t,j}\|^2, \tag{4}$$

where B, W, and J are batch size, window size, and keypoints count, respectively. Weights w_j emphasize key regions (e.g., spine and legs) over arms. The $\hat{p}_{b,t,j}$ represents the predicted 3D coordinates and the $p_{b,t,j}$ refers to the true 3D coordinates.

Angle Constraint Loss. To avoid unrealistic joint distortion, the cosine difference between predicted and true bone angles is penalized:

$$\mathcal{L}_{\text{angle}} = \frac{1}{|\mathcal{P}|} \sum_{((a,b),(c,d)) \in \mathcal{P}} \frac{1}{BW} \sum_{b=1}^{B} \sum_{w=1}^{W} \left(\cos \theta^{\text{pred}}_{(a,b),(c,d)}(b,w) - \cos \theta^{\text{true}}_{(a,b),(c,d)}(b,w) \right)^2 \tag{5}$$

$\mathcal{P}$ is a set containing multiple pairs of bones, and all bone pairs that require angle error calculation are included in it. Similar to the reconstruction loss, the calculation of joint angle constraints also excludes body parts such as the arms and shoulders.

Total Loss. Due to the scale difference between reconstruction loss and angle constraint loss, balancing their influence is necessary. Common methods include manual weighting, loss normalization, and automatic weight learning, each with drawbacks such as poor generalization, slower convergence, or increased complexity. Since these methods have limited impact on overall performance, this paper uses simple manual weighting, setting the weights to maintain a 10:1 ratio—0.1 for reconstruction loss (w_1) and 1 for angle constraint loss (w_2). The total loss is defined in Eq. 6.

$$\mathcal{L}_{total} = w_1 \mathcal{L}_{\text{recon}} + w_2 \mathcal{L}_{\text{angle}} \tag{6}$$

2.4 Error Accumulation Mitigation

To address error drift in sequential prediction, three techniques are adopted: Gaussian Noise Injection, Multi-step Skeleton Prediction and Random Restting of Temporal Information.

Adding Gaussian Noise. Since foot pressure data and skeleton keypoints are continuous rather than discrete, directly mapping inputs to ground truth may limit the model to training values, leading to errors on unseen inputs. To enhance robustness and reduce error accumulation, we follow the VAE [3] approach by adding Gaussian noise (mean 0, variance 0.1) to both encoder and decoder inputs of the Transformer, transforming each input from a fixed point into a neighborhood distribution.

Multi-step Skeleton Prediction. Building on the Action-Chunking method [1,7], the model predicts skeleton states over a multi-step horizon and aggregates them via weighted averaging. This design mitigates error accumulation by fusing multiple future references to correct trajectory drift. To balance accuracy and stability, higher weight is given to predictions aligned with current insole pressure, while others are down-weighted according to the weighting equation:

$$w_i = \frac{e^{-mi}}{\sum_{i=0}^{ws-1} e^{-mi}} \tag{7}$$

Here, m represents the exponential decay factor. A larger value of m leads to a faster attenuation of the weights assigned to past time steps. In the proposed model, m is set to 1. When m = 1, the weighting scheme ensures that the majority of information is derived from the current predicted skeleton data, while only a small portion incorporates references to past predictions. And ws refers to the window_size, which is mentioned above.

Random Resetting of Temporal Information. Unlike methods that only slow error accumulation, Random Resetting of Temporal Information effectively reduces the accumulated error itself. The idea is simple: since errors build up over time, the model occasionally discards past skeleton states and predicts solely from pressure data. During training, past skeleton inputs are masked with a probability of 0.05, meaning that in each step there is a 5% chance the model relies only on pressure. This setting reflects the observation that errors become significant after 20 steps, while still allowing sufficient use of temporal information. As a result, the model periodically resets its context, improving long-term stability.

2.5   Evaluation Criteria

To evaluate the predicted skeleton quality, besides visual inspection, this paper uses two quantitative metrics: MSED and FID. MSED (Mean Squared Euclidean Distance) measures the average squared distance between predicted keypoints and ground truth, defined as:

$$\mathrm{MSED} = \frac{1}{N} \sum_{i=1}^{N} \|\mathbf{p}_i - \hat{\mathbf{p}}_i\|^2 \tag{8}$$

Here, N is the number of keypoints, $\mathbf{p}_i$ and $\hat{\mathbf{p}}_i$ are the ground truth and predicted keypoint positions respectively, and $\|\cdot\|$ is the Euclidean norm. A larger MSED indicates greater deviation, while a smaller value means closer alignment to the ground truth, providing a quantitative accuracy measure.

FID (Fréchet Inception Distance) evaluates the similarity between two data distributions, commonly used to assess generative model outputs. Its formula is:

Using MSED and FID together provides a quantitative, comprehensive assessment of predicted skeleton quality, enabling more objective model comparison (Table 1).

Table 1. Result

Seq_Length	Window_Size	MSED(cm)	FID
1	1	2.0808	1.7680
1	3	1.6993	1.5665
1	5	1.8228	1.4984
3	1	1.8909	1.7163
3	2	1.6860	1.4744
3	3	1.5791	1.3574
3	4	1.6874	1.6972
3	5	1.7490	1.6032
VAE Model		7.0724	3.0189
GAN Model		6.4029	2.8832
(3,3) Diffusion(UNet Backbone) Model		2.8348	2.0102
(3,3) Without Randomly Resetting of Temporal Information		3.6251	2.3227

As shown in the table, the best performance was achieved when seq_length was set to 3, with minimal improvement observed for other values. Similarly, the optimal window_size was found to be 3, balancing prediction accuracy and stability, as reflected by the lowest FID and favorable MSED results.

To validate the effectiveness of the proposed Diffusion-Transformer model, baseline comparisons were conducted with GAN and VAE models. The Diffusion-Transformer significantly outperformed both, achieving an MSED of 1.5791 compared to 7.0724 (GAN) and 6.4029 (VAE).

Further ablation studies confirmed the importance of the Transformer module and the Random Resetting mechanism. Removing either led to a marked drop in performance, underscoring their critical roles in maintaining prediction accuracy.

3 Conclusion

In summary, this paper proposes a Diffusion-Transformer model that predicts skeleton structures from plantar pressure data. The model leverages reconstruction and angle constraint losses to ensure anatomically consistent predictions. To address error accumulation in long-term prediction, we introduce Gaussian noise and random temporal resets, enabling more realistic motion generation. Future work will extend the framework to multi-modal inputs and broader applications, incorporating visual and sensor data to predict skeleton states, motion patterns, and behavior-related targets.

References

1. Fu, Z., Zhao, T.Z., Finn, C.: Mobile aloha: learning bimanual mobile manipulation with low-cost whole-body teleoperation. arXiv preprint arXiv:2401.02117 (2024)
2. Ho, J., Jain, A., Abbeel, P.: Denoising diffusion probabilistic models. Adv. Neural. Inf. Process. Syst. **33**, 6840–6851 (2020)
3. Kingma, D.P., Welling, M.: Auto-encoding variational bayes. arXiv preprint arXiv:1312.6114 (2013)
4. Sohl-Dickstein, J., Weiss, E., Maheswaranathan, N., Ganguli, S.: Deep unsupervised learning using nonequilibrium thermodynamics. In: International Conference on Machine Learning, pp. 2256–2265. PMLR (2015)
5. Vaswani, A., et al.: Attention is all you need. In: Advances in Neural Information Processing Systems, vol. 30 (2017)
6. Watanabe, A., Aisuwarya, R., Jing, L.: P2P-Insole: human pose estimation using foot pressure distribution and motion sensors. arXiv preprint arXiv:2505.00755 (2025)
7. Zhao, T.Z., Kumar, V., Levine, S., Finn, C.: Learning fine-grained bimanual manipulation with low-cost hardware. arXiv preprint arXiv:2304.13705 (2023)

LightVideoRAG: Low-Resource Long Video Question-Answering via Adaptive Sampling and Context-Aware Retrieval

Zifeng Shi and Mizuho Iwaihara[✉]

Graduate School of Information, Production and Systems, Waseda University, 2-7 Hibikino, Wakamatsu-ku, Kitakyushu-shi, Fukuoka, Japan
shizifeng@suou.waseda.jp, iwaihara@waseda.jp

Abstract. Retrieving relevant information from long videos remains a significant challenge due to high computational costs, semantic redundancy, and the need for temporal reasoning. We propose LightVideoRAG, a lightweight retrieval framework tailored for long-video question answering. LightVideoRAG combines adaptive frame sampling, which filters out redundant frames while preserving key semantic content, with context-aware retrieval modules that integrate both local neighborhood signals and global temporal information. This design enables efficient temporal grounding without processing entire video sequences. Unlike existing methods that rely on dense captioning or proprietary APIs, our system operates entirely on a locally deployed Vision-Language Model (VLM), ensuring strong data privacy and low latency. Evaluations on the LongVideoBench and Video-MME benchmarks show that LightVideoRAG achieves substantial gains in QA accuracy while requiring only a fraction of the computational resources, outperforming the base model and approaching the performance of larger size models. This demonstrates its potential as a scalable and accessible solution for efficient video understanding in resource-constrained environments. Our code is available at https://github.com/linshys/lightvideoRAG.

Keywords: Long-video understanding · Retrieval-Augmented Generation · Adaptive Sampling · Video Question Answering

1 Introduction

1.1 Background

Retrieval-Augmented Generation (RAG) has emerged as a powerful framework to enhance the factual accuracy and reasoning ability of Large Language Models (LLMs) by retrieving relevant external knowledge [9]. While early RAG methods focused on text-based retrieval from large-scale corpora using methods like BM25 or Dense Passage Retrieval (DPR) [8,16], recent advances in Vision-Language Models (VLMs), such as CLIP, BLIP, and LLaVA [10,11,14], have enabled multimodal RAG systems that incorporate both visual and textual signals.

© The Author(s), under exclusive license to Springer Nature Switzerland AG 2026
P. Delir Haghighi et al. (Eds.): MoMM 2025, LNCS 16329, pp. 10–24, 2026.
https://doi.org/10.1007/978-3-032-11768-7_2

However, extending RAG to video data introduces new challenges due to the temporal dimension, visual redundancy, and multimodal complexity. Long-video understanding requires not only spatial comprehension but also long-range temporal reasoning. Benchmarks such as LongVideoBench [18] and Video-MME [4] highlight the importance of fine-grained reasoning across temporally distant segments.

Meanwhile, the growing demand for data privacy and accessibility in AI systems has raised the importance of open-source and local deployment [3]. Moreover, as model sizes grow, the computational barrier excludes small labs and individual users from accessing advanced capabilities [7]. This calls for lightweight, efficient, and fully self-contained video RAG solutions.

1.2 Limitations of Existing Video RAG Systems

Despite recent progress, existing video RAG systems suffer from key limitations:

- **Redundant Visual Tokens and Resource Cost:** Many Video RAG methods extract frames at fixed intervals [1,22], resulting in redundant visual tokens that increase memory usage and computational load while contributing minimal semantic value. Additionally, interprocessing steps on frames, such as caption-based pipelines [13], further increase latency and resource overhead.
- **Distortion of Caption-based Retrieval:** Caption-based retrieval methods use VLMs to generate sentences per fixed-length clip [2,23]. This abstraction strips away frame-level visual fidelity, omitting fine-grained spatial details and subtle visual cues essential for accurate interpretation. Since clips are segmented at uniform time intervals rather than semantic boundaries, contextual dependencies across clips are often lost, disrupting the continuity of events and hindering accurate interpretation. Captions are also subject to typical VLM issues such as hallucination, ambiguity, and language bias, further degrading retrieval precision.
- **Proprietary Dependence:** Several methods, such as MM-REACT [21] and VideoRAG [15], rely on closed-source models (e.g., GPT-4o, Gemini) for inference or interprocessing, restricting their usability in resource-constrained or privacy-sensitive environments.

In response to these limitations, we propose **LightVideoRAG**—a lightweight, privacy-preserving retrieval framework for long-video QA. LightVideoRAG combines adaptive frame sampling, frame-level multimodal matching, and global-local context fusion, and is designed for full local execution on a single consumer-grade GPU. Our system provides an efficient and scalable alternative to existing methods, enabling high-quality long-video understanding without reliance on proprietary APIs or cloud infrastructure.

2   LightVideoRAG

LightVideoRAG pipeline includes stages of index construction, retrieval and inference, and answer generation, as shown in Fig. 1.

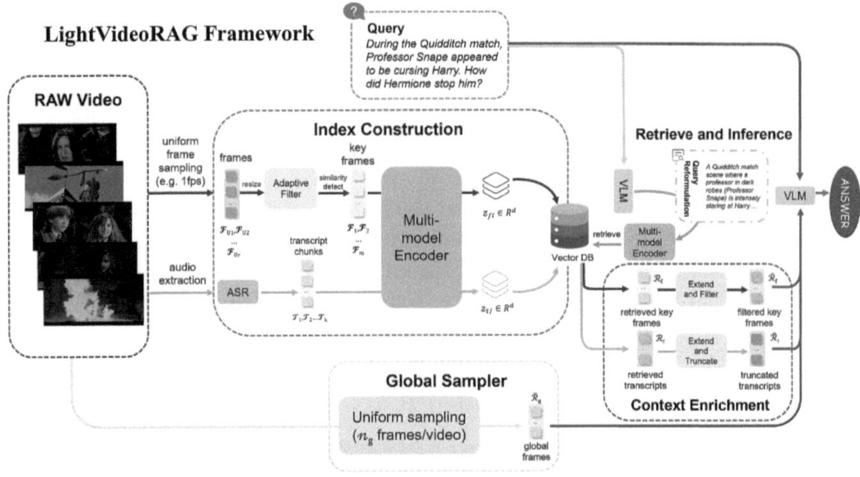

Fig. 1. LightVideoRAG Framework: The pipeline consists of Index Construction, Retrieval and Inference, and Answer Generation.

2.1   Core Design

Adaptive Frame Sampling. Processing all frames in a long video is ineffi-cient due to redundancy. LightVideoRAG applies adaptive sampling to select a compact yet informative set of frames using similarity filtering, reducing visual token load while preserving key semantic content. This improves both efficiency and retrieval quality by focusing on visually distinctive frames.

Frame-Level Matching. LightVideoRAG retrieves directly from raw video frames and text in a shared embedding space, to some extent preserving fine-grained visual cues and mitigating the abstraction and information loss typically introduced by caption-based methods.

Context-Enriched and Globally-Aware Retrieval. LightVideoRAG enhances temporal and semantic context through two complementary modules: context enrichment and global sampling. The context enrichment module uses nearby frames and transcripts within a set window to recover local continuity. The global sampler injects uniformly spaced frames across the video timeline to capture long-range evidence. Together, these components improve temporal coherence and coverage without compromising efficiency.

Fully Local Execution. LightVideoRAG is designed for full local execution on a single consumer-grade GPU, such as the RTX 4090, without relying on external APIs or cloud-based services. This enables secure and low-latency pro-cessing, making the system suitable for small-scale users under privacy-sensitive applications.

2.2   Resource Efficiency Considerations

LightVideoRAG is designed to achieve high accuracy under limited computational resources. Unlike prior systems that rely on exhaustive frame encoding or dense temporal modeling, it adopts a selective and modular strategy.

Adaptive frame sampling reduces visual token load by identifying semantically rich regions, avoiding the need to process hundreds of uniformly sampled frames.

Strategic retrieval passes only the most relevant visual and textual context to the base model, lowering memory usage and inference latency.

These optimizations enable a streamlined pipeline that runs efficiently on a single GPU.

3   Proposed Method

LightVideoRAG extends the retrieval-augmented generation (RAG) paradigm to long-video question answering with a focus on efficiency and adaptability to long and complex video inputs. The method consists of three main stages: preprocessing, index construction, and retrieval with inference.

3.1   Preprocessing

Given a video V with N frames, we uniformly sample it every Δ frames to obtain a reduced set of candidate frames. To eliminate redundancy, we compute pairwise similarity using Structural Similarity Index (SSIM):

$$\text{SSIM}(f_i, f_j) = \frac{(2\mu_i\mu_j + C_1)(2\sigma_{ij} + C_2)}{(\mu_i^2 + \mu_j^2 + C_1)(\sigma_i^2 + \sigma_j^2 + C_2)} \tag{1}$$

Frames with SSIM above a threshold γ are removed, resulting in a compact set of informative keyframes.

We also extract transcripts using automatic speech recognition (ASR), segmenting the audio into time-aligned textual chunks.

3.2   Index Construction

Both keyframes and transcript segments are embedded into a shared semantic space using a multimodal encoder E:

$$\mathbf{z}f_i = E(f_i), \quad \mathbf{z}t_j = E(t_j) \tag{2}$$

The resulting embeddings, along with metadata (e.g., timestamps), are stored in a vector database for efficient retrieval.

3.3   Retrieval and Inference

Query Reformulation with VLM. To maintain cross-modal consistency, the user query q is reformulated by the vision-language model (VLM) into a visual prompt q_v and a transcript prompt q_t:

$$q_v, q_t = \mathrm{VLM}_{\mathrm{rewrite}}(q) \tag{3}$$

The visual query q_v is designed to emphasize spatial features such as objects, actions, and scene context, enabling more accurate keyframe selection. In contrast, the transcript query q_t focuses on linguistic elements like dialogue semantics and speaker intent, improving the retrieval of relevant textual segments. Together, they enable modality-specific retrieval aligned with the original question intent.

Nearest Neighbor Retrieval. Using cosine similarity, we retrieve relevant frames and transcripts:

$$
\begin{aligned}
R_v(q) &= \{k \mid \mathrm{sim}(z_{q_v}, z_k) \geq \tau_v, (z_k, \mathrm{meta}_k) \in \mathcal{I}\}, \\
R_t(q) &= \{k \mid \mathrm{sim}(z_{q_t}, z_k) \geq \tau_t, (z_k, \mathrm{meta}_k) \in \mathcal{I}\}.
\end{aligned}
\tag{4}
$$

τ_v and τ_t are separate similarity thresholds for visual and textual retrieval, allowing modality-specific control over retrieval precision.

Context Expansion and Filtering. Each retrieved frame is expanded with neighboring frames within a temporal window δ, and transcripts are extended within a context window θ. We apply redundancy filtering to retain only distinctive content:

$$\tilde{R}_f = \{f_i \in R_f^+ \mid \forall f_j, \mathrm{sim}(f_i, f_j) < \gamma\}, \quad \tilde{R}_t = \{t_j \in R_t^+ \mid \mathrm{tokens}(t_j) \leq \tau\} \tag{5}$$

Global Sampler. To enhance temporal coverage, we uniformly sample a fixed number of global frames, denoted by n_g, across the entire video timeline. These frames serve to improve robustness by compensating for missed content during query-based retrieval and to increase contextual diversity, particularly in short videos where local evidence is limited. The resulting global set $\tilde{R}_g$ is combined with $\tilde{R}_f$ and $\tilde{R}_t$ to provide a more comprehensive input for inference.

Final Answer Generation. The VLM processes the refined keyframes, global context, and transcripts to generate the final answer:

$$A = \mathrm{VLM}(q, \tilde{R}_f, \tilde{R}_g, \tilde{R}_t) \tag{6}$$

The model fuses visual and textual features, aligns cross-modal semantics, and ensures temporal coherence by accounting for sequential dependencies across frames and transcripts. This enables accurate and contextually grounded responses to complex long-video queries.

4   Demonstration on Visual Question Answering

To demonstrate the effectiveness of LightVideoRAG on visual question answering, we present a demonstrative example over a video query sample from the Video-MME [4] benchmark. This example highlights how our system integrates query-driven retrieval, local frame expansion, and global context sampling to answer a long-form, multimodal question accurately.

```
Video: Mortal Combat (Full Episode) | Animal Fight Night¹
(44:23)
    Query: According to the video, what does the cougar fight with?
    Options: A. A tiger  B. A lion  C. A hippo  D. A grizzly
```

This video presents multiple animal combat narratives divided into thematic chapters, each depicting a different animal matchup. To correctly answer the query, the system must identify and focus on the specific segment—"Grizzly vs Cougar"—among the many unrelated chapters such as "Nile Crocodile vs Hippo" and "Frigate Bird vs Incomer." This illustrates the importance of precise multimodal retrieval in the presence of distracting but thematically similar content.

4.1   Retrieve Based on Query

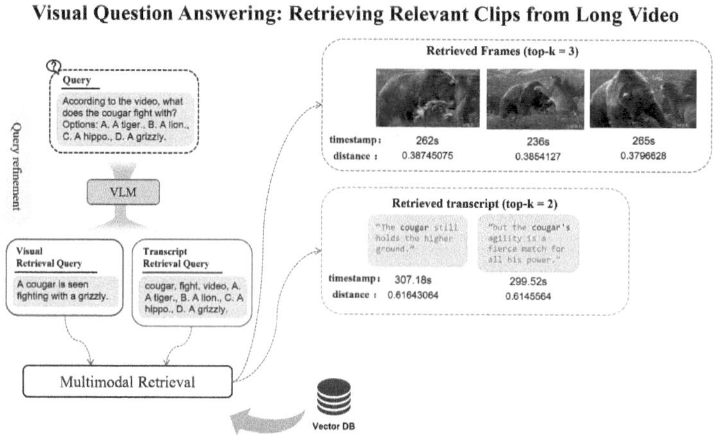

Fig. 2. Multimodal retrieval results based on refined visual and transcript queries.

We skip the index construction stage here and assume the vector database is already built. To initiate the inference process, we begin with query refinement. The original user question is transformed into two distinct retrieval prompts: a

---

¹ https://www.imdb.com/title/tt7371642.

visual query (e.g., "A cougar is seen fighting with a grizzly.") aimed at matching visual content, and a *transcript query* composed of relevant keywords and phrases likely to appear in spoken narration.

Both queries are used to independently search the vector database for top-matching frames and transcript chunks. Figure 2 shows the top-3 retrieved visual frames and top-2 transcript segments, along with their associated timestamps and cosine similarity scores.

The visual retrieval clearly captures the correct answer context: each selected frame depicts the cougar in combat with the grizzly. Likewise, the transcript retrieval effectively surfaces semantically aligned sentences mentioning the cougar's position or agility. This step demonstrates the high recall and alignment capability of our retrieval pipeline.

Although these results may be sufficient in this case, LightVideoRAG proceeds to a context enrichment stage to ensure robustness for harder queries.

4.2 Context Enrichment

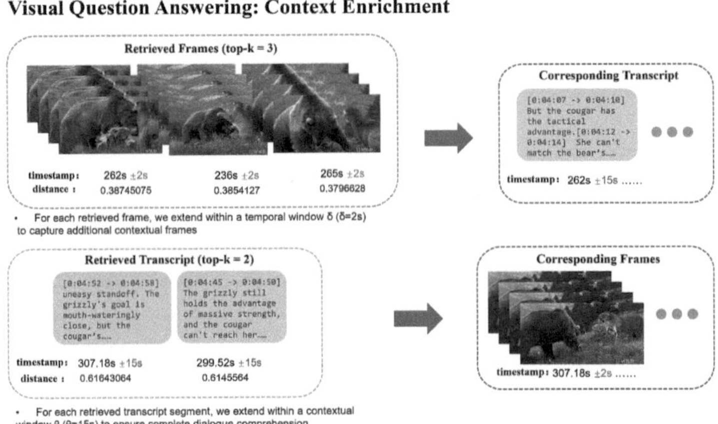

Fig. 3. Context enrichment stage. Bidirectional mapping ensures both modalities support each other.

After the initial retrieval, LightVideoRAG enhances interpretability through context enrichment. Due to the temporal structure of videos, isolated frames or brief transcript segments may lack sufficient context for reasoning.

As illustrated in Fig. 3, each retrieved keyframe is extended by a temporal window of $\delta = \pm 2$ seconds to include nearby frames with supporting content. Transcript segments are similarly expanded by $\theta = \pm 15$ seconds to capture full sentences and maintain narrative flow.

To align modalities, we cross-reference timestamps: visual segments are paired with matching transcripts, and transcript segments are also enriched with aligned visual frames. This bidirectional grounding ensures robust integration of visual and textual context for improved reasoning.

4.3 Answer Generation

After retrieval and enrichment, LightVideoRAG combines keyframes, transcript segments, and a fixed number of global frames with the original query to generate the final answer, as shown in Fig. 4

In this example, the system correctly selects "D. A grizzly" based on the retrieved context. In more challenging cases, global frames enhance robustness by offering broader grounding. This process illustrates LightVideoRAG's ability to integrate multimodal context and produce accurate responses efficiently.

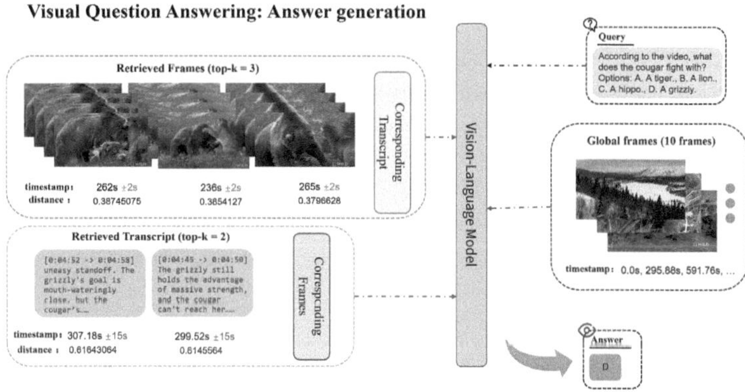

Fig. 4. Answer generation using retrieved context and global frames.

Through step-by-step visualization, we show that our system can precisely locate and interpret relevant segments, bridge visual and textual modalities, and robustly synthesize final answers with minimal redundancy.

5 Performance Evaluation

To evaluate the effectiveness of LightVideoRAG, we conduct experiments on two VideoQA benchmarks: LongVideoBench [18] and Video-MME [4]. LongVideoBench serves as our primary evaluation benchmark due to its focus on long-context video-text reasoning and its inclusion of referring reasoning questions, which closely align with the design of our system. Video-MME complements this by covering a wide range of domains, durations, and modalities, offering a broader assessment of general multimodal performance. These benchmarks together allow us to validate the scalability and retrieval precision of LightVideoRAG across diverse scenarios. In addition to retrieval accuracy, we also evaluate system efficiency using a typical long video to simulate real-life usage, (in Sect. 5.4).

5.1   Environment Setup

All experiments are conducted on a single RTX 4090 GPU with 24GB VRAM. The base model used is Ovis2, a Multi-Modal Large Language Model (MLLM) derived from Qwen2.5 [12,20]. Decoding temperature is fixed at 0 to ensure deterministic outputs.

During index construction, videos are uniformly sampled at 1 frame per second (FPS). To reduce redundancy, Structural Similarity Index (SSIM) [17] filtering is applied with a threshold of 0.8. Automatic speech recognition (ASR) transcripts are extracted using Faster-Distil-Whisper-Large-v3 [5]. We employ ImageBind [6] as our unified multimodal encoder to embed both visual frames and textual segments into a shared semantic space. Its unified representation facilitates cross-modal alignment between video content and text queries, thus improving retrieval precision.

In inference, the top-3 most relevant visual frames and top-2 transcript segments are retrieved based on cosine similarity. Each retrieved keyframe is temporally extended with a ± 2-second window, resulting in up to 5 frames per visual retrieval. In addition, 10 uniformly sampled frames are added as global detail frames to enhance long-range context. Consequently, the total number of input frames per query ranges from 15 to 35, depending on the semantic relevance of the query and the density of adjacent informative frames. The model processes up to 1280 tokens of transcript per query to balance contextual completeness and computational efficiency.

5.2   Evaluation Metrics

We evaluate LightVideoRAG along two key dimensions: retrieval accuracy and efficiency. Retrieval accuracy is measured by question answering (QA) accuracy, reflecting how well the system retrieves relevant multimodal segments to answer a query. Efficiency is assessed by the total time required for index construction and inference, normalized by video duration. These metrics separately demonstrate the system's long-range reasoning ability and its efficiency under complex multimodal scenarios.

5.3   Results and Analysis

We present the experimental results of LightVideoRAG, focusing on its performance in question answering accuracy, runtime efficiency.

Accuracy and Effectiveness. To isolate the effect of our retrieval-augmented framework, we compare Ovis2 (8B) with and without the integration of LightVideoRAG. This controlled comparison enables a direct assessment of how LightVideoRAG enhances retrieval quality and reasoning accuracy under the same base model. The average input length of LightVideoRAG ranges from 15 to 35 frames, dynamically adjusted based on semantic relevance, while the non-RAG version uses a fixed 32-frame input to ensure fair comparison.

Results on LongVideoBench. Our experiments are conducted on the validation set, which includes 753 videos and 1,334 human-annotated question-answer pairs. Table 1 shows the performance of Ovis2 (8B) with and without LightVideoRAG across four video duration groups. Our system consistently outperforms the plain Ovis2 (8B), especially for longer videos where sparse, uniform sampling fails to capture critical events.

Table 1. QA accuracy(%) on LongVideoBench

Duration Group	15 s	60 s	600 s	3600 s	Overall
Ovis2 (8B)	69.8	68.6	57.5	51.4	58.1
Ovis2 (8B) + LightVideoRAG	**70.4**	**75.0**	**63.1**	**56.9**	**63.1**

The performance gap widens as video length increases. For 10-minute and 1-hour videos, LightVideoRAG achieves +5.6% and +5.5% gains respectively. This demonstrates its strength in navigating visual sparsity and semantic diffusion common in long-form content. Instead of treating all frames equally, our system dynamically selects informative frames via adaptive sampling and filters out redundancy using SSIM-based similarity thresholds.

As shown in Table 2, LightVideoRAG achieves a validation accuracy of 63.1%, which would place it at Rank 5 on the LongVideoBench leaderboard as of July 2025. Compared to similarly sized models, our method delivers comparable or better performance using *fewer input frames* (35 vs. 128/256). Compared to systems using the same number of input frames, LightVideoRAG relies on a significantly smaller base model (8B vs. 72B), highlighting the efficiency and robustness introduced by the RAG pipeline. This demonstrates that strategic retrieval and adaptive sampling can substantially compensate for scale in resource-constrained environments.

Table 2. Leaderboard comparison on LongVideoBench (as of July 2025) [19]

Rank	Model	Max Frames	Open-Source	Test Total	Val Total	Model Size
1	GPT-4o (0513)	256	No	66.7	66.7	–
2	Aria	256	Yes	65.0	64.2	25.3B
3	LLaVA-Video-72B-Qwen2	128	Yes	64.9	63.9	72B
4	Gemini-1.5-Pro (0514)	256	No	64.4	64.0	–
5	LLaVA-OneVision-Qwen2-72B-OV	32	Yes	63.2	61.3	72B
6	LLaVA-Video-7B-Qwen2	128	Yes	62.7	61.1	7B
7	Gemini-1.5-Flash (0514)	256	No	62.4	61.6	–
8	GPT-4-Turbo (0409)	256	No	60.7	59.1	–
–	Ovis2-8B	32	Yes	–	58.1	8B
–	**LightVideoRAG (Ovis2-8B)** (ours)	35	Yes	–	**63.1**	8B

Results on Video-MME. We also evaluate LightVideoRAG on the Video-MME benchmark to assess its generalizability across a wide range of video types and modalities. As shown in Table 3, LightVideoRAG consistently outperforms the plain Ovis2 (8B) across all duration groups. Notably, the largest improvement is observed for long videos (30–60 min), where visual sparsity and temporal dispersion challenge uniform sampling approaches.

Table 3. QA accuracy(%) on Video-MME Benchmark

Duration	Short (<2 min)	Medium (4–15 min)	Long (30–60 min)	Overall
Ovis2 (8B)	71.6	58.6	53.7	61.3
Ovis2 (8B) + LightVideoRAG	**75.4**	**63.6**	**59.2**	**66.1**

Compared to the plain Ovis2 (8B), LightVideoRAG yields an overall gain of 4.8%, with consistent improvements from short to long durations. The +5.5% enhancement on long videos demonstrates the advantage of incorporating adaptive frame sampling, contextual enrichment, and multimodal retrieval into the video QA pipeline.

5.4   Efficiency Analysis

To evaluate the runtime performance of LightVideoRAG under practical conditions, we conduct a comparative analysis against VideoRAG [15] using a full-length commercial film (2h38m, 9,531 s), which reflects typical user behavior—of posting open-domain queries over long duration content in a personal computing environment.

VideoRAG [15] serves as an appropriate comparison point because (i) it is a high-performing, publicly available caption-based RAG system, and (ii) its multi-stage pipeline—clip-level captioning, entity–relation graph construction, and hybrid indexing—illustrates a markedly different design philosophy from ours. The method processes many uniformly sampled frames without adaptive reduction and depends on both local models and cloud services. Reasoning is carried out on generated captions rather than raw video, introducing a modality gap and extra latency that accentuates the advantages of LightVideoRAG's fully local, frame-adaptive workflow.

To approximate usage conditions, we used one open-ended question that targets a specific scene. Since both systems returned the correct answer, accuracy comparison would not reveal additional insights. Therefore, we focus on end-to-end latency.

Both systems are run on the same machine to ensure a fair comparison. LightVideoRAG employs Ovis2 (8B), while VideoRAG [15] is executed using the official configuration described in its original paper, which combines a local VLM with remote OpenAI services. In our setting, we followed the same setup by calling the specified remote endpoints: `gpt-4o-mini-2024-07-18` for caption generation and `text-embedding-3-small` for text embedding. The execution time of VideoRAG includes API request latency. Network conditions during testing remained stable and did not reach OpenAI's speed limits, ensuring that the measurement closely reflects real-world system behavior. We report the total time for index construction (frame sampling, embedding, and database setup) and inference (retrieval and answer generation), reflecting end-to-end latency from the user's perspective. Table 4 summarizes the results.

Table 4. Efficiency comparison on a 2h38m video. LightVideoRAG (based on Ovis2, 8B) processes the entire video in only 2.53% of its length, compared to 22.86% for VideoRAG [15].

System	Index Time (s)	Inference Time (s)	Total (% of Video)
LightVideoRAG (Ovis2-8B)	**210.82**	**30.19**	**2.53**
VideoRAG [15]	2129.58	50.23	22.86
Video Duration	2h 38 m 51 s (9531 s)		

LightVideoRAG achieves over $8\times$ speedup in total processing time. Indexing completes in just 210.82 s (2.2% of video duration), while VideoRAG requires over 35 min. For inference, LightVideoRAG is also faster (30.19 s vs. 50.23 s) despite maintaining high retrieval quality. This efficiency results from a tightly integrated design that minimizes unnecessary computation. Adaptive frame sampling eliminates redundant visual data, similarity-based filtering selects only salient content, and all components are optimized for end-to-end execution without external dependencies. As a result, LightVideoRAG achieves fast processing on a single consumer-grade GPU while preserving answer quality.

5.5 Discussion

Our results indicate that LightVideoRAG can transform a modest-performing base model into a competitive solution with only minimal additional computational overhead. Instead of scaling up model parameters or expanding context length, we optimize the input through adaptive frame selection and multimodal retrieval. This approach is especially well-suited for edge deployment and privacy-preserving applications, where computational resources are limited and data locality is crucial. LightVideoRAG opens the door for building high-performing video understanding systems that can operate securely on personal or sensitive video content without relying on cloud-based large-scale infrastructure.

6 Ablation Study

To further evaluate the effectiveness of LightVideoRAG, we conduct ablation studies on the LongVideoBench validation set. The goal is to assess the contribution of three key components: (1) **Adaptive Frame Sampling**, (2) **Global**

Sampler, and (3) **Context Enrichment**. We use controlled experiments by disabling one component at a time, while keeping all other settings identical.

6.1   Results

All ablation experiments are conducted using the same inference pipeline described in Sect. 5. We evaluate our proposed system, LightVideoRAG (Ovis2-8B), alongside several ablated variants to quantify the contribution of each component. The evaluation is performed on the LongVideoBench validation set, which is publicly available. Table 5 presents the accuracy comparison between the full pipeline and ablated variants.

Table 5. Ablation results on LongVideoBench (accuracy in percentage)

Configuration	15 s	60 s	600 s	3600 s	Overall
LightVideoRAG (proposed)	70.4	75.0	63.1	56.9	63.1
w/o Adaptive Frame Sampling	71.4	75.6	62.9	56.7	63.1
w/o Global Sampler	67.7	75.0	64.1	55.7	62.5
w/o Context Enrichment	71.4	74.4	60.3	53.0	60.6
Ovis2 (8B)	69.8	68.6	57.5	51.4	58.1

6.2   Analysis

The ablation results confirm the distinct role each module plays in enhancing long-video QA performance:

- **Adaptive Frame Sampling.** Removing this module has negligible impact on overall accuracy, with the model still achieving 63.1%. This indicates that adaptive sampling effectively reduces input redundancy and computational cost without compromising accuracy. Notably, a slight performance gain in the 3600-second group suggests that filtering out irrelevant frames helps reduce retrieval noise, potentially increasing the diversity and relevance of returned results.
- **Global Sampler.** The absence of the global sampler leads to the most noticeable drop in the 15 s group (from 70.4% to 67.7%). This suggests that global sampling enhances temporal diversity and provides supplemental context that complements top-k retrieval. For longer videos, the performance gap narrows, indicating diminishing marginal utility as duration increases.
- **Context Enrichment.** This component proves to be the most critical. Accuracy drops significantly with increasing duration when it is removed, particularly in the 3600 s group (from 56.9% to 53.0%). This highlights the growing importance of local temporal and textual coherence in longer videos, where

a single frame or caption may be insufficient for comprehensive understanding. Without enrichment, the model struggles to establish semantic continuity across retrieved segments.

The results emphasize the complementary nature of LightVideoRAG's components. **Adaptive Sampling** ensures focused and efficient retrieval, **Global Sampler** introduces scene-level diversity, and **Context Enrichment** reinforces local coherence.

7   Conclusion

In this paper, we introduced LightVideoRAG, a lightweight and privacy-preserving framework for long-video understanding. By combining adaptive frame sampling, unified multimodal embeddings, and local retrieval-augmented inference, the system addresses key challenges in efficiency, relevance, and user data protection. The entire pipeline is designed for deployment on a single device without reliance on cloud platforms or heavyweight models.

Rather than increasing model size or input length, LightVideoRAG focuses on improving the quality of retrieved context, showing that smart retrieval and minimal input can enable effective reasoning even with modest computational resources.

Acknowledgement. This work was in part supported by JSPS KAKENHI Grant Number 25K03230.

References

1. Arefeen, M.A., Debnath, B., Uddin, M.Y.S., Chakradhar, S.: IRAG: advancing rag for videos with an incremental approach. In: Proceedings of the 33rd ACM International Conference on Information and Knowledge Management, pp. 4341–4348 (2024)
2. Arefeen, M.A., Debnath, B., Uddin, M.Y.S., Chakradhar, S.: Vita: an efficient video-to-text algorithm using VLM for rag-based video analysis system. In: Proceedings of the IEEE/CVF Conference on Computer Vision and Pattern Recognition (CVPR) Workshops, pp. 2266–2274 (2024)
3. Das, B.C., Amini, M.H., Wu, Y.: Security and privacy challenges of large language models: a survey. ACM Comput. Surv. **57**(6), 1–39 (2025)
4. Fu, C., et al.: Video-MME: the first-ever comprehensive evaluation benchmark of multi-modal LLMs in video analysis. arXiv preprint arXiv:2405.21075 (2024)
5. Gandhi, S., von Platen, P., Rush, A.M.: Distil-whisper: robust knowledge distillation via large-scale pseudo labelling. arXiv preprint arXiv:2311.00430 (2023)
6. Girdhar, R., et al.: ImageBind: one embedding space to bind them all. In: Proceedings of the IEEE/CVF Conference on Computer Vision and Pattern Recognition, pp. 15180–15190 (2023)
7. Hadi, M.U., et al.: A survey on large language models: applications, challenges, limitations, and practical usage. Authorea Preprints **3** (2023)

8. Karpukhin, V., et al.: Dense passage retrieval for open-domain question answering. In: EMNLP, vol. 1, pp. 6769–6781 (2020)

9. Lewis, P., et al.: Retrieval-augmented generation for knowledge-intensive NLP tasks. Adv. Neural. Inf. Process. Syst. **33**, 9459–9474 (2020)

10. Li, J., Li, D., Xiong, C., Hoi, S.: BLIP: bootstrapping language-image pre-training for unified vision-language understanding and generation. In: International Conference on Machine Learning, pp. 12888–12900. PMLR (2022)

11. Liu, H., Li, C., Wu, Q., Lee, Y.J.: Visual instruction tuning. Adv. Neural. Inf. Process. Syst. **36**, 34892–34916 (2023)

12. Lu, S., et al.: OVIS: structural embedding alignment for multimodal large language model. arXiv preprint arXiv:2405.20797 (2024)

13. Luo, Y., et al.: Video-Rag: visually-aligned retrieval-augmented long video comprehension. arXiv preprint arXiv:2411.13093 (2024)

14. Radford, A., et al.: Learning transferable visual models from natural language supervision. In: International Conference on Machine Learning, pp. 8748–8763. PmLR (2021)

15. Ren, X., Xu, L., Xia, L., Wang, S., Yin, D., Huang, C.: VideoRag: retrieval-augmented generation with extreme long-context videos. arXiv preprint arXiv:2502.01549 (2025)

16. Robertson, S., Zaragoza, H., et al.: The probabilistic relevance framework: BM25 and beyond. Found. Trends® Inf. Retrieval **3**(4), 333–389 (2009)

17. Wang, Z., Bovik, A.C., Sheikh, H.R., Simoncelli, E.P.: Image quality assessment: from error visibility to structural similarity. IEEE Trans. Image Process. **13**(4), 600–612 (2004)

18. Wu, H., Li, D., Chen, B., Li, J.: LongVideoBench: a benchmark for long-context interleaved video-language understanding. Adv. Neural. Inf. Process. Syst. **37**, 28828–28857 (2024)

19. Wu, H., Li, D., Chen, B., Li, J.: LongVideoBench leaderboard (2025). https://longvideobench.github.io/index.html#leaderboard. Accessed 24 June 2025

20. Yang, A., et al.: Qwen2. 5 technical report. arXiv preprint arXiv:2412.15115 (2024)

21. Yang, Z., et al.: MM-React: prompting ChatGPT for multimodal reasoning and action. arXiv preprint arXiv:2303.11381 (2023)

22. Yuan, H., et al.: Memory-enhanced retrieval augmentation for long video understanding. arXiv preprint arXiv:2503.09149 (2025)

23. Zhang, L., Zhao, T., Ying, H., Ma, Y., Lee, K.: OmAgent: a multi-modal agent framework for complex video understanding with task divide-and-conquer. arXiv preprint arXiv:2406.16620 (2024)

Exploring the Design of Context-Aware Widget Recommender System in Mixed Reality

Yiming Sun, Yang Zhan$^{(\boxtimes)}$, and Tatsuo Nakajima$^{(\boxtimes)}$

Department of Computer Science and Engineering, Waseda University, Tokyo, Japan
{ysun60,yang.zhan,tatsuo}@dcl.cs.waseda.ac.jp

Abstract. Mixed Reality (MR), which overlays virtual user interfaces (UIs) onto physical environments, necessitates UI adaptation to complex scenes and tasks. While prior work focused on adaptive spatial UI layout in MR, functional adaptation such as widget recommendation remains underexplored. We present a user study ($n = 16$) using a Large Language Models (LLMs)-powered widget recommender system (RS) as a technology probe to investigate how context-aware recommendations affect user experience. The system uses LLMs with contextual data (reading text, video transcript and typed data) to suggest MR widgets. Results show that widget recommendations facilitated access to context-relevant functionalities and simplified task workflows, thus enhancing the user experience and reducing workload. However, the usability of the widget RS depends on appropriate widget design and recommendation strategies that enable personal customization. This study serves as an initial step toward MR widget RSs and offers insights for adaptive user-RS interactions.

Keywords: Mixed Reality · Context awareness · Widget Recommendation · Large Language Models

1 Introduction

In recent years, the development of Mixed Reality (MR) has shown its potential to improve users' productivity and become an everyday wearable product. By expanding user interfaces (UIs) into 3D space, MR applications can arbitrarily overlay virtual UIs onto the real world, offering greater mobility compared to conventional laptops and phones. Moreover, MR displays multi-dimensional information simultaneously and enables intuitive interactions [17], which are widely used in programming [29] and education [28]. Although MR systems present novel experiences, their design and implementation are challenging due to complex real-world environments and dynamic user statuses. For instance, it

---

Y. Sun and Y. Zhan—These authors contributed equally to this work.

P. Delir Haghighi et al. (Eds.): MoMM 2025, LNCS 16329, pp. 25–39, 2026.
https://doi.org/10.1007/978-3-032-11768-7_3

is time-consuming for users to manually place virtual interfaces to avoid occlusion by real-world surroundings and adjust UI layouts when switch physical workspaces [5].

Previous research has emphasized the value of adaptive systems in MR environments. Studies examined how environmental factors affect user experience [12,23] and how UI placement can align with semantic features of physical objects [5]. Adaptive interfaces have also responded to user states such as mental workload [20]. However, most of these works focus on layout-level adaptation and overlook the recommendation of MR applications based on user needs. In dynamic environments and user activities, repeated app selection can be burdensome. Prior work [6] found that users prefer function-oriented UIs, such as widgets, over application-based ones. Yet, widgets—lightweight tools derived from specific app—may lead to an overwhelming number of options. These findings underscore the need for adaptive widget recommendation to streamline interaction and improve usability in MR.

Motivated by above research gap, this paper takes an initial step toward exploring the user experience and design considerations of widget recommender system (RS) on MR devices. Specifically, we aim to investigate the following two research questions:

- **(RQ1)** How does the recommendation of MR widgets affect users' experience and perception during tasks?
- **(RQ2)** What system features influence the usability of widget RS in MR?

To address our research questions, we conducted a within-subject study ($n = 16$), and designed an open-ended task using an MR widget RS in conjunction with a PC workspace, forming a hybrid workspace [27], which is a common scenario in MR productivity applications [5,6]. We implemented a technology probe [16] that leverages Large Language Models (LLMs) to recommend task-relevant widgets on MR head-mounted displays (HMDs). Three types of contextual inputs—reading texts, video transcripts, and typed data—were incorporated to investigate how context influences recommendations and user experience. Our main contributions are:

(1) extending MR context-aware adaptation from UI layout adjustments to functionality-based adaptation,
(2) evaluating its impact on user experience and perception through a user study, and
(3) deriving design insights for future RSs and broader MR applications.

2   Related Work

2.1   Adaptive Designs in MR

MR encompassing Virtual Reality (VR) and Augmented Reality (AR), offers high mobility and has been applied across daily scenarios for flexible UIs and efficient interaction. To support dynamic environments, prior studies optimized

MR interface placement in offices [22], classrooms [2], and stores [35]. Shin et al. [31] showed that room size affected AR game experience, suggesting space-adaptive UIs for indoor contents. SemanticAdapt [5] aligned UIs with physical objects via contextual cues. For dynamic contexts, Du et al. [10] enabled anchoring UIs to everyday objects, and FingerSwitches [25] introduced UI switching principles across static and dynamic surroundings. While the physical environment is critical in MR interface design, user status and ongoing activities are equally important considerations. Grubert et al. [14] emphasized the necessity of developing context-aware AR systems to support continuous and multi-purpose user experiences. When users transition between contexts, such as tasks or environments, associated changes in cognitive load can be leveraged to optimize both the amount of information displayed and the positioning of MR UIs [20]. To understand UI preferences across activities, MineXR [6] collected personalized UI layouts across four daily XR scenarios, producing 109 layouts tailored to tasks. The findings revealed a preference for functionality UI over complete application, supporting widget-centric designs in XR productivity. Despite the advancement, most existing studies concentrated on adapting UI layouts to environments and users. It remains unclear how adaptive widgets, the functionality of the UI, can enhance user experience in MR.

2.2   App Recommendation

The rapid growth of mobile apps has driven the development of automatic app RS to aid app selection and optimize system operations such as memory management. For example, Baeza-Yates et al. [1] treated app prediction as a classification task, using sensor data and sequential usage patterns to enhance precision. Bayesian and Markov models have been widely used to analyze contextual data and predict subsequent app usage [15,24]. Despite achieving reasonable accuracy, traditional methods often fail to capture sufficient features from complex contextual data. To address this, Shen et al. [30] applied deep reinforcement learning to reduce app loading time and improve user satisfaction. Likewise, WhatsNextApp [18] used an LSTM model to mitigate the cold-start problem when users set up new devices. The rise of LLMs offers new opportunities for app recommendation by enabling better reasoning over contextual cues and understanding semantic app descriptions. LLMs have proven effective as RSs in various applications, such as open-world recommendation [33] with both fine-tuned [34] and prompt-based approaches [7]. Khaokaew et al. [19] utilized a pre-trained LLM to predict top-k apps using contextual data such as app details and points of interest, outperforming traditional models in standard and cold-start cases.

While prior research has explored app recommendation for real-time task adaptation, few have addressed its application in MR environments, especially regarding user–RS interaction. The distinct characteristics of 3D MR spaces challenge the usability of approaches designed for 2D screens. The most related work focuses on selecting MR apps and adapting UI based on task type and cognitive load [20]. In contrast, we leverages richer contextual information to recommend widgets and explores multiple context-aware mechanisms in everyday tasks, offering new insights into app recommendation in MR.

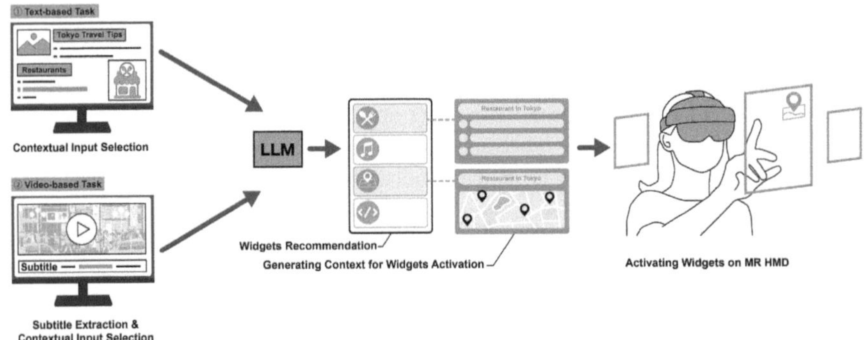

Fig. 1. System pipeline with three main components: context-aware mechanisms (*left*), an LLM-powered RS backend (*middle*), and MR widgets (*right*). *Left*: Passive and proactive mechanisms capture context for the RS (Sect. 3.1). *Middle*: The RS uses WRC to recommend widgets and WAC to adapt their functions (Sect. 3.2). *Right*: Recommended widgets appear in predefined MR areas to support user tasks (Sect. 3.3).

3   System Overview

We developed a functional system prototype specifically for the user study. Rather than aiming to build a fully mature system, we employed the prototype as a technology probe to gather user insights and design implication for the MR widgets recommendation.

Our system comprises three main components: *context-aware mechanisms* built into computer interfaces that capture on-screen content and treat it as contextual input (see Sect. 3.1), an *LLM-powered RS backend* for widget prediction and activation (see Sect. 3.2), and *MR widgets* for task assistance (see Sect. 3.3). The system pipeline is shown in Fig. 1. Three contexts, including reading texts, video transcripts, and typed data, are captured proactively and passively by the context-aware mechanism and fed into the RS. The LLM-powered RS consists of two core features: Widget Recommendation based on Context (WRC) and Widget Activation driven by Context (WAC). WRC focuses on recommending the most suitable widgets based on the current user contexts, whereas WAC enables the selected widgets to autonomously perform relevant functions or guide users to specific functionalities by applying the contextual parameters to the widgets. For example, when viewing a travel video, the WRC recommends a map widget, and the WAC automatically displays information related to the point of interest on the widget.

Our implementation consists of three components that communicate via WebSocket: (1) computer interfaces developed with React, (2) a server that hosts a GPT-4o-powered RS backend and widget services, and (3) a MR application developed in Unity with MRTK3, integrating 11 widgets. The relevance of widgets is task-dependent and thus are described in Sect. 4.3.

(a) Context-aware mechanisms: (1) passive text selection, (2) passive subtitle selection, and (3) proactive title input.

(b) User interacting with MR widgets during the task.

Fig. 2. Context-aware mechanisms and MR interface usage.

3.1 Context-Aware Mechanisms

Although technologies like eye tracking and text recognition may enable MR headsets to autonomously capture context, they risk introducing bias and inconsistency in user studies. Therefore, we extract contextual input on PC. Contextual information is acquired through **passive** and **proactive** mechanisms. The passive mechanism relies on user-selected content. For the text-based contexts (Fig. 2a-(1)), users select text content as contextual input, then activates the blue button to send the contexts. For video contexts (Fig. 2a-(2)), users extracts interest points from subtitles by pressing the blue button and then selects one to transmit the contextual information. It also incorporates typed input to enrich recommendation context. In contrast, the proactive mechanism automatically captures after title input (Fig. 2a-(3)). Our LLM-based RS primarily uses the passive mechanism, as it offers greater precision and fosters user trust [21].

3.2 LLM-Powered Widget RS

The LLM-based RS backend analyzes the current context, recommends relevant widgets, and activates their functionalities accordingly. It operates via structured prompts refined through pilot testing, incorporating techniques such as few-shot prompting [3] and task decomposition [32]. Each prompt includes: AI role assignment, task explanation, widget/context descriptions, output format, and a one-shot example (Fig. 3). Square-bracketed fields are dynamically replaced with task-specific content during the study.

The RS generates two outputs: (1) WRC results, identifying context-relevant widgets; and (2) refined context parameters ($<$ keyword $>$) for WAC, enabling each selected widget to function with appropriate inputs.

Prompt: Now you act as a helpful [assistant]. You will read the user's [contexts], recommend multiple important widgets and fill in the keyword fields for the widgets tagged by $<$ keyword $>$ in the predefined library with the correct information. Using this text, please fill in the following library structure, $<$ library $>$[...]$<$ /library $>$. The user's [typed input] is tagged by [$<$ tag $>$], and the user is currently focusing on the content delimited by $<$ focus $>$. The focus content could be the [reading context] or [typed input]. You should always recommend 3 to 4 widgets. Your answer must end with a JSON format using the following template: [...]. Below is an example for user's travel description: [...], Your answer could be: [...].

Output: [{ "widget": "...", "keywords": "..."}, ...]

Fig. 3. Example of the LLM prompt and output. Task-specific content is enclosed in square brackets. The output includes selected widgets ($<$ library $>$) for WRC and refined context parameters ($<$ keyword $>$) for WAC.

3.3 MR Widgets

MR widgets are supported by the WAC, activating their features based on users' contextual input. To accommodate diverse functionalities, we adopted a Web Widget deployment strategy: these widgets rely on external web content and do not run natively on the MR headset. Instead, they display simplified information in MR and include navigation buttons for accessing full content via a linked desktop browser. This approach accelerates development and enables rapid deployment of task-relevant widgets. To improve awareness and predictability, users can predefine widget display areas during system initialization.

4 User Study

To answer the research questions, we conducted a within-subject study with two conditions: *Widget RS* and *PC-only*. In the Widget RS condition, the participants wore HoloLens 2 MR headsets and completed the assigned task on a computer with assistance from the RS and MR widgets. In contrast, the PC-only condition required participants to perform the same task merely on the computer without assistance, serving as the baseline. We selected a PC-only condition as the baseline because this familiar paradigm and workflow introduce no additional variables and therefore allow more intuitive comparisons with the MR-based RS. We recruited 16 participants (6 females, 10 males), aged 19–35 ($M = 25.3$, $SD = 3.3$). One participant used MR weekly, 9 less than monthly, and 6 had no prior MR experience.

4.1   Task

Travel planning, a cognitively demanding task involving various types of contextual information [26], was chosen to evaluate the system across diverse contexts. Its open-ended nature better mirrors real-world MR usage than goal-driven tasks. To limit study duration, participants compiled a travel note rather than a full itinerary. They selected points of interest from text and video materials, searched for related details, recorded supplementary information, and identified a hotel and restaurants within given constraints. Use of conversational LLMs was prohibited to ensure comparability across participants. Two destinations, Vienna and Florence, were assigned in a fixed order while the two system conditions were counterbalanced. None participants had visited the assigned cities.

4.2   Procedure

The entire study lasted around two hours. Upon arrival, participants were briefed on the research goals, signed a consent form, and completed a demographic questionnaire. They then performed a training task to familiarize themselves with the system. Next, they proceeded to complete the travel planning task under either the PC-only or Widget RS condition, presented in counterbalanced order. After each task, the participants completed several questionnaires. Finally, a 15-min semi-structured interview was conducted, and participants were offered a $20 Amazon gift card as compensation. The study was exempted from review by the local IRB.

4.3   Widget Description

In the user study, eleven widgets were designed to support specific types of contextual information or user needs associated with the travel planning task. A list of these widgets is presented in Table 1, with visual examples shown in Fig. 2b. The selection and design of these widgets were informed by common travel planning requirements, as well as frequently used widget types identified in the MineXR dataset [6]. Each widget features buttons that can be operated via direct finger interaction.

4.4   Measures

We adopted a mixed-method evaluation combining objective and subjective metrics. Objective data included task completion time and the number of passive recommendations across all context types. Subjective evaluation focused on perceived productivity, user experience (measured using the User Experience Questionnaire, UEQ), and workload (measured using the NASA Task Load Index, TLX). Productivity was assessed using four items rated on a 7-point Likert scale: two addressing system usability ("I can quickly find the information I need." and "I am willing to explore more information."), and two adapted from prior research on perceived usefulness [8] ("Using this system in my daily work will

Table 1. Overview of widgets used in the study. Asterisks denote widgets without WAC support due to API or crawling limitations.

Name	Description	Content
Local Restaurant	A list of three restaurants from Google Local	Restaurant's name, cuisine type, price range, and rating
Result from Google	A list of three websites retrieved via Google Search	Website title
Top Hotel Picks	A list of three most-viewed hotels retrieved from Google Hotels	Hotel's name, price, rating, and photos
Google, Google Maps, Wikipedia, YouTube, OpenTable*, Red Note*, The Fork*, Trip*	A context-aware website of the corresponding widget, which is arranged as an item of *More Widgets You May Like*	Widget icon and context-related parameters

improve my productivity." and "...my job performance."). Higher scores indicate better perceived productivity. In the semi-structured interview, we asked participants for general feedback, including preferences, their experiences, and perceptions of the RS and the MR widgets.

5   Results

This section presents the quantitative and qualitative findings of our user study. For quantitative data, including objective measures and questionnaire responses, we conducted paired-samples t-tests when the normality assumption was satisfied. When normality was not met, the Wilcoxon signed-rank test was used as a non-parametric alternative. All other statistical assumptions were verified before analysis, and significance levels were set at $\alpha = .05, .01$, and $.001$. Questionnaire scores were reported as averages of the items within each subscale. For qualitative data, we performed open coding on interview transcripts, followed by affinity mapping to group codes. Key findings were synthesized through team discussions to identify novel and meaningful insights.

5.1   Objective Measures

For task completion time, participants spent an average of 21.66 min ($SD = 8.46$) in the PC-only condition and 22.73 min ($SD = 9.98$) in the RS condition, with no significant differences confirmed ($t(15) = -0.565, p = 0.580$). A Friedman test revealed no significant differences among the three contextual sources ($\chi^2(2) = 0.623$, $p = 0.732$), although more passive recommendations were triggered on average when reading text ($M = 4.25$, $SD = 3.56$), with similar mean values observed in the video ($M = 2.94$, $SD = 1.77$) and the note contexts ($M = 3.00$, $SD = 3.31$).

5.2   Questionnaire Responses

Productivity was measured through system usability and perceived usefulness (Fig. 4a). Usability scores were significantly higher in the MR RS condition ($M = 5.28$, $SD = 1.25$) than in the PC-only condition ($M = 4.19$, $SD = 1.15$; $W = 4.0$, $p = 0.004$). Perceived usefulness showed a marginal increase for the MR RS ($M = 4.94$, $SD = 1.29$) over PC-only ($M = 4.00$, $SD = 1.24$; $t(15) = -1.996$, $p = 0.064$). UEQ showed significant improvements in four subscales: *attractiveness* ($t(15) = -4.086$, $p < 0.001$), *efficiency* ($t(15) = -2.948$, $p = 0.009$), *novelty* ($W = 0$, $p < 0.001$), and *stimulation* ($t(15) = -6.141$, $p < 0.001$). No differences were found in *dependability* or *perspicuity*. For the NASA-TLX, overall workload was marginally lower in the MR RS condition ($t(15) = 2.126$, $p = 0.051$). Among subscales (Fig. 4b), significant reductions were observed in *performance* ($t(15) = 2.875$, $p = 0.012$), *effort* ($t(15) = 2.375$, $p = 0.031$), and *frustration* ($t(15) = 2.916$, $p = 0.011$). No differences were found in *mental, physical,* or *temporal* demand.

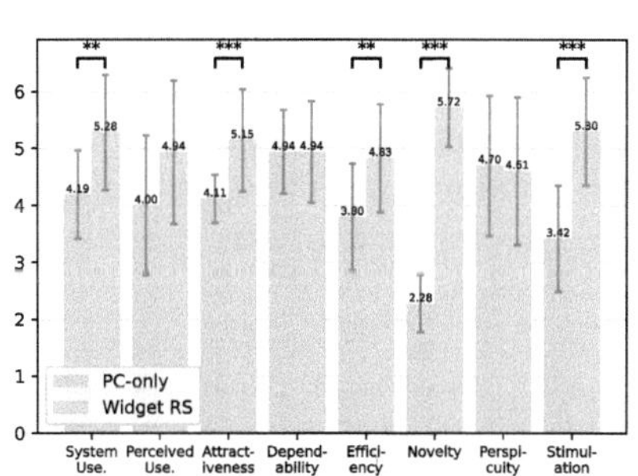

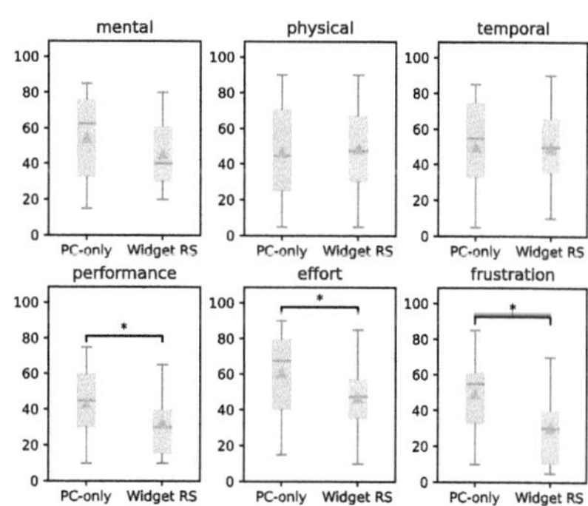

(a) Mean and SD of productivity and UEQ. "System Use." denotes System Usability; "Perceived Use." denotes Perceived Usefulness. Significance: * $p < 0.05$, ** $p < 0.01$, *** $p < 0.001$.

(b) Boxplots of raw NASA-TLX subscales. Green triangles: means; orange lines: medians. * ($p < 0.05$) indicates significance.

Fig. 4. a: Productivity and UEQ, b: NASA-TLX results.

5.3   Interview

User Experience with PC-only Vs. MR System. Participants compared their task experiences using the Widget RS in MR versus the PC-only condition. Over half ($n = 9$) cited operational familiarity as the main advantage of using a PC. However, the PC-only condition required high cognitive overload when processing abundant information ($n = 4$). P15 noted the lack of task guidance, requiring more mental effort to organize thoughts. In contrast, the MR system was praised for its convenience and time-saving features, with most participants ($n = 7$) noting that recommended widgets reduced search effort. Participants appreciated the centralized layout ($n = 6$), guidance served by RS ($n = 3$), and familiar icons that increased trust and usability (P11, P16). Reported drawbacks of the MR system included its learning curve ($n = 3$), and physical fatigue from interactions and the headset ($n = 7$). A few participants ($n = 2$) also found an excess of widgets overwhelming.

MR Widgets. Regarding widget usability, most participants ($n = 13$) preferred widgets that supported WAC, such as Google Map or Local Restaurant. About half ($n = 6$) noted that WAC simplified their workflow and reduced workload. As P1, P6, and P16 remarked, *"Not having to input the search query is convenient."* However, the majority ($n = 13$) found widget functionality insufficient. Participants attributed this to dependence on external webpages (P1, P7, P11) or widgets merely redirecting to main pages (P4, P14, P15). In terms of content richness, most participants ($n = 11$) felt the displayed information was lacking, with several requesting more comprehensive results, especially for hotel ($n = 3$) and restaurant widgets ($n = 2$).

Context-Based RS. When evaluating RS performance across the context-aware mechanisms, most participants ($n = 11$) favored the video-based passive mechanism, highlighting its convenience and accuracy in reflecting points of interest. P15 emphasized the contrast with the PC-only condition: *"you need to manually type in the names ... but MR can automatically search and provide the key results."* However, some ($n = 3$) noted that pausing videos to extract subtitles disrupted their workflow. As improvements, participants suggested adding support for image frame extraction as context ($n = 9$). The text-based passive mechanism was also well received, with participants appreciating its selection accuracy ($n = 10$) and seamless integration into the reading flow ($n = 4$). P11 noted that selecting and searching in text was more convenient than pausing video. However, some users expected the system to better anticipate their focus and recommend related content automatically (P10). The proactive mechanism, triggered by title input, was considered helpful by most participants ($n = 10$). Still, concerns were raised about mismatches due to abstract or inconsistent titles ($n = 6$). Participants stressed the importance of recommendation timing based on context sequences, suggesting the system should anticipate next steps in the planning process (P1, P13).

User Perception. Several participants ($n = 7$) expressed a strong willingness to explore the MR system, citing its interactivity (P5, P15), novelty (P2), and reduced time (P7) and effort (P14). Some ($n = 3$) noted its suitability for open-ended tasks, as it *"suggests things I hadn't originally thought of"* (P3). Most participants ($n = 14$) reported a smooth transition between the MR and PC environments, particularly in interaction and attention switching. Proactive recommendations were generally non-intrusive ($n = 4$), but occasionally ignored

($n = 2$) due to their peripheral positioning around the PC monitor and the need for head movement (P14). As P2 explained, participants could disregard them, especially when *"the timing was wrong."*

6   Discussion

For **RQ1**, participants reported enhanced efficiency, streamlined workflows, and increased exploratory motivation with the MR system. Regarding **RQ2**, key usability features included widget functionality, the intuitiveness of the context-aware mechanisms, and the RS capacity to interpret contextual input. These findings are further discussed in Sects. 6.1 and 6.2. We also outline potential applications beyond the hybrid workspace scenario explored in this study.

6.1   User Experience and Perception

Although objective performance did not significantly differ, users reported improved usability and experience with the Widget RS. Factors such as task characteristics or prior experience with PC workflows may have influenced the outcome. UEQ results showed that the MR condition was perceived as more attractive, stimulating, and novel, with higher efficiency. However, no significant improvement was observed in completion time or temporal demand, suggesting that RS contributed to a high perceived performance, even if it was not reflected in task completion time, it may be driven by the workflow simplification. Lower effort and frustration scores in TLX further reflected the system's supportive role on inspiration and motivation. For example, P2 described the experience as engaging and curiosity-driven. However, mental demand remained unchanged, We believe that this is due to limitations in widget functionality. Specific tasks like booking still required users to access external websites, which required users to invest additional mental effort.

6.2   Design Implications

Prioritizing Context-Activated Widgets over Icons. Participants strongly preferred context-activated MR widgets with WAC support, as these enabled direct access to relevant information without additional navigation. In contrast, icon-type widgets linking to static websites were rarely used, differing from prior findings [6]. This shift may be attributed to the combined cognitive load of MR HMD usage and the travel-planning task since reported workload scores (PC-only: $M = 50.7$; MR RS: $M = 42.1$) fall within cognitively intensive ranges [13]. We suggest future MR systems prioritize widgets with immediately accessible content. Extending prior research [20], our results emphasize context-aware interface design over mere simplification.

Balancing Recommendation Complexity and Workload. The RS exploited 3D space to display multiple widgets, but users often prioritized only a few, underscoring the need to avoid redundant recommendations. Some participants also noted limited functionality in individual widgets. However, adding too many features can increase ergonomic burden [11]. Designers should focus on core functionality and reduce unnecessary interaction frequency to balance utility and cognitive load.

Incorporating Users Into the Recommendation Loop. Low-level contextual input helped narrow recommendations but lacked precision due to limited understanding of user goals. Variations in title writing and user knowledge affected the accuracy of outcomes. Future systems should support preference customization and interactive feedback to better align with user intent. Research in human-AI interaction has underscored the importance of personalization [21] and user autonomy [4] for user experience, which is echoed and extended in our results.

6.3 MR Widget RS in Broader Scenarios

Although the study was conducted on a hybrid workspace, our findings highlight two key advantages of widget RS for broader MR scenarios:

Motivation for Continuous Exploration. The RS promotes engagement by suggesting context-relevant widgets that simplify tasks and reduce workload (Sect. 5.3, Sect. 6.1), fostering motivation similarly to personalized educational recommendations [9]. For example, the RS could recommend explanatory widgets during MR reading. In such cases, designers should aim to balance recommendation complexity and personalize suggestions (Sect. 6.2).

Inspiration for Problem-Solving and Creativity. The RS guides users during uncertain task stages by suggesting relevant widgets, particularly beneficial for creative or open-ended tasks (Sect. 5.3). For example, in MR shopping, the RS could suggest coupons or alternative products to enhance user decisions. To support this, proactive recommendations should consider task progress and cognitive load, balancing usability and cognitive demands (Sect. 6.2).

6.4 Limitations and Future Work

Application Scenarios. Due to time constraints, our task design focused on a single scenario and did not fully simulate real-world travel exploration, and also the small sample size limited the generalizability of results. Future research should investigate long-term use of the widget RS across multiple task types. Moreover, the hybrid workspace setting may not reflect the full potential of RS in more immersive MR environments. We encourage applying the system to diverse scenarios as discussed in Sect. 6.3 to support generalizable MR design.

Diverse Contexts. Contextual input in our study was extracted via PC rather than MR devices. Although we included text, video, and typed data, other rich inputs—such as gaze tracking and live video—were not explored. Future systems should leverage native MR sensors to enable richer, real-time context capture.

Usability of Widget and RS. Some widgets were limited by the lack of public APIs, restricting full WAC support. Integration at the OS level (e.g., visionOS) and more interactive 3D UIs may improve usability. For the RS, proactive mechanisms depend heavily on the quantity and quality of contextual input. Enhancing prompt design or incorporating fine-tuned models [19] may lead to more intelligent and personalized recommendations.

7 Conclusion

This work explored how an MR widget RS supports users in daily tasks and offers design insights for future applications. Through a user study, we examined its impact across different contextual inputs and mechanisms on user experience and perception. Results showed that the RS streamlined workflows and enhanced user satisfaction. Based on qualitative findings, we proposed design implications to improve system usability. Although the study was conducted in a hybrid workspace, its findings extend to broader MR contexts and contribute to advancing adaptive MR system design.

References

1. Baeza-Yates, R., Jiang, D., Silvestri, F., Harrison, B.: Predicting the next app that you are going to use. In: Proceedings of the Eighth ACM International Conference on Web Search and Data Mining, pp. 285–294 (2015)
2. Broussard, D.M., Rahman, Y., Kulshreshth, A.K., Borst, C.W.: An interface for enhanced teacher awareness of student actions and attention in a vr classroom. In: 2021 IEEE Conference on Virtual Reality and 3D User Interfaces Abstracts and Workshops (VRW), pp. 284–290. IEEE (2021)
3. Brown, T., et al.: Language models are few-shot learners. Adv. Neural. Inf. Process. Syst. **33**, 1877–1901 (2020)
4. Chen, W., et al.: Investigating context-aware collaborative text entry on smartphones using large language models. In: Proceedings of the 2025 CHI Conference on Human Factors in Computing Systems, pp. 1–20 (2025)
5. Cheng, Y., Yan, Y., Yi, X., Shi, Y., Lindlbauer, D.: Semanticadapt: optimization-based adaptation of mixed reality layouts leveraging virtual-physical semantic connections. In: The 34th Annual ACM Symposium on User Interface Software and Technology, pp. 282–297 (2021)
6. Cho, H., et al.: Minexr: mining personalized extended reality interfaces. In: Proceedings of the 2024 CHI Conference on Human Factors in Computing Systems, pp. 1–17 (2024)
7. Dai, S., et al.: Uncovering chatgpt's capabilities in recommender systems. In: Proceedings of the 17th ACM Conference on Recommender Systems, pp. 1126–1132 (2023)

8. Davis, F.D.: Perceived usefulness, perceived ease of use, and user acceptance of information technology. MIS Q. 319–340 (1989)
9. Drissi, S., Chefrour, A., Boussaha, K., Zarzour, H.: Exploring the effects of personalized recommendations on student's motivation and learning achievement in gamified mobile learning framework. Educ. Inf. Technol. **29**(12), 15463–15500 (2024)
10. Du, R., et al.: Opportunistic interfaces for augmented reality: transforming everyday objects into tangible 6dof interfaces using ad hoc ui. In: CHI Conference on Human Factors in Computing Systems Extended Abstracts, pp. 1–4 (2022)
11. Evangelista Belo, J.A.M., Feit, A.M., Feuchtner, T., Grønbæk, K.: Xrgonomics: facilitating the creation of ergonomic 3d interfaces. In: Proceedings of the 2021 CHI Conference on Human Factors in Computing Systems, CHI '21. Association for Computing Machinery, New York (2021). https://doi.org/10.1145/3411764.3445349
12. Gal, R., Shapira, L., Ofek, E., Kohli, P.: Flare: fast layout for augmented reality applications. In: 2014 IEEE International Symposium on Mixed and Augmented Reality (ISMAR), pp. 207–212. IEEE (2014)
13. Grier, R.A.: How high is high? A meta-analysis of nasa-tlx global workload scores. In: Proceedings of the Human Factors and Ergonomics Society Annual Meeting. vol. 59, pp. 1727–1731. Sage Publications, Los Angeles (2015)
14. Grubert, J., Langlotz, T., Zollmann, S., Regenbrecht, H.: Towards pervasive augmented reality: context-awareness in augmented reality. IEEE Trans. Visual Comput. Graph. **23**(6), 1706–1724 (2016)
15. Huang, K., Zhang, C., Ma, X., Chen, G.: Predicting mobile application usage using contextual information. In: Proceedings of the 2012 ACM Conference on Ubiquitous Computing, pp. 1059–1065 (2012)
16. Hutchinson, H., et al.: Technology probes: inspiring design for and with families. In: Proceedings of the SIGCHI Conference on Human Factors in Computing Systems, CHI '03, pp. 17–24. Association for Computing Machinery, New York (2003). https://doi.org/10.1145/642611.642616
17. Irshad, S., Rambli, D.R.B.A.: User experience of mobile augmented reality: a review of studies. In: 2014 3rd International Conference on User Science and Engineering (i-USEr), pp. 125–130. IEEE (2014)
18. Katsarou, K., Yu, G., Beierle, F.: Whatsnextapp: LSTM-based next-app prediction with app usage sequences. IEEE Access **10**, 18233–18247 (2022)
19. Khaokaew, Y., Xue, H., Salim, F.D.: Maple: mobile app prediction leveraging large language model embeddings. Proc. ACM Interact. Mobile Wearable Ubiq. Technol. **8**(1), 1–25 (2024)
20. Lindlbauer, D., Feit, A.M., Hilliges, O.: Context-aware online adaptation of mixed reality interfaces. In: Proceedings of the 32nd Annual ACM Symposium on User Interface Software and Technology, pp. 147–160 (2019)
21. Lu, F., Xu, Y., Xu, X., Jones, B., Malamed, L.: Exploring the impact of user and system factors on human-ai interactions in head-worn displays. In: 2023 IEEE International Symposium on Mixed and Augmented Reality (ISMAR), pp. 109–118. IEEE (2023)
22. Luo, W., Lehmann, A., Widengren, H., Dachselt, R.: Where should we put it? Layout and placement strategies of documents in augmented reality for collaborative sensemaking. In: Proceedings of the 2022 CHI Conference on Human Factors in Computing Systems, pp. 1–16 (2022)
23. Macedo, M.C., Apolinario, A.L.: Occlusion handling in augmented reality: past, present and future. IEEE Trans. Visual Comput. Graph. **29**(2), 1590–1609 (2021)

24. Natarajan, N., Shin, D., Dhillon, I.S.: Which app will you use next? Collaborative filtering with interactional context. In: Proceedings of the 7th ACM Conference on Recommender Systems, pp. 201–208 (2013)
25. Pei, S., Kim, D., Olwal, A., Zhang, Y., Du, R.: Ui mobility control in xr: switching ui positionings between static, dynamic, and self entities. In: Proceedings of the 2024 CHI Conference on Human Factors in Computing Systems, pp. 1–12 (2024)
26. Peng, Y., et al.: Navigating the unknown: a chat-based collaborative interface for personalized exploratory tasks. In: Proceedings of the 30th International Conference on Intelligent User Interfaces, IUI '25, p. 1048–1063. Association for Computing Machinery, New York (2025). https://doi.org/10.1145/3708359.3712093
27. Plasson, C., Blanch, R., Nigay, L.: Selection techniques for 3d extended desktop workstation with ar hmd. In: 2022 IEEE International Symposium on Mixed and Augmented Reality (ISMAR), pp. 460–469 (2022). https://doi.org/10.1109/ISMAR55827.2022.00062
28. Prit Kaur, D., Mantri, A., Horan, B.: Design implications for adaptive augmented reality based interactive learning environment for improved concept comprehension in engineering paradigms. Interact. Learn. Environ. 30(4), 589–607 (2022)
29. Segura, R.J., del Pino, F.J., Ogáyar, C.J., Rueda, A.J.: Vr-ocks: a virtual reality game for learning the basic concepts of programming. Comput. Appl. Eng. Educ. 28(1), 31–41 (2020)
30. Shen, Z., Yang, K., Du, W., Zhao, X., Zou, J.: Deepapp: a deep reinforcement learning framework for mobile application usage prediction. In: Proceedings of the 17th Conference on Embedded Networked Sensor Systems, pp. 153–165 (2019)
31. Shin, J.E., Kim, H., Parker, C., Kim, H.I., Oh, S., Woo, W.: Is any room really ok? the effect of room size and furniture on presence, narrative engagement, and usability during a space-adaptive augmented reality game. In: 2019 IEEE International Symposium on Mixed and Augmented Reality (ISMAR), pp. 135–144. IEEE (2019)
32. Wu, T., Terry, M., Cai, C.J.: Ai chains: transparent and controllable human-ai interaction by chaining large language model prompts. In: Proceedings of the 2022 CHI Conference on Human Factors in Computing Systems, pp. 1–22 (2022)
33. Xi, Y., et al.: Towards open-world recommendation with knowledge augmentation from large language models. In: Proceedings of the 18th ACM Conference on Recommender Systems, pp. 12–22 (2024)
34. Yang, F., Chen, Z., Jiang, Z., Cho, E., Huang, X., Lu, Y.: Palr: personalization aware llms for recommendation. arXiv preprint arXiv:2305.07622 (2023)
35. Zhan, Y., Nakajima, T.: Effect of presentation methods on user experiences and perception in vr shopping recommender systems. In: Proceedings of the 2024 Annual International ACM SIGIR Conference on Research and Development in Information Retrieval in the Asia Pacific Region, pp. 241–248 (2024)

System to Support Acquiring Midfoot Strike Running through Intermittent Feedback of Foot Pressure Balance

Ryo Nakamura, Ayumi Ohnishi⑩, Tsutomu Terada$^{(\boxtimes)}$⑩,
and Masahiko Tsukamoto⑩

Graduate School of Engineering, Kobe University, Kobe, Hyogo 657-8501, Japan
`ryo-nakamura@stu.kobe-u.ac.jp`, {`ohnishi,tsutomu,tuka`}`@eedept.kobe-u.ac.jp`

Abstract. This study proposes a system to support the establishment of midfoot strike (MFS), a foot strike pattern where the heel and forefoot contact the ground simultaneously. While MFS is considered to reduce injury risk and improve running performance, it is difficult to acquire and maintain consistently. To promote MFS acquisition, runners must become aware of their ground contact balance and the distribution of plantar pressure during running. The proposed system enhances this awareness by providing intermittent visual feedback, which consists of insoles with pressure sensors placed at the heel and the ball of the foot and an LED mounted on the brim of a cap. When pressure values exceed a threshold, the LED lights up in red (heel) or blue (ball of the foot). Rather than delivering constant feedback, the system provides feedback at fixed intervals, encouraging users to estimate their foot strike internally and later verify its accuracy. This cycle of estimation and correction helps runners gradually learn to identify and correct deviations from MFS on their own. Even after the system is removed, users are expected to have learned to maintain MFS independently. An experiment was conducted to evaluate the system's effectiveness. The results showed that participants who used the system could detect and correct deviations from MFS earlier than those who did not. This suggests that the intermittent feedback is effective for supporting the acquisition and retention of MFS during running.

Keywords: Wearable device · Running · Ground contact balance

1 Introduction

Sports are essential activities for daily life due to their significant health benefits, and among them, long-distance running and marathons are particularly familiar to many people. However, long-distance running carries a high risk of injury, and it has been reported that the injury incidence rate during continuous long-distance running over two years exceeds 50% [1].

P. Delir Haghighi et al. (Eds.): MoMM 2025, LNCS 16329, pp. 40–52, 2026.
https://doi.org/10.1007/978-3-032-11768-7_4

One of the major causes of injury in long-distance running is improper foot strike patterns. These are generally classified into three types: rear foot strike (RFS), where the heel contacts the ground first; mid foot strike (MFS), where the heel and the forefoot contact the ground simultaneously; and fore foot strike (FFS), where the forefoot contacts the ground first. Due to the structure of most modern running shoes, many runners adopt the RFS pattern [2]. However, RFS has been associated with an increased risk of knee injuries and repetitive stress injuries [3]. Similarly, FFS has been reported to increase the risks of injuries to the Achilles tendon and ankles [4]. In contrast, MFS is considered to reduce the risk of injury and is also associated with the potential for improved running performance [5,6]. Therefore, establishing an MFS pattern is generally recommended. However, it has been noted that Asian runners tend to have smaller anterior pelvic tilt angles compared to African American and Caucasian runners, making it more difficult for them to adopt MFS [7].

Various devices have been proposed to support the correction from RFS to MFS. For example, Hassan et al. proposed a system that applies electrical muscle stimulation to the user's calves, forcibly correcting RFS to MFS [8]. With this system, all participants were able to acquire MFS. Other studies have introduced insole devices with lower heel and toe heights [9]. However, these devices have only been evaluated for short-term effectiveness, and not for the long-term establishment of MFS. In this study, the establishment of MFS refers to the ability to maintain MFS over a long period, even without using any system. Specifically, it means that when a runner deviates from MFS during running, they can independently correct their foot strike back to MFS. In contrast, temporary acquisition refers to a state in which the runner cannot correct deviations from MFS without external assistance.

To support long-term MFS establishment, we propose a system that enhances the runner's ability to detect deviations from MFS and correct their foot strike accordingly. To do this, runners must be aware of the distribution of plantar pressure at the moment of ground contact—hereafter referred to as ground contact balance. The proposed system provides intermittent rather than continuous-feedback on ground contact balance. Specifically, feedback is presented every few steps, encouraging users to estimate their foot strike pattern during feedback-free intervals and then verify the accuracy of their estimation when feedback is provided. Through this cycle of estimation and confirmation—thinking about whether MFS is being performed and verifying it afterward—users gradually develop an internal sense of their ground contact balance. As a result, even when they are no longer using the system and no feedback is available, users are expected to detect deviations from MFS and correct their foot strike accordingly.

In this study, we first conducted preliminary experiments to determine the placement of pressure sensors in the insole and the most effective type of feedback. Based on these findings, the proposed system provides users with feedback on ground contact balance, helping them perceive their foot strike and acquire MFS. In the evaluation experiment, we investigated whether participants who used the proposed system for five minutes could correct their foot strike back to MFS after deviating from it.

The remainder of this paper is organized as follows. Section 2 introduces related work. Section 3 describes the proposed system and the preliminary experiments conducted to determine its configuration. Section 4 presents the evaluation of the system's effectiveness and the corresponding results. Finally, Sect. 5 concludes the paper.

2 Related Work

2.1 Studies on Foot Strike Patterns in Long-Distance Running

Foot strike patterns in long-distance running can be categorized into three types: RFS, MFS, and FFS. These strike patterns are closely related to the incidence of injuries in long-distance running. Patellofemoral pain in runners is primarily caused by RFS [10]. Additionally, it has been reported that runners with RFS experience approximately twice the incidence of repetitive stress injuries compared to runners with FFS [3]. Studies on FFS indicate that running with this pattern places significant stress on the ankle joints and Achilles tendon, increasing the risk of injury [4]. In contrast, MFS has been shown to reduce loading on areas prone to stress fractures [5], resulting in a lower risk of injury compared to the other two strike patterns.

Foot strike patterns are also closely related to running speed. Various studies have reported that runners using MFS or FFS tend to run faster than those using RFS. Ardigo et al. and Ogueta-Alday et al. demonstrated that FFS theoretically enables faster running due to its shorter ground contact time compared to RFS [11,12]. Similarly, MFS is associated with faster running speed, and athletics coaches often instruct their students to transition to MFS [6]. In practice, many fast runners adopt MFS or FFS, whereas approximately 70% of general runners still use RFS [2]. From the perspective of improving running speed, it is therefore important to encourage general runners to transition from RFS to MFS or FFS.

Given this background, the present study proposes a system for acquiring MFS, which not only holds promise for improving running speed but also reducing injury risk.

2.2 Studies on the Correction of Foot Strike Patterns

Several studies have proposed devices aimed at correcting RFS to MFS, targeting a broad range of runners regardless of ethnicity. FootStriker, proposed by Hassan et al., is a device that uses electrical muscle stimulation to promote MFS acquisition [8]. In their study, three types of feedback were compared: video-based feedback on foot strike, weak electrical stimulation, and FootStriker. The results showed that only the participants using FootStriker were able to run with MFS. Giandolini et al. developed an insole called the flat midsole, characterized by low drop and low heel height. They reported that wearing this device reduced heel acceleration and shock wave propagation speed, suggesting successful correction to MFS [9].

According to Arima et al., Asian individuals tend to have a smaller anterior pelvic tilt angle compared to African Americans and Caucasians [7]. This anatomical difference may make it more difficult for some Japanese runners to acquire MFS, which requires a more forward-leaning posture during running. Therefore, the use of such corrective systems may be especially beneficial for these individuals.

These studies suggest that temporary acquisition of MFS through device-based correction is possible. However, runners may deviate from MFS due to changes in running speed or environmental conditions. With only temporary acquisition, runners may fail to notice such deviations, highlighting the need for the establishment of MFS.

Therefore, this study proposes a system that supports the long-term establishment of MFS.

2.3   Studies on Correction Through Feedback

Several studies have investigated the effectiveness of correction using feedback in motor tasks. McNair et al. provided auditory feedback on landing sounds to participants during jumping exercises and instructed them to land more softly in subsequent jumps based on the feedback. As a result, they reported a reduction in landing impact forces [13]. Similarly, Cronin et al. demonstrated that both visual and auditory feedback can reduce landing impact during volleyball play [14]. These studies suggest that feedback-based correction is effective in motor tasks. Ohnishi et al. proposed a device designed to improve left-right plantar pressure balance during running by providing frequency-modulated auditory feedback. However, their study observed no significant improvement [15].

Regarding the timing of feedback, Ikegami et al. investigated the effect of visual feedback on error correction in rhythmic movement. In their study, participants performed a rhythmic one-handed movement task, in which they were instructed to swing their arm in time with a metronome. They observed that providing visual feedback every 4 to 5 cycles, rather than every cycle, significantly improved participants' ability to correct timing errors [16]. These findings suggest that intermittent-feedback presentation may be effective in enhancing the user's ability to perceive ground contact balance. The system proposed in this study aims to improve the user's ability to correct to MFS through intermittent feedback.

3   Proposed System

3.1   Overview and Objectives

This study aims to develop a system that enables users to correct deviations from MFS and eventually internalize the ability to maintain MFS without relying on external feedback. To achieve this, the system provides the following three key functions.

1: Detection of ground contact balance.
2: Real-time feedback to inform users of their foot strike pattern.
3: intermittent-feedback to support self-estimation and internalization of MFS.

3.2 Sensor Placement

To determine appropriate pressure sensor placement for the proposed system, a preliminary experiment was conducted using a high-resolution multi-point plantar pressure sensor. The goal of this experiment was to identify whether it is possible to distinguish between foot strike patterns (RFS and MFS) using only two pressure sensors, one at the heel and one at the ball of the foot. While the multi-point sensor provides detailed pressure distribution across the entire foot, such high-resolution hardware is not practical for lightweight, low-power wearable systems. Therefore, we aimed to determine the optimal sensor positions that could be transferred to a simplified insole design using only two sensors. Three participants were recruited for the experiment: one male in his twenties with six years of long-distance running experience who had already acquired MFS, and two male participants in their twenties who had not acquired MFS. All participants wore the multi-point pressure insole and ran on a treadmill using both RFS and MFS foot strike patterns. For participants who had not acquired MFS, the MFS trial was performed based on a prior explanation and instruction, and their attempts were recorded for analysis. It was found that:

- The participant who had acquired MFS showed a contact timing difference of 63.8 ms during RFS and 12.4 ms during MFS.
- A participant who had not acquired MFS showed 48.3 ms during RFS and 49.8 ms when attempting MFS.

Based on this analysis, it was determined that placing sensors in the proposed system at the positions corresponding to sensor 15 (heel) and sensor 77 (ball of the foot) in the multi-point pressure insole would be appropriate. These locations reliably captured the contact timing necessary to distinguish MFS from other foot strike patterns. Figure 1 shows the sensor layout of the multi-point pressure insole used in the preliminary experiment. Sensors 15 and 77 were chosen as they recorded the highest average pressure values in the heel and toe regions, respectively. The final implementation adopts the placement shown in Fig. 2, where actual FSR 402 sensors are positioned at the selected sites on the insole to capture contact events.

Figure 3 shows the procedure for measuring the difference in contact timing using the pressure sensor values obtained with the sensors used in the proposed system. The proposed system employs FSR 402 pressure sensors and a microcontroller module (M5StickC Plus) to sample pressure values at 100 Hz. When the heel sensor exceeds a threshold of 3000, it is interpreted as heel contact, and the same applies to the ball of the foot.

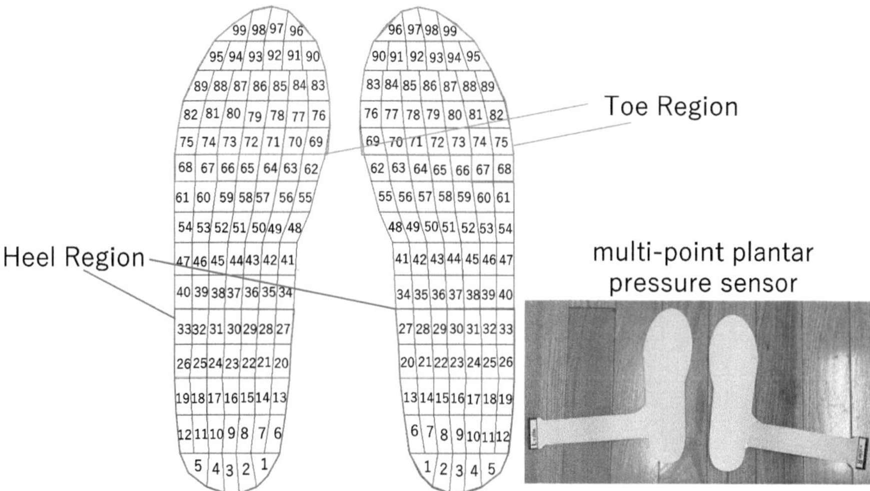

Fig. 1. Sensor layout on multi-point pressure insole for premininary experiment

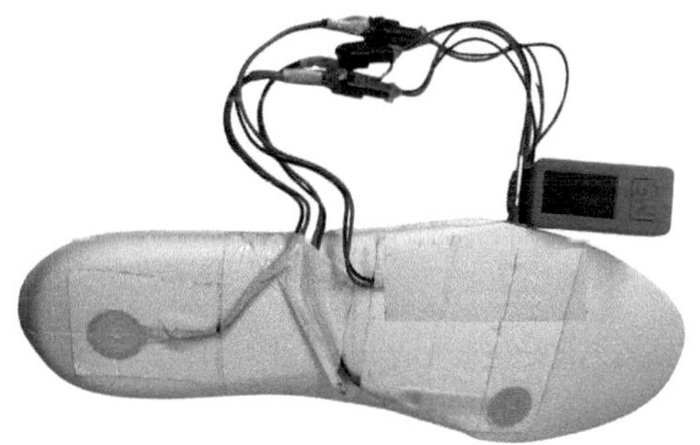

Fig. 2. Pressure sensor placement on the insole

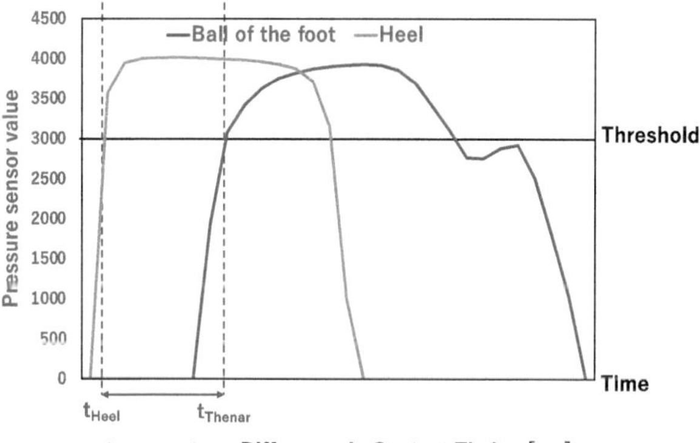

Fig. 3. Measurement procedure for contact timing difference

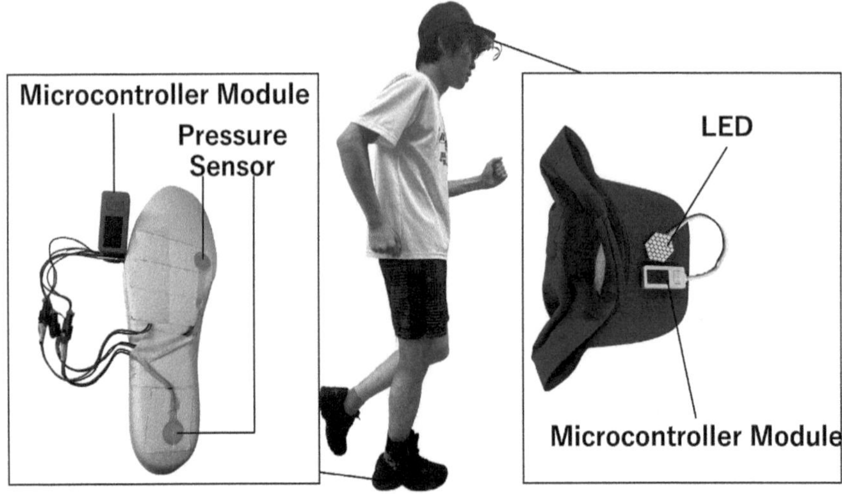

Fig. 4. Proposed System

3.3 System Configuration and Feedback Implementation

To determine the optimal feedback modality to be implemented in the proposed system, a preliminary experiment was conducted. This experiment aimed to evaluate which type of feedback is most effective in promoting accurate and timely correction toward MFS. The experiment involved a total of eight male participants in their twenties who had not acquired MFS. Each of the four feedback modalities—visual presentation, visual instruction, auditory presentation, and auditory instruction—was tested by two participants. In the experimental procedure, participants first ran without feedback for one minute to record the baseline difference in contact timing between the heel and the ball of the foot. Then, they ran for three minutes with one of the feedback types. Finally, they ran for an additional one minute without feedback, during which the post-intervention contact timing difference was measured. The effectiveness of each feedback modality was evaluated based on the amount of reduction in contact timing difference before and after feedback.

As a result, the visual presentation feedback showed the greatest improvement and was thus selected for use in the proposed system. Figure 4 shows the configuration of the proposed system. The final system consists of an insole and a cap. The insole contains two pressure sensors (Interlink Electronics, FSR402), and the cap includes a hexagonal RGB LED board (M5Stack Unit HEX, NeoPixel-compatible). During the swing phase, the LEDs remain off. When the heel sensor is triggered, the front half of the LED panel lights up blue. When the ball of the foot sensor is triggered, the other half lights up red.

When MFS is correctly performed, both colors illuminate simultaneously. Feedback is shown for 2 s every 7 steps, encouraging the user to estimate their own contact balance during the off-period and verify their accuracy once feedback resumes. This cycle of estimation and confirmation helps users internalize MFS. To reduce device complexity and improve usability, the insole is worn only on the right foot. The LED cap is controlled using M5StickC Plus (M5Stack).

This streamlined system effectively supports both the acquisition and autonomous maintenance of MFS in runners.

4   Evaluation

In this section, we describe an experiment conducted to investigate whether users can acquire the ability to correct their foot strike back to MFS when deviating from it, using the proposed system. This experiment was approved by the Human Ethics Committee of Graduate School of Engineering, Kobe University (Permission number: 06–35) and was carried out according to the guidelines of the Declaration of Helsinki.

4.1   Experimental Design

The proposed system alternates between periods with and without feedback, introducing intentional intervals between feedback presentations. This design encourages users to explore how to improve their ground contact balance during the feedback-free periods, thereby enhancing their ability to perceive it independently. This experiment aimed to examine whether the presence or absence of such feedback intervals affects the user's ability to correct their foot strike pattern when deviating from MFS.

The experimental setup is shown in Fig. 5. Participants used the proposed system while running on a treadmill. The participants were ten males in their twenties who had not acquired MFS and had not participated in the preliminary experiments.

To evaluate the effect of feedback intervals, we compared two conditions: a continuous-feedback condition with no interval, and an intermittent-feedback condition with intentional feedback intervals. Five participants were assigned to each condition.

4.2   Experimental Procedure

The flow of the experiment is illustrated in Fig. 6. To assess each participant's baseline ground contact balance, they first ran for one minute without any feedback. This condition is referred to as *Before Feedback (FB-before)*. Next, participants ran for five minutes while receiving visual feedback according to their assigned condition (continuous or intermittent). This is referred to as *During Feedback (FB-during)*. After that, participants again ran for three minutes without feedback, referred to as *After Feedback (FB-after)*. The treadmill speed was initially set to 9 km/h for all conditions. However, during the FB-during (5 min) and FB-after (3 min) periods, the speed was changed at a specific timing: when 2 min remained in each phase, the speed was increased to 12 km/h. After running

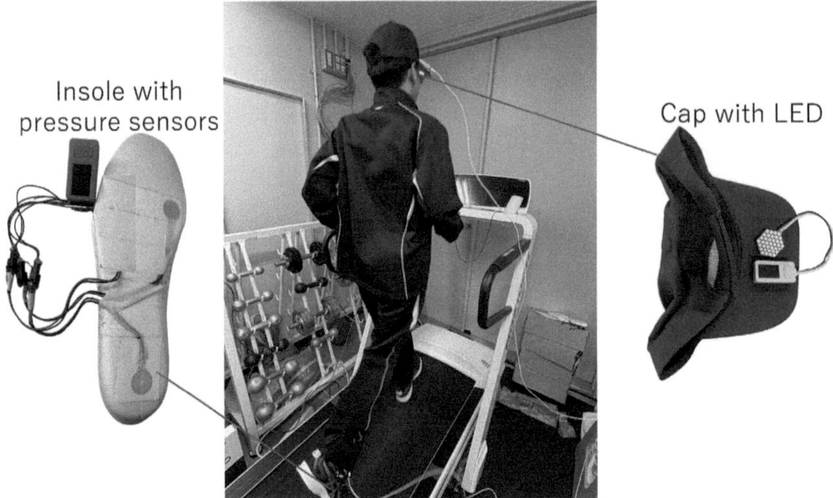

Fig. 5. Experimental setup

at 12 km for 1 min, the speed was returned to 9 km/h for the remaining 1 min. The state before the speed change is referred to as *Pre-change*, the period at 12 km/h as *Post-increase*, and the final period after returning to 9 km/h as *Post-decrease*. This manipulation aimed to determine whether participants could correct their foot strike back to MFS after being disturbed by changes in running speed. It was expected that participants receiving intermittent feedback would be able to quickly adjust back to MFS even after disruption caused by the speed change. Therefore, under the intermittent condition, the difference in contact timing during the Post-increase and Post-decrease phases was expected to decrease compared to FB-before. Each participant completed the experiment twice under the same condition, with a one-week interval between sessions. After completing the experiment, participants responded to a questionnaire asking whether they noticed any deviations from MFS during feedback or speed changes.

Condition	FB-before	FB-during			FB-after		
State		Pre-change	Post-increase	Post-decrease	Pre-change	Post-increase	Post-decrease
Time	1 min	3 min	1 min	1 min	1 min	1 min	1 min
Speed	9 km/h	9 km/h	12 km/h	9 km/h	9 km/h	12 km/h	9 km/h

Fig. 6. Experimental Procedure

4.3   Evaluation Metrics

In this experiment, the evaluation was based on the same metric used in the preliminary experiment for selecting the feedback type: the difference in contact timing. The contact timing difference was measured under each condition, and the average value was calculated.

4.4   Experimental Results

Table 1 shows the average contact timing difference for each condition. The values represent the averages from two experimental sessions conducted by five participants per condition. From the table, it can be observed that, compared to the continuous-feedback condition, the intermittent-feedback condition resulted in a greater reduction in contact timing difference from FB-before to FB-after. In addition, under the continuous-feedback condition, the contact timing difference increased progressively across the three phases of the FB-after period. In contrast, under the intermittent-feedback condition, the value decreased in the Post-decrease phase compared to the Post-increase phase.

The average contact timing difference for each of the five participants was calculated for each step during the 1-min periods after speed increase and after speed decrease in the FB-after phase. The data were further separated by feedback interval type and trial number. Figures 7 and 8 present graphs of these results based on a total of 55 steps. The vertical axis represents the contact timing difference in milliseconds, and the horizontal axis indicates the number of right foot contacts. In both graphs, the contact timing difference was initially high immediately after the speed change. While the values remained high under the continuous feedback condition, the values began to decreases around the 20th step under the intermittent feedback condition.

Table 1. Mean difference in contact timing for each condition [ms]

Condition	FB-before	FB-after		
		Pre-change	Post-increase	Post-decrease
Continuous	45.5	33.7	37.3	41.2
Intermittent	44.7	24.4	29.8	28.9

4.5   Discussion

This experiment was conducted to investigate whether the proposed system could help users acquire the ability to correct their foot strike back to MFS after deviation. The results showed that the average contact timing difference after feedback (FB-after) was smaller in the intermittent-feedback condition compared

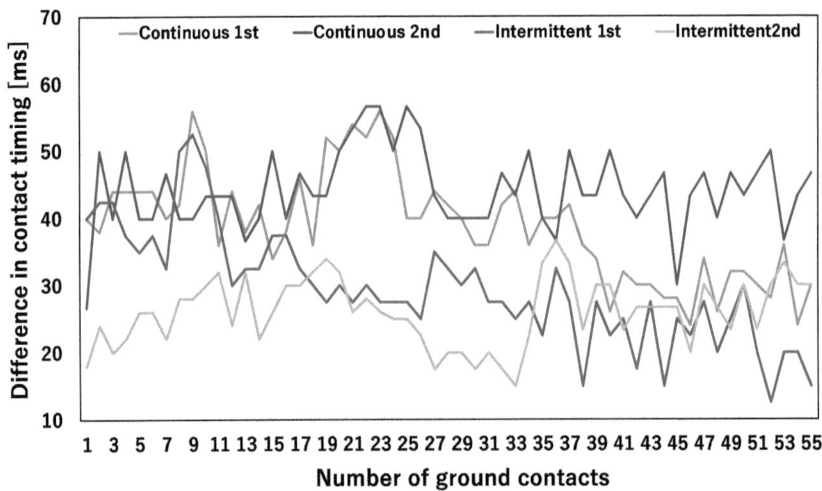

Fig. 7. Difference in contact timing (FB-after, Post-increase)

to the continuous-feedback condition. This indicates that intermittent-feedback presentation is more effective in developing the ability to run with MFS.

The objective of this experiment was to intentionally disrupt MFS by changing the running speed, and to evaluate whether participants could recognize the deviation and make corrections accordingly. The results suggested that MFS tended to be disrupted across all conditions following speed changes. Under the intermittent condition, participants appeared to correct their MFS deviation after approximately 20 steps. In contrast, under the continuous condition, participants generally did not demonstrate a clear return to MFS within the observed timeframe.

Furthermore, linear approximation was applied to all lines in Figs. 7 and 8, and the slopes of the fitted lines were calculated. In Fig. 7, the slope for the first trial under continuous feedback was –0.335, and for the second trial it was 0.015. Under intermittent feedback, the first trial yielded a slope of –0.431, and the second trial yielded 0.047. In Fig. 8, the slope under continuous feedback was –0.250 in the first trial and –0.470 in the second trial. For intermittent feedback, the slopes were –0.507 and –0.129 in the first and second trials, respectively.

These values indicate that while the proposed system with intermittent feedback did not consistently outperform continuous feedback across all trials, it tended to show more favorable trends in the first trial under intermittent conditions. In particular, a relatively large negative slope was observed in the first intermittent-feedback trial, suggesting that contact timing differences decreased more rapidly in that condition. Although the results are not entirely conclusive, they provide partial support for the effectiveness of intermittent feedback in enhancing users' ability to self-correct toward MFS.

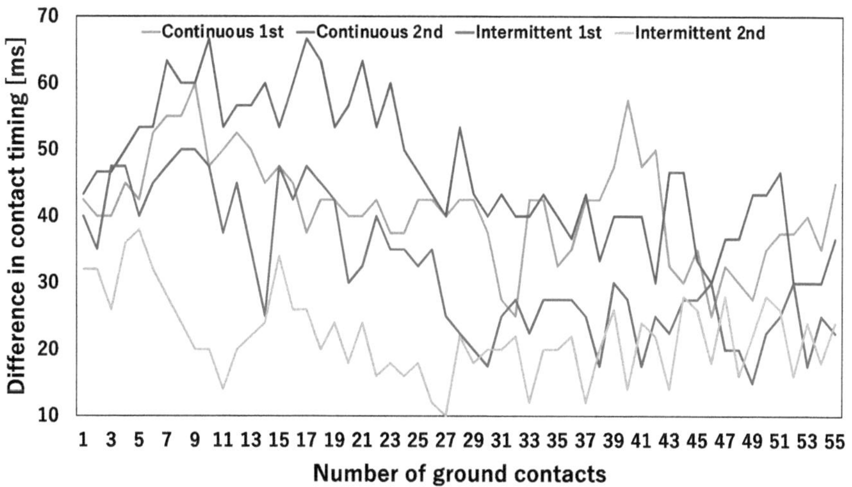

Fig. 8. Difference in contact timing (FB-after, Post-decrease)

5   Conclusion

In this study, we proposed a system designed to enhance a runner's ability to recognize and correct deviations from MFS during running through intermittent-feedback presentation. We conducted preliminary experiments to determine the optimal placement of pressure sensors on the insole and to identify the most effective feedback content for supporting the correction to MFS. As a result, the proposed system consists of an insole with pressure sensors placed at the ball of the foot and heel, and an LED mounted on the brim of a cap that provides visual feedback at regular intervals. When the pressure value from the heel sensor exceeds a predefined threshold, the front half of the LED lights up red; when the pressure value from the ball of the foot sensor exceeds the threshold, the remaining half lights up blue. The evaluation assessed whether the system enables users to regain MFS after deviation. The results showed that the proposed system successfully supported correction to MFS and helped users acquire the ability to restore their foot strike pattern. Therefore, it was found that intermittent-feedback is more effective than continuous-feedback for establishing MFS.

In future work, we plan to develop an insole with sensors placed in positions that more accurately distinguish foot strike patterns. Additionally, we aim to reexamine feedback methods better suited for improving ground contact balance awareness and upgrade the system to support low-latency wireless communication.

Acknowledgement. This work was supported in part by JST Moonshot R&D Program Grant Number JPMJMS229C.

References

1. Messier, S.P., et al.: A 2-year prospective cohort study of overuse running injuries: the runners and injury longitudinal study (TRAILS). Am. J. Sports Med. **46**(9), 2211–2221 (2018)
2. Hasegawa, H., Yamauchi, T., Kraemer, W.J.: Foot strike patterns of runners at the 15-km point during an elite-level half marathon. J. Strength Cond. Res. **21**(3), 888–893 (2007)
3. Daoud, A.I., Geissler, G.J., Wang, F., Saretsky, J., Daoud, Y.A., Lieberman, D.E.: Foot strike and injury rates in endurance runners: a retrospective study. Med. Sci. Sports Exerc. **44**(7), 1325–1334 (2012)
4. Xu, Y., Yuan, P., Wang, R., Wang, D., Liu, J., Zhou, H.: Effects of foot strike techniques on running biomechanics: a systematic review and meta-analysis. Sports Health **13**(1), 71–77 (2020)
5. Giandolini, M., et al.: Impact reduction during running: efficiency of simple acute interventions in recreational runners. Eur. J. Appl. Physiol. **113**(3), 599–609 (2012)
6. Abran, G., et al.: Current perception and practice of athletics coaches about the modification of footstrike pattern in endurance runners: a survey. Int. . Sports Sci. Coach. **17**(6), 1345–1353 (2022)
7. Arima, H., et al.: Differences in lumbar and pelvic parameters among African American, caucasian and Asian populations. Eur. Spine J. **27**(12), 2990–2998 (2018)
8. Hassan, M., Daiber, F., Wiehr, F., Kosmalla, F., Krüger, A.: FootStriker: an EMS-based foot strike assistant for running. ACM Interact. Mobile Wearable Ubiq. Technol. **1**(1), 1–18 (2017)
9. Giandolini, M., Horvais, N., Farges, Y., Samozino, P., Morin, J.: Impact reduction through long-term intervention in recreational runners: midfoot strike pattern versus low-drop/low-heel height footwear. Eur. J. Appl. Physiol. **113**(8), 2077–2090 (2013)
10. Santos, A.F., Nakagawa, T.H., Serrão, F.V., Ferber, R.: Patellofemoral joint stress measured across three different running techniques. Gait Post. **68**, 37–43 (2019)
11. Ardigo, L.P., Lafortuna, C., Minetti, A.E., Mognoni, P., Saibene, F.: Metabolic and mechanical aspects of foot landing type, forefoot and rearfoot strike, in human running. Acta Physiol. Scand. **155**(1), 17–22 (1995)
12. Ogueta-Alday, A., Rodríguez-Marroyo, J.A., García-López, J.: Rearfoot striking runners are more economical than midfoot strikers. Med. Sci. Sports Exerc. **46**(3), 580–585 (2014)
13. McNair, P.J., Prapavessis, H., Callender, K.: Decreasing landing forces: effect of instruction. Br. J. Sports Med. **34**(4), 293–296 (2000)
14. Cronin, J.B., Bressel, E., Finn, L.: Augmented feedback reduces ground reaction forces in the landing phase of the volleyball spike jump. J. Sport Rehabil. **17**(2), 148–159 (2008)
15. Ohnishi, A., Nishiyama, I., Terada, T., Tsukamoto, M.: An auditory feedback system to improve the foot pressure balance for runners. In: 17th International Conference on Advances in Mobile Computing & Multimedia, pp. 94–101 (2020)
16. Ikegami, T., Hirashima, M., Osu, R., Nozaki, D.: Intermittent visual feedback can boost motor learning of rhythmic movements: evidence for error feedback beyond cycles. J. Neurosci. **32**(2), 653–657 (2012)

Ear Canal Pressure-Based Oral Gesture Recognition for Saxophone Performance

Ayana Hamagawa[1], Hiroki Watanabe[1]([⊠]), Hiroya Miura[2], and Yoshinari Takegawa[1]

[1] Future University Hakodate, 116-2 Kamedanakano-cho, Hakodate, Hokkaido 041-8655, Japan
hwata@fun.ac.jp
[2] RIKEN Center for Advanced Intelligence Project, 1-4-1 Nihonbashi, Chuo-ku, Tokyo 103-0027, Japan

Abstract. In saxophone performance, the shape of the mouth and the use of breath are crucial factors. However, because these elements are not visually observable, mastering the instrument can be challenging. This study proposes a method for recognizing mouth movements during saxophone playing by focusing on changes in ear canal pressure. Since ear canal pressure varies depending on the positional relationship between the mandible and the ear canal, it serves as an effective non-contact means of measuring mouth movement. We developed a classification model to distinguish four representative types of mouth movements used in saxophone performance. Features were extracted from the pressure data and classified using base models including SVM, KNN, and Random Forest. Logistic regression was applied to integrate the outputs of these classifiers. An evaluation experiment involving five participants achieved classification F-scores ranging from 89.9% to 98.3%, demonstrating the effectiveness of the proposed method. The results of this study provide a foundation for a performance support system that enables saxophonists to objectively recognize their mouth usage.

Keywords: Ear canal pressure · Saxophone · Hearable · Earable · Performance learning support

1 Introduction

The saxophone is a woodwind instrument that produces sound by vibrating a thin wooden piece called a reed, as shown in Fig. 1(b). Since players produce sound by placing the mouthpiece in their mouth, as illustrated in Fig. 1(b), properly forming the shape of the mouth is a crucial factor that significantly affects the quality of performance. The shape of the player's mouth and how they use the surrounding muscles is referred to as the embouchure [14], and it has a major impact on musical elements such as tone and pitch.

P. Delir Haghighi et al. (Eds.): MoMM 2025, LNCS 16329, pp. 53–67, 2026.
https://doi.org/10.1007/978-3-032-11768-7_5

However, the embouchure is difficult to observe and self-aware of, which increases the barriers to learning. Current learning methods include instructional books, video tutorials, and face-to-face lessons with experienced instructors. However, these methods come with constraints such as cost, location, and time, and also present difficulties in reproducing the same embouchure during self-practice. Xu has pointed out that demonstrations and corrections by instructors are effective for acquiring proper playing techniques, and that it is difficult to achieve this through self-study alone [19]. Moreover, methods for objectively and quantitatively measuring mouth movements during performance are limited, and it has been reported that there is a lack of effective teaching materials or tools that can provide useful feedback, particularly for beginners [14].

To address these challenges, this study proposes a method for recognizing mouth movements based on changes in ear canal pressure, focusing on the deformation of the ear canal that occurs in response to head and jaw movements. By utilizing ear canal pressure, it becomes possible to measure mouth motion in a quantitative and non-invasive manner. In this study, we use OpenEarable [15], an earphone-type smart device equipped with an ear canal pressure sensor (Fig. 1(a)), to measure pressure changes inside the ear canal associated with mouth movements. The barometric sensor embedded in OpenEarable allows for continuous acquisition of ear canal pressure data. The obtained pressure data reflects changes in the shape of the ear canal caused by mouth movements, and these patterns exhibit characteristic variations depending on the specific motion. We extract features from these pressure variations and apply machine learning techniques to classify and recognize different types of mouth movements.

In the experiment, participants wore OpenEarable on one ear and reproduced four types of mouth movements commonly used during saxophone performance. Data were collected and used to develop a classification model, and its recognition performance was evaluated. This study introduces a non-invasive and simple measurement method using ear-mounted devices to support musical instrument performance, capturing data on mouth movements during saxophone playing, which are difficult to observe from the outside, and quantitatively evaluating them. This is expected to provide musicians with objective feedback and serve as a new foundation for supporting the acquisition of appropriate embouchure. The main contributions of this study are summarized as follows:

- We demonstrated the potential for non-invasive and quantitative measurement of mouth movements during saxophone performance by utilizing changes in ear canal pressure.
- Using a machine learning-based classification model, we confirmed that four representative mouth movements in saxophone playing can be recognized with an accuracy of 90%–98%.
- The proposed method has the potential to be applied to support systems that objectively assess embouchure and assist players in acquiring proper playing form.

– We are the first to apply ear-canal pressure sensing to saxophone embouchure recognition, extending in-ear sensing research from general motion recognition into the domain of music performance learning support.

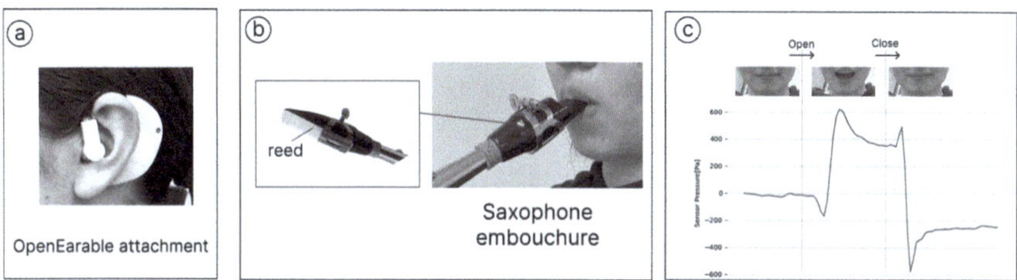

Fig. 1. a) OpenEarable is an earphone-type hearable device [15]. The sensor part can be easily worn by hooking it to the ear. b) Examples of saxophone embouchure and reed c) Examples of face-related movements and the ear canal pressure values observed during these movements.

2   Related Work

2.1   Embouchure Acquisition and Analytical Methods

The formation and control of the embouchure are essential skills in saxophone performance, influencing tone quality, pitch, and expressiveness. However, mastering the embouchure requires significant time and experience. Teal noted that it is one of the most difficult aspects for beginners, requiring sustained practice [17], and Xu demonstrated its acoustic impact on reed vibration and airflow [18]. While its importance is widely recognized, beginners often struggle to evaluate their own embouchure. To address this, studies have explored embouchure analysis using MRI [9] and thermography [5]. However, these methods involve bulky equipment and restrict natural performance conditions. In this study, we estimate mouth movements using ear canal pressure data measured via an in-ear sensor. This approach enables simple, quantitative, and non-intrusive evaluation of embouchure during natural playing, overcoming limitations of prior methods.

2.2   Motion Recognition with Hearables

Research has been conducted on head and motion recognition using hearable devices [1,3,13]. CanalSense, proposed by Ando et al., measures pressure changes in the ear canal using a pressure sensor worn in the ear, and has demonstrated the ability to classify 11 types of movements—including facial expressions, jaw motion, and head posture—with an average recognition accuracy of 87.6% [2]. In addition, the system achieved a recognition accuracy of 87.6% in a task that classified mouth opening into four levels. This study highlights the strong correlation between ear canal pressure and head movement, suggesting the potential for motion recognition using compact and non-invasive sensor devices.

2.3 Comparison Between Ear Canal Pressure Sensing and Other Methods

To classify mouth movements during saxophone performance, we compared cameras, electromyography (EMG) sensors, and accelerometers. This study adopted an external auditory canal pressure sensor. Cameras offer high spatial resolution but depend on lighting conditions and field-of-view, and raise privacy concerns [11,12]. EMG can directly measure muscle activity but is susceptible to noise and requires complex, stable attachment [6–8]. Accelerometers are compact and easy to handle, but they must be placed near the lips to capture fine movements and may interfere with playing [10,16]. In contrast, the external auditory canal pressure sensor can be used simply by placing it in the ear. It is unaffected by lighting or visual obstructions, enables natural playing while protecting privacy, and is therefore the most suitable choice for this study.

3 Proposed Method

3.1 Overview

This study aims to establish a method for recognizing mouth movements to support embouchure acquisition in saxophone performance. To this end, we focus on ear canal pressure data obtained from an earphone-type sensor worn in the ear. Features are extracted from this data, and the mouth state is classified and predicted using machine learning techniques. The proposed method allows for measurement without interfering with oral movements during performance and can capture pressure variations corresponding to specific mouth actions.

Potential applications of this method include providing feedback on the embouchure state to performers, enabling early detection of incorrect habits and supporting effective practice. Additionally, by recording desirable mouth movements during lessons and comparing them with those during individual practice, performers can objectively assess their current state and better acquire proper embouchure techniques. For instructors, presenting objective data may facilitate more accurate guidance and support.

In this paper, as a first step toward supporting embouchure training, we focus on whether four key types of mouth movements in saxophone performance can be successfully distinguished.

3.2 Principle of Ear Canal Pressure Sensing

The ear canal is a narrow tubular structure that extends from the entrance of the ear to the eardrum, and its shape undergoes slight changes due to the movement of surrounding muscles and bones (Fig. 2). Facial movements such as jaw opening and closing, lip motion, and expressions affect the shape of the ear canal through these musculoskeletal structures [4]. In this study, we focus on the dynamic response characteristics of ear canal pressure and attempt to classify mouth movements inferred during saxophone performance (Fig. 3) into four major motion categories, based on the corresponding patterns of pressure variation.

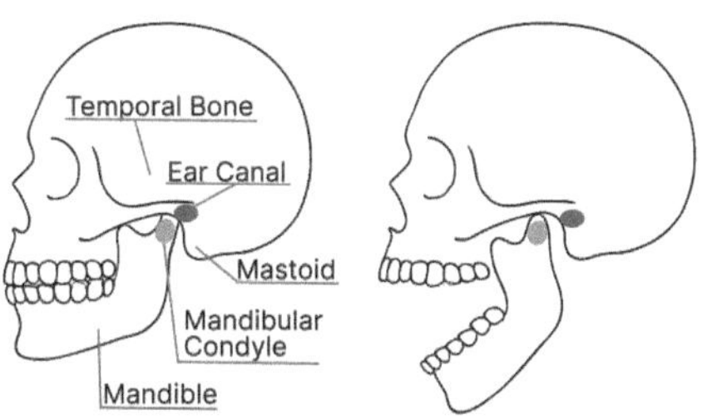

Fig. 2. Skeletal structure around the ear canal

3.3 Targeted Mouth Movements for Classification

In this study, we focused on mouth-area movements involved in saxophone performance and targeted the four types of motion patterns shown in Fig. 3. All of these are deeply related to fundamental aspects of saxophone playing, such as embouchure formation and jaw control. Below, we describe the significance of each movement.

Pattern 1: Open Mouth → Close Mouth
This movement constitutes a critical factor that exerts substantial influence on pitch, tone quality, and overall performance stability.
Pattern 2: Bring Chin Forward → Pull Chin Back
This jaw movement regulates reed pressure and angle, indispensable for flexible performance.
Pattern 3: Bring Chin Forward → Open Mouth
This action adjusts airflow and reed contact, enabling flexible embouchure and dynamic variation.
Pattern 4: Bring Chin Forward → Close Mouth
This movement stabilizes the embouchure and increases reed pressure; tongue and palate positioning plays a role in shaping tonal quality.

These four motion patterns should not be regarded merely as physical movements, but rather as integral components of the physical control structure that underpins performance technique. By treating them as classification targets, we aim to establish a foundation for indirectly capturing mouth movements during performance through variations in ear canal pressure.

3.4 Ear Canal Pressure Waveforms Corresponding to Mouth Movements

Ear canal pressure exhibits characteristic changes depending on the type of movement. To illustrate this, Fig. 3 shows examples of facial movements measured in this study and the corresponding ear canal pressure waveforms. As shown in the figure, each type of movement results in a distinct waveform.

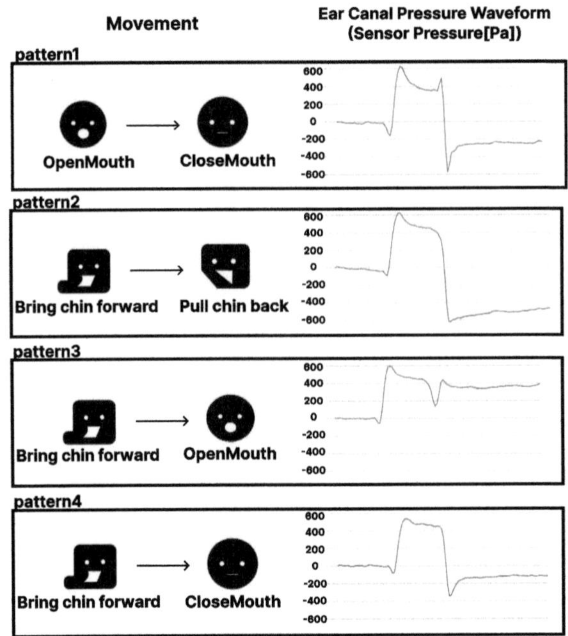

Fig. 3. Mouth Movement Patterns and Corresponding Ear Canal Pressure Waveforms

Open Mouth → Close Mouth

The waveform dips slightly, then rises and falls sharply before stabilizing, reflecting jaw movement which changes the volume of the ear canal, increasing pressure as the jaw drops while the mouth is open.

Bring Chin Forward → Pull Chin Back Movement

This movement generates a waveform characterized by a gradual rise in pressure followed by a smooth decline, suggesting that while skeletal movement due to jaw displacement significantly affects ear canal pressure, delayed recovery due to muscle elasticity also contributes to the waveform shape.

Combined Movements (Bring Chin Forward → Open/Close Mouth)

When multiple actions occur in sequence, the waveform exhibits complex variations. This implies that different movements impose distinct mechanical effects on the ear canal, resulting in superimposed waveform changes.

As demonstrated above, ear canal pressure waveforms exhibit distinct variation patterns depending on the movement type, and these contain valuable information for distinguishing movements. Therefore, by extracting features from these waveforms and applying machine learning, it becomes possible to estimate the corresponding mouth movements.

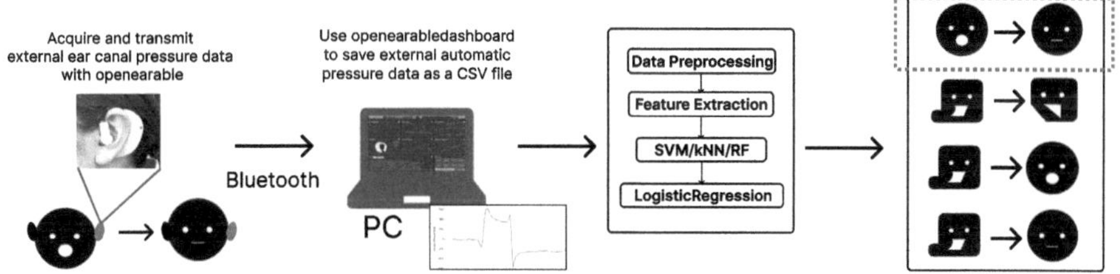

Fig. 4. System configuration

3.5   System Configuration

The overall processing flow of the proposed system is illustrated in Fig. 4. This system is designed to non-invasively and naturally record and recognize mouth movements during saxophone performance. To acquire ear canal pressure data, we employed OpenEarable [15], an ear-hook-type smart device equipped with an air pressure sensor that can be comfortably worn inside the ear without interfering with performance. The sensor was consistently worn on the left ear for all participants to reduce variability in sensor placement. In addition, multiple sizes of earpieces were prepared, and each participant selected the most suitable size to ensure proper sealing and improve the reliability of pressure measurements. This setup was intended to enable stable acquisition of subtle pressure fluctuations inside the ear canal. The collected ear canal pressure data were transmitted via Bluetooth to a PC connected to OpenEarableDashboard and stored in CSV format. The data were sampled at a frequency of 30 Hz. Since mouth movements alter the shape of the ear canal, the corresponding ear canal pressure also exhibits characteristic fluctuation patterns depending on the type of movement. This study leverages this relationship by extracting statistical features from the pressure waveforms and applying a machine learning model to classify the motions.

To reduce the influence of initial sensor pressure and environmental factors, a preprocessing step was applied to normalize the data based on the baseline pressure measured immediately after device attachment. This differential normalization effectively suppresses the impact of noise caused by environmental pressure changes or differences in earpiece fit, allowing for more accurate extraction of movement-induced pressure variations.

3.6   Classification Model

In this study, we constructed a supervised learning model to classify mouth movement patterns based on ear canal pressure waveforms, using statistical features as input. The pressure fluctuation patterns differ depending on the type of movement, in terms of amplitude, rate of change, trends, and the frequency of local extrema. To quantitatively capture these differences, a set of statistical features was designed and extracted (Table 1). For the classification model, we employed

Table 1. Summary of Extracted Features

Feature
Average of differential waveform per data
Standard deviation pressure per data
Range of maximum to minimum pressure per data
Mean of the 10 largest pressure per utterance
Mean of the 10 lowest pressure per utterance

a stacking ensemble learning approach that combines multiple base classifiers. Specifically, Support Vector Machine (SVM), k-Nearest Neighbors (KNN), and Random Forest were used as base learners, and their prediction results were fed into a logistic regression model as meta-features. This architecture allows the system to complement the different learning biases and representational abilities of each method, thereby improving classification performance beyond what is achievable with a single model. All models were implemented using scikit-learn library[1], a machine learning library for Python. The detailed parameter settings for the classifier are as follows:

- Support Vector Machine (SVM): radial basis function (RBF) kernel, $C = 1.0$, $\gamma = $ `scale`, probability estimation enabled, `random_state` $= 42$.
- k-Nearest Neighbors (kNN): number of neighbors $k = 3$.
- Random Forest: number of trees $n\_estimators = 100$, `random_state` $= 42$.
- Meta model: Logistic Regression with scikit-learn default parameters (L2 regularization, $C = 1.0$, solver $= $ `lbfgs`, max_iter $= 100$).

For evaluation, we adopted 5-fold Stratified K-Fold cross-validation with shuffle enabled and `random_state` $= 42$.

4   Evaluation

4.1   Experimental Procedure

In this study, we examine whether it is possible to classify the mouth movements assumed during saxophone playing using the ear canal pressure data acquired from OpenEarable. This is intended to be applied as a technological basis for recognizing mouth movements during saxophone playing, and this experiment aims to clarify the classification performance. Five participants (two with saxophone experience and three with no experience) between the ages of 22 and 25 participated in the experiment. The subjects performed the measurements while sitting on a chair. At the beginning of the experiment, the four target mouth movements shown in Fig. 3 were explained to the participants using both the figure and verbal instructions to ensure they could accurately reproduce

---

[1] https://scikit-learn.org/stable/.

each movement. Each participant was then asked to select the earpiece(11 mm, 12 mm, or 13 mm in diameter) that best fits his or her ears, and to wear the OpenEarable over his or her left ears. The sampling frequency of the air pressure sensor was set to 30 Hz, and four seconds of air pressure data were collected in one trial. All measurements were taken with the mouth closed, changing the shape of the mouth every second and ending with the mouth closed. Each movement was repeated 30 times, for a total of 120 sets of data for the four types of movements. A total of 600 trials (30 rounds of 4 different face-related movements by 5 participants) of barometer values were collected in this experiment.

4.2   Result

To evaluate the performance of the classification model, an individual classifier was developed for each participant, and the discrimination accuracy for four types of mouth movements was verified. For the evaluation, we used five-fold cross-validation with Stratified K-Fold. All motion data (4 classes × 30 times) were equally divided into 5 groups, and in each division, 4 groups were used for training and the remaining 1 group was used for validation. The main evaluation index for classification accuracy is the percentage of correct responses.

As a result, a high discrimination accuracy was obtained for all five participants, as shown in Table 2. The highest F-score was obtained by P1 with 98.3%, and the lowest by P5 with 89.9%. The overall average F-score was 93.6%, indicating consistently high performance across participants. In order to confirm the classification tendencies of each of the four classes in more detail, the confusion matrix is shown in Fig. 5. It is suggested that this method effectively captures the pattern of ear canal pressure fluctuation in response to each participant's movement.

Table 2. Classification performance for each participant. P1 and P2 are experienced saxophone players, and P3–P5 are non-experienced. All metrics are shown as macro-averages over four classes.[%]

Group	Participant	Accuracy	Precision	Recall	F-score
Experienced saxophone player	P1	98.3	98.3	98.3	98.3
	P2	90.8	90.9	90.8	90.8
No saxophone playing experience	P3	97.5	97.7	97.5	97.5
	P4	91.6	91.6	91.6	91.6
	P5	90.0	90.3	90.0	89.9
Average		93.6	93.7	93.6	93.6
Standard Deviation		3.52	3.61	3.68	3.72

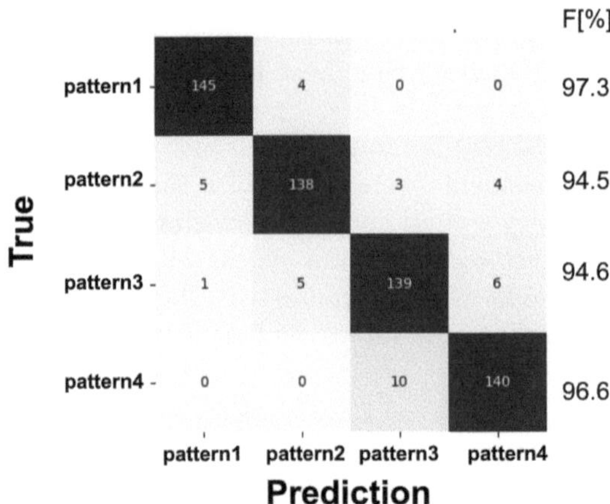

Fig. 5. Confusion Matrix and Per-Class F-scores for mouth movement patterns

5   Discussion

5.1   Analysis and Discussion Based on Experimental Results

In this study, we developed a model to classify mouth movements during saxophone performance using an ear canal pressure sensor and evaluated it with five participants. As a result, we achieved a high average F-score of 93.6%, with all participants reaching F-score of over 89.9%. This indicates that each mouth movement produced distinct variation patterns in the ear canal pressure waveform, which were successfully captured as statistical features, and that the stacking-based classification model effectively learned the differences between the movements with high precision.

Variations in classification accuracy were observed among participants. In particular, P5 showed slightly lower accuracy compared to the others. This may be attributed to differences in the sealing performance of the earpieces, which could have affected the accuracy of pressure fluctuation measurements. In fact, P5 used an earpiece with a diameter of 11 mm, which was smaller than those used by other participants (12 mm). This likely resulted in relatively lower airtightness within the ear canal, potentially degrading the quality of pressure sensing.

Table 3 shows the F-score for each movement class, comparing experienced and inexperienced saxophone players. Focusing on the movement patterns, those that end with "Close Mouth" as the second action (e.g., Open Mouth → Close Mouth, Bring Chin Forward → Close Mouth) yielded relatively high F-score for both experienced and inexperienced participants. This may be because the "Close Mouth" action produces a clear and converging change in the pressure waveform, providing a consistent endpoint that is easier for the machine learning model to identify. In contrast, patterns in which the second action is "Open Mouth" or "Bring Chin Forward" (e.g., Bring Chin Forward → Open Mouth, Bring Chin Forward → Pull Chin Back) tended to result in lower F-score among

Table 3. Comparison of F-score per pattern between experienced and inexperienced saxophonists [%]

Pattern	Experienced	No Experienced
Open Mouth→ Close Mouth	94.0	98.3
Bring chin forward→ Pull chin back	95.0	91.3
Bring chin forward→ Open Mouth	95.0	89.7
Bring chin forward→ Close Mouth	94.0	93.0

inexperienced participants. These movements may lack a clearly defined endpoint, making it more difficult for inexperienced individuals to reproduce them consistently compared to mouth-closing actions. As a result, the corresponding pressure waveforms are less stable and harder to classify. On the other hand, experienced players reproduced unclear movements more consistently, resulting in more stable waveforms and improved classification performance.

The confusion matrix results indicate that misclassifications frequently occurred between Bring Chin Forward → Close Mouth and Bring Chin Forward → Open Mouth. These two movements share the common action of bringing the chin forward, resulting in similar rising patterns in the pressure waveform during the initial phase. Although the subsequent actions—Open Mouth and Close Mouth—are fundamentally different, their directions of oral change are opposite. Therefore, while the latter parts of the waveforms do show clear differences, the classification model may have been more strongly influenced by the similar initial patterns, leading to confusion between the two.

Regarding differences in device fit, this study employed baseline pressure calibration during measurement to correct for environmental pressure. However, challenges remain in mitigating the impact of earpiece sealing and stability on classification accuracy. From a user interface perspective, incorporating earpieces that better match individual users may enable more reliable sensing in future implementations. In addition, to address confusion between similar movements, it would be effective to supplement the current set of statistical features with features that capture more detailed temporal patterns. For example, dividing the waveform into multiple segments over a one-second interval and extracting dynamic features from each segment could help the model better capture differences that appear in the latter part of the waveform. Such an approach is expected to enhance classification accuracy by incorporating the temporal context of mouth movements.

Table 4. Examples of prediction probability distributions for Pattern 4 classification

Example	True Label	Predicted Label	Pattern 1	Pattern 2	Pattern 3	Pattern 4
Example 1	Pattern 4	Pattern 4	1.3%	1.9%	1.0%	**95.7%**
Example 2	Pattern 4	Pattern 4	42.7%	2.3%	0.8%	**54.1%**

5.2 Probabilistic Evaluation of Classification Confidence and Its Potential Applications

The stacking classification model constructed in this study can be extended to output prediction probabilities for each class, enabling a quantitative evaluation of classification confidence. By utilizing these probability scores, it becomes possible to interpret the degree of ambiguity and certainty in motion classification, going beyond binary judgments of correct or incorrect predictions. Table 4 presents two representative examples extracted from the data of participant P3, in which both the true and predicted labels are Pattern 4. In Example 1, the model assigned a high probability of 95.7% to the correct class, indicating a highly confident classification. In contrast, Example 2 shows a case where the correct class (Pattern 4) received only 54.1% probability, while a substantial competing score of 42.7% was assigned to another class (Pattern 1), suggesting that the model's internal decision-making was more ambiguous despite the correct classification. These differences in probability distributions indicate that even when the predicted labels are the same, the level of confidence can vary significantly. These findings highlight the potential for applying prediction probabilities to performance learning support systems. Specifically, possible applications include adjusting the strength of feedback based on classification confidence, alerting users to ambiguous movements, and quantitatively assessing skill proficiency.

5.3 Limitation

The experiments in this study were conducted under static conditions, with participants reproducing four predetermined mouth movements at a constant tempo. Such verification under controlled settings is an important step toward demonstrating the effectiveness of the proposed method. However, in actual saxophone performance, mouth movements occur more continuously and in a more complex manner, with no clear boundaries between actions. Moreover, because subtle adjustments are repeated over short periods in response to musical expression, real-world conditions present challenges distinct from the classification of isolated movements targeted in this study. In addition, this study involved five subjects, of whom only two had playing experience. Due to the limited number of subjects, it is possible that individual differences related to ear canal shape and movement reproducibility were not sufficiently covered. Furthermore, although high recognition accuracy was achieved when individual classification models were constructed for each subject, the average F-score rate was significantly low at 0.23 in the Leave-One-Participant-Out cross-validation conducted to evaluate the model's generalizability, suggesting that the current model has difficulty generalizing to unknown performers. In the future, it will be necessary to collect data from a more diverse range of subjects, redesign features that can absorb movement variability, and introduce learning methods that can adapt to individual differences. In addition, as a comparison with other sensor methods, we performed a similar classification using an ear-worn IMU (accelerometer and gyroscope). As a result, the macro-average F-score under conditions involving forward and backward body movements was only 0.19, and most predictions were biased toward a single class. On the other hand, using the present method with external ear canal pressure, an F-score of 0.36 was achieved under the same conditions, suggesting that it is capable of distinguishing multiple classes compared to the IMU. This result indicates that pressure sensing may have relatively higher sensitivity to changes in oral movements associated with embouchure compared to inertial sensors around the ear. Furthermore, with a view to practical application in real-world environments, the following technical issues can be identified:

Maintaining Classification Accuracy for Continuous and Implicit Movements: In continuous performance, there are no explicit boundaries between movements. Therefore, methods for automatic segmentation of motion intervals and the introduction of time-series models should be considered.

Expanding the Range of Recognizable Movements While Maintaining Accuracy: This study targeted four specific movements: however, real performance involves a much wider variety of actions. Thus, a key challenge is to expand the set of movement definitions while preserving classification performance.

Ensuring Stability and Comfort of Sensor Attachment During Extended Performance: During prolonged performance, shifts in earpiece position or changes in ear canal sealing due to individual ear shapes may lead to signal degradation.

Implementing Real-Time Estimation and Minimizing Latency: Although classification was conducted offline in this study, real-time processing and feedback will be essential for practical use during actual performance.

By addressing these challenges, the proposed method has the potential to become a useful tool that enables performers to objectively assess their embouchure states. Possible use cases include providing feedback for beginners, comparing current embouchure states with recorded practice data, and offering quantitative support for instructors during lessons. Moreover, by recording and accumulating performance-related states, the system may also support applications such as learning history management and skill proficiency assessment. In future work, we aim to address these technical issues and develop the system into a comprehensive support tool for embouchure skill acquisition.

6 Conclusion

In this study, we proposed a method for recognizing mouth movements during saxophone playing based on ear canal pressure. The method recognizes mouth movements by measuring the pressure of the ear canal using the air pressure sensor built into OpenEarable. As a result of evaluation experiments, we have confirmed that the system can recognize mouth movements with an F-score ranging from 89.9% to 98.3%.

Acknowledgments. This work was supported by JSPS KAKENHI Grant Numbers JP23K22318, JP24K02988.

References

1. Amesaka, T., Watanabe, H., Sugimoto, M.: Facial expression recognition using ear canal transfer function. In: Proceedings of the 2019 ACM International Symposium on Wearable Computers (ISWC'19), pp. 1–9. Association for Computing Machinery, New York (2019). https://doi.org/10.1145/3341163.3347747
2. Ando, T., Kubo, Y., Shizuki, B., Takahashi, S.: Canalsense: face-related movement recognition system based on sensing air pressure in ear canals. In: Proceedings of the 30th Annual ACM Symposium on User Interface Software and Technology, UIST'17, pp. 679–689. Association for Computing Machinery, New York (2017). https://doi.org/10.1145/3126594.3126649
3. Bedri, A., Byrd, D., Presti, P., Sahni, H., Gue, Z., Starner, T.: Stick it in your ear: building an in-ear jaw movement sensor. In: Adjunct Proceedings of the 2015 ACM International Joint Conference on Pervasive and Ubiquitous Computing and the 2015 ACM International Symposium on Wearable Computers (UbiComp/ISWC'15 Adjunct), pp. 1333–1338. Association for Computing Machinery, New York (2015). https://doi.org/10.1145/2800835.2807933
4. Brenman, H.S., Mackowiak, R.C., Friedman, M.H.F.: Condylar displacement recordings as an analog of mandibular movements. J. Dent. Res. **47**(4), 599–602 (1968). https://doi.org/10.1177/00220345680470041501
5. Cerqueira, J., et al.: Thermographic evaluation of the saxophonists' embouchure. In: Tavares, J.M.R.S., Natal Jorge, R.M. (eds.) ECCOMAS 2017. LNCVB, vol. 27, pp. 1069–1078. Springer, Cham (2018). https://doi.org/10.1007/978-3-319-68195-5_119
6. Chowdhury, R.M., Reaz, M.B.I., Ali, M.A., Bakar, A.R.A., Chellappan, K., Chang, T.G.: Surface electromyography signal processing and classification techniques. Sensors **13**(9), 12431–12466 (2013). https://doi.org/10.3390/s130912431. https://www.mdpi.com/1424-8220/13/9/12431
7. Colonna, A., Noveri, L., Ferrari, M., Bracci, A., Manfredini, D.: Electromyographic assessment of masseter muscle activity: a proposal for a 24 h recording device with preliminary data. J. Clin. Med. **12**(1), 247 (2023). https://doi.org/10.3390/jcm12010247. https://www.ncbi.nlm.nih.gov/pmc/articles/PMC9821195/
8. Iltis, P.W., Givens, M.W.: Emg characterization of embouchure muscle activity: reliability and application to embouchure dystonia. Med. Prob. Perfor. Artists **20**(1), 25–34 (2005). https://doi.org/10.21091/mppa.2005.1005
9. Iltis, P.W., Schoonderwaldt, E., Zhang, S., Frahm, J., Altenmüller, E.: Real-time MRI comparisons of brass players: a methodological pilot study. Hum. Mov. Sci. **42**, 132–145 (2015). https://doi.org/10.1016/j.humov.2015.04.013
10. Jucevičius, M., Ožiūnas, R., Mažeika, M., Marozas, V., Jegelevičius, D.: Accelerometry-enhanced magnetic sensor for intra-oral continuous jaw motion tracking. Sensors **21**(4), 1409 (2021). https://doi.org/10.3390/s21041409
11. Küntzler, T., Höfling, T.T.A., Alpers, G.W.: Automatic facial expression recognition in standardized and non-standardized emotional expressions. Front. Psychol. **12**, 627561 (2021). https://doi.org/10.3389/fpsyg.2021.627561

12. Lozano-Monasor, E., López, M.T., Fernández-Caballero, A., Vigo-Bustos, F.:
    Facial expression recognition from webcam based on active shape models and sup-
    port vector machines. In: Pecchia, L., Chen, L.L., Nugent, C., Bravo, J. (eds.)
    IWAAL 2014. LNCS, vol. 8868, pp. 147–154. Springer, Cham (2014). https://doi.
    org/10.1007/978-3-319-13105-4_23
13. Matthies, D.J.C., Strecker, B.A., Urban, B.: Earfieldsensing: A novel in-ear elec-
    tric field sensing to enrich wearable gesture input through facial expressions. In:
    Proceedings of the 2017 CHI Conference on Human Factors in Computing Systems
    (CHI'17), pp. 1911–1922. Association for Computing Machinery, New York (2017).
    https://doi.org/10.1145/3025453.3025692
14. Morris, B.C.: Saxophone methods and pedagogical materials: a literature review
    (2022)
15. Röddiger, T., King, T., Roodt, D.R., Clarke, C., Beigl, M.: Openearable: open
    hardware earable sensing platform. In: Proceedings of the 1st International Work-
    shop on Earable Computing, EarComp'22, pp. 29–34. Association for Computing
    Machinery, New York (2023). https://doi.org/10.1145/3544793.3563415
16. Severin, I.C., Dobrea, D.M., Dobrea, M.C.: Head gesture recognition using a 6dof
    inertial imu. Int. J. Comput. Commun. Control **15**(3), 3856 (2020). https://doi.
    org/10.15837/ijccc.2020.3.3856
17. Teal, L.: The Art of Saxophone Playing. Alfred Music (1963)
18. Xu, N.: Factors affecting the saxophone in tone. In: Proceedings of the 2018 1st
    International Conference on Internet and e-Business (ICIEB'18), pp. 369–371.
    Association for Computing Machinery, Singapore (2018). https://doi.org/10.1145/
    3230348.3230439
19. Xu, X.: Analysis of common problems and solutions in saxophone teaching. In: Pro-
    ceedings of the 2019 International Conference on Education Management (ICEM
    2019). ESSP (2019). https://doi.org/10.25236/icem.2019.133

Step-Based Sensor Data Segmentation Using Foot Pressure Sensors

Yue Zhang, Ayumi Ohnishi, Tsutomu Terada[✉],
and Masahiko Tsukamoto

Kobe University, 1-1, Rokkodai-cho, Nada-ku, Kobe 657-8501, Japan
zhangyue@stu.kobe-u.ac.jp, {ohnishi,tsutomu,tuka}@eedept.kobe-u.ac.jp

Abstract. When calculating features in activity recognition, applying a fixed-length sliding window to time series data without considering the timing of activity transitions (hereinafter referred to as activity change points) may result in multiple activities being mixed within a single window, thereby reducing recognition accuracy. To address this issue, we propose a segmentation method that utilizes plantar pressure sensors placed on the foot to automatically detect moments of foot-ground contact. Since these contact moments often correspond to the boundaries between distinct lower-body movements, they can be used to segment continuous activity data into more homogeneous segments. This approach helps reduce the likelihood of mixed activities within a single analysis window. In our evaluation, we compared the proposed method with a conventional segmentation approach based on the spectral transition measure of acceleration data. Although the proposed method did not outperform the conventional method in terms of overall segmentation or activity recognition accuracy, it showed better segmentation performance in specific transitions characterized by distinct foot-ground contact patterns, such as transitions from sitting to walking or from walking to ascending stairs. These findings suggest that plantar pressure–based segmentation can serve as a valuable supplement to existing approaches, particularly in scenarios involving lower-limb activity transitions.

Keywords: Data Segmentation · Human Activity Recognition · Wearable Sensor · Plantar Pressure Sensor

1 Introduction

Human activity recognition (HAR) aims to classify human activities from sensor data and is widely applied in fields such as rehabilitation, sports analysis, and human-computer interaction. To achieve accurate recognition, it is necessary to divide long sequences of sensor data into segments that correspond to individual activities, so that meaningful features can be extracted for model training.

Among the various segmentation techniques, the sliding-window method has been widely adopted in many HAR studies [1,2]. This method divides the continuous sensor data into fixed-length, often overlapping windows, from which time

P. Delir Haghighi et al. (Eds.): MoMM 2025, LNCS 16329, pp. 68–82, 2026.
https://doi.org/10.1007/978-3-032-11768-7_6

or frequency domain features are extracted. Its simplicity and general applicability make it suitable for activity recognition tasks.

However, a known limitation of the sliding-window approach is that a single window may span multiple activity transitions, especially when activity boundaries do not align with window borders. This can introduce noisy or mixed features and negatively affect classification accuracy.

To address this, methods like the spectral transition measure (STM) [3] detect change points based on signal transitions. Yet, these methods can be sensitive to sensor placement, leading to inconsistent segmentation.

In this study, we propose an automatic segmentation method that leverages plantar pressure data, which is less affected by sensor placement and upper-body noise. The method detects valley points in plantar pressure data corresponding to foot-ground contact events to segment the data. Adjacent segments are then compared using cross-correlation; segments with high similarity are merged, while low similarity indicates an activity boundary.

By combining structural features of plantar pressure with a similarity-based refinement, the proposed method achieves more robust segmentation and improves the quality of features used for activity recognition.

The structure of this paper is as follows: Sect. 2 introduces related research, Sect. 3 describes the proposed method, Sect. 4 describes the evaluation experiments, Sect. 5 describes the experimental results, and Sect. 6 concludes the paper.

2   Related Research

2.1   Research on Human Activity Recognition

Human activity recognition (HAR) has traditionally been studied using either vision-based or sensor-based approaches. However, vision-based methods often raise privacy concerns, require substantial computational resources, and are constrained by limited recognition range, leading to a growing preference for sensor-based alternatives.

Among the various sensors employed in HAR, two types of wearable sensors are particularly common. The first is inertial measurement unit (IMU) sensors, such as accelerometers and gyroscopes. These sensors are capable of capturing dynamic full-body movements and transitional activities with high temporal resolution. Due to their compact size and ease of integration, they are widely embedded in smartphones and wearable devices.

The second type is plantar pressure sensors, which are typically installed in insoles or socks. These sensors offer robust measurement of foot-ground contact patterns and are relatively unaffected by upper-body movement noise. This makes them especially effective for recognizing repetitive lower-limb activities, such as walking, running, or stair climbing.

Many studies have achieved high recognition accuracy using these sensors. For instance, Lara et al. [4] combined a chest-mounted accelerometer with biometric data, reaching 95.7% accuracy. Bao et al. [5] used multiple biaxial accelerometers placed on different body parts to classify daily activities.

Tsukamoto et al. [6] embedded hundreds of IMUs in garments, showing that optimal placement improves accuracy. Similarly, plantar pressure sensors have enabled accurate recognition: Sugimoto et al. [7] reported nearly 100% accuracy for lower-limb activities; Fukabori et al. [8] achieved 99.4% with sock-type sensors; and Ohnishi et al. [9] recognized 22 activities using high-resolution in-shoe sensors. Moreover, Hegde et al. [10] combined IMUs and pressure sensors to achieve over 94% accuracy.

However, most prior works have not explicitly addressed the challenge of **automatic segmentation** of continuous activity data. Accurate segmentation is essential: if windows contain mixed activities, feature extraction and recognition performance degrade significantly.

In this study, we propose a method that combines the complementary strengths of IMU and plantar pressure sensors for HAR. Crucially, we also tackle the segmentation problem by extracting structural features from plantar pressure data to automatically identify activity boundaries. This approach aims to improve recognition accuracy and robustness, particularly around transitions where conventional fixed-window methods often fail.

2.2   Research on Segmentation Methods

Conventional Segmentation Approaches. In HAR, early studies often relied on manual segmentation, where activity boundaries were annotated using synchronized video or metadata. While manual segmentation yields accurate boundaries, it is time-consuming, labor-intensive, and subject to human bias.

Many HAR studies have instead adopted sliding-window techniques [1,2], which divide continuous sensor data into fixed-length or variable-length windows for feature extraction and classification. However, it is important to note that sliding-window schemes are not segmentation methods per se; they do not explicitly identify activity boundaries but process the data in chunks without ensuring alignment with actual transitions.

In contrast, strict segmentation aims to automatically detect precise change points between different activities. Recent research has therefore focused on dedicated segmentation methods, such as change-point detection, clustering, or spectral analysis. These approaches seek to address the limitations of sliding windows-such as label mixing and temporal ambiguity-and improve the quality of segmented data for downstream recognition tasks.

Spectral Transition Measure Based Segmentation. Segmentation methods based on the **STM** have recently gained attention as effective alternatives to conventional time-domain approaches. The central idea is that transitions between human activities are often accompanied by changes in the frequency characteristics of sensor data, which can be captured through spectral analysis.

STM was originally proposed for speech segmentation [11,12], where it quantifies the degree of spectral variation over time. Murao et al. [3] extended this method to the domain of human activity recognition, applying STM to acceleration data for automatic activity segmentation. Their findings demonstrated that

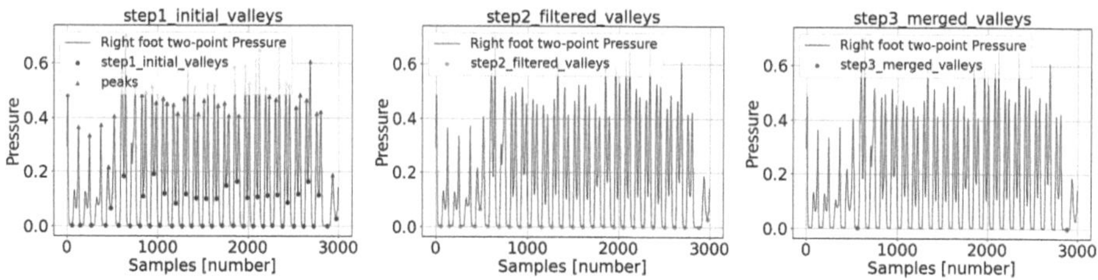

Fig. 1. Three-step procedure of the proposed method for detecting activity change points

STM values remain low within a single activity, indicating temporal stability, but increase significantly at boundaries between different activities.

In this study, we adopt STM as a baseline for segmenting acceleration data and compare its performance with our proposed method.

The STM value $G(t)$ at time t is computed as:

$$G(t) = \frac{1}{p} \sum_{i=1}^{p} a_{i,t}^2 \tag{1}$$

Here, p is the number of cepstral coefficients, and $a_{i,t}$ represents the temporal change of the ith coefficient, computed as:

$$u_{i,t} = \frac{\sum_{n=-M}^{M} C_{i,t+n} \cdot n}{\sum_{n=-M}^{M} n^2} \tag{2}$$

Here, $C_{i,t}$ denotes the i-th cepstral coefficient at time t, obtained from the log spectrum of the signal. M represents the window size used to compute temporal derivatives, and p is the number of cepstral coefficients retained, typically the lower-order coefficients.

3 Proposed Method

Conventional segmentation methods based on acceleration data, such as STM, are often affected by sensor placement, as acceleration signals are sensitive to body position and orientation. These methods may also fail to detect subtle or slow lower-body movements, and their performance tends to degrade in non-periodic or complex activities where acceleration features are ambiguous. In contrast, plantar pressure sensors provide stable, position-insensitive measurements that directly reflect foot-ground interaction and gait phases. Motivated by this, we propose a segmentation approach based on plantar pressure data.

3.1 Automatic Activity Segmentation

We propose an **automatic segmentation method** that leverages the cyclical nature of foot-ground contact to divide continuous data into meaningful activity units. The process consists of three stages, illustrated in Fig. 1.

Step 1: Peak and Valley Detection. We first detect local peaks in the normalized composite pressure signal (from heel and forefoot sensors) using scipy's find peaks with a prominence threshold near the global mean (0.12). Between each pair of peaks, the lowest point (valley) is extracted as a candidate segmentation point, marking the start of a new motion cycle.

Step 2: Refinement. During walking or stair-related activities, we observed sharp downward spikes between adjacent valleys (Fig. 1). These are caused by brief pressure surges during heel-to-toe transitions.

As our goal is to detect the true moment of foot-ground contact-typically characterized by slight fluctuations rather than sharp spikes-we refine the valleys by checking the slope between each valley and points six samples before and after it. If both slopes exceed a threshold of 0.002, the point is considered a transitional spike and removed.

We further eliminate false valleys near peaks by checking whether both neighboring points are lower than the current valley. After these two steps, we obtain a cleaner set of contact points, as illustrated in Step 2.

Step 3: Similarity-Based Merging. We compute the Sliding Normalized Cross-Correlation (SNCC) between two adjacent segments S_n and S_{n+1} to evaluate their similarity:

$$\text{SNCC}(x, y) = \max_{i=0}^{L-n} \left(\frac{(x - \bar{x}) \cdot (y_{i:i+n} - \bar{y}_{i:i+n})}{\|x - \bar{x}\| \cdot \|y_{i:i+n} - \bar{y}_{i:i+n}\|} \right) \tag{3}$$

Equation (3) defines SNCC, where x is the shorter of the two adjacent signal segments and y is the longer one. Both signals are first zero-mean normalized by subtracting their respective means. Then, the shorter segment x is compared with each window of equal length within y using cosine similarity. Specifically, for each window $y_{i:i+n}$, we calculate the dot product between x and the window, normalized by the product of their Euclidean norms. The maximum of these values is used as the SNCC score.

This value ranges from zero to one, with higher values indicating stronger shape similarity. If the SNCC score exceeds a predefined threshold, the segments are considered similar and merged; otherwise, a boundary is maintained.

To avoid over-merging distinct activities into the same segment, a relatively high threshold is selected to ensure finer segmentation granularity. Based on extensive empirical evaluation, a threshold of 0.75 was chosen, balancing the trade-off between over-segmentation and under-segmentation, and ensuring that each segment maintains behavioral consistency.

The proposed method offers several advantages. First, it exploits the cyclical nature of plantar pressure patterns to guide segmentation, allowing for more accurate detection of activity boundaries. Additionally, the use of similarity-based merging between adjacent segments enhances accuracy, particularly near activity transitions. By combining data from both heel and forefoot sensors, the

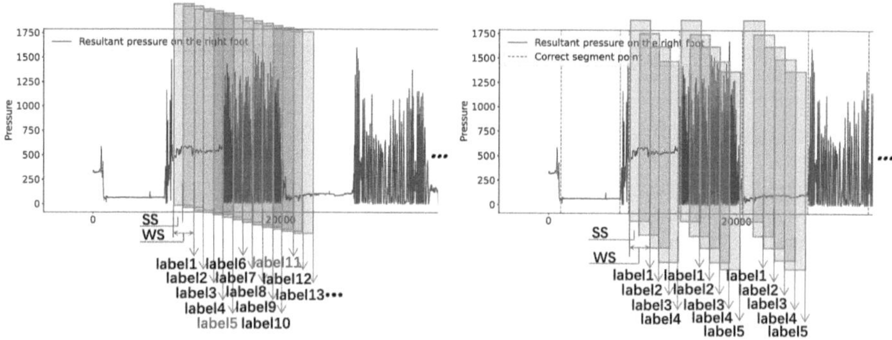

Fig. 2. Comparison of label assignment using conventional sliding-window method (left) and the proposed segmentation method (right)

method can robustly handle various postures and activity types. Moreover, the application of adaptive thresholding mechanisms enables the method to account for individual differences across subjects. As a result, it produces cleaner and more consistent segments, which in turn contribute to improved performance in downstream activity recognition tasks.

3.2   Label Correction

After the automatic segmentation step, the data is further divided into overlapping windows for feature extraction using a sliding window of size $WS = 100$ samples and a step size of $SS = 50$ samples.

As illustrated in Fig. 2, the left side demonstrates the conventional sliding-window approach, which applies fixed-length windows across the entire sequence without considering activity boundaries. In this case, some windows (e.g., windows 5 and 11) span multiple activities, leading to mixed labels and inconsistent feature representations, which can negatively impact recognition accuracy.

In contrast, the right side of Fig. 2 shows our proposed method. Here, red dashed lines represent segmentation points, and the sliding windows are constrained within each segment. This ensures that windows do not cross activity boundaries, resulting in more coherent features and improved classification performance.

However, due to the step size of 50 samples, not all data points are covered by a window. Gaps may occur between windows, especially at the beginning of each segment. To ensure that every time step has a corresponding label in the final prediction sequence, we fill in these missing points using the first predicted label from the corresponding window.

Finally, to evaluate segmentation accuracy, we compare the reconstructed predicted labels with ground truth at known activity boundaries. If predicted labels change across an automatic segmentation point, it indicates that the method correctly identified an actual activity transition. By reducing feature contamination at boundaries and accurately capturing transitions, the proposed segmentation-aware approach improves overall recognition robustness.

4   Evaluation Experiment

4.1   Subject Information

Height, weight, sex, and other participant information are summarized as follows. The study included ten participants (nine males and one female). Nine participants were in their 20 s and one was in their 30 s. Nine participants were in their 20 s and one was in their 30 s. The participants had an average height of 171.5 ± 5.5 cm an average weight of 67.3 ± 11.4 kg and an average BMI of 22.9 ± 4.4.

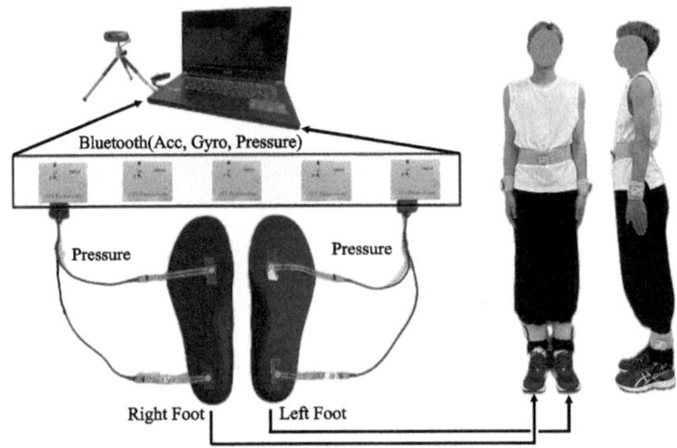

Fig. 3. System configuration and sensor position

4.2   Sensor Configuration

As shown in Fig. 3, five nine-axis IMU sensors (TSND151, ATR-Promotion [13]) were used to collect motion data. Sensors were attached to both wrists, both ankles, and the lower abdomen using elastic bandages to reduce motion artifacts. Although the IMUs can record gyroscope and magnetometer data, only tri-axial acceleration was used in this study.

In addition, four pressure sensors (Model A201, FlexiForce [14]) were attached to the ball and heel of each foot, following the design of Ohnishi et al. [9]. Each sensor has an active area of approximately 0.72 cm^2 and can measure forces up to 440 N, covering about 0.8% of the plantar surface.

IMU data were transmitted via Bluetooth, and pressure sensor data were sent through cables connected to the ankle-mounted IMUs. Both data streams were synchronized and recorded using Altima software [15]. A webcam connected

Table 1. Collection of 16 activities

ID	Objects	ID	Objects
0	Upstairs	8	Cleaning the floor with a vacuum cleaner
1	Downstairs	9	Walking while carrying heavy objects
2	Sitting	10	Running
3	Jumping and throwing the ball	11	Squatting
4	Kicking the ball	12	Cycling
5	Standing	13	Walking
6	Opening the door	14	Lying
7	Standing while holding heavy objects	15	Transition

to the PC simultaneously recorded video, which was synchronized with the sensor data to enable manual annotation of activity boundaries. This experiment was conducted with the approval of the Research Ethics Review Committee for Human Research Directly Involving the Graduate School of Engineering, Kobe University (approval number 06–27).

4.3   Parameter Settings

Since human daily activities are usually lower than 20 Hz, the Nyquist frequency sampling definition allows recording data of daily activities as long as the frequency is 40 Hz or higher. Therefore, the sampling frequency of the sensor is set to 100 Hz in this study. In addition, since the range of acceleration in human daily activities usually does not exceed ± 4 g, the range of acceleration is set to ± 8 g in this study.

4.4   Experimental Contents

In this study, we collected plantar pressure data from five subjects who each performed two different sequences consisting of the same set of 16 daily activities, with each sequence repeated twice.

Sequence 1 (Original Order): Participants began by sitting quietly on a chair for one minute, then stood up to pick up two four-kilogram objects and held them while standing still for another minute. They walked around the room carrying the objects for one minute, set them down, squatted for one minute, and stood still again for one minute. Next, they cleaned the room with a vacuum cleaner for one minute, ran on a treadmill at eight km/h for one minute, and cycled on a stationary bike (resistance level five) for one minute. Afterward, they jumped and threw a ball upward with both hands ten times, kicked a ball with the dominant foot ten times, and lay flat on a mattress for one minute. Finally, they opened the door, exited the room, descended two floors, walked about 30 m, returned via the same route, and sat back on the chair-opening four doors on each round trip. The entire sequence was repeated twice per participant.

Sequence 2 (Reversed Order): Participants began by exiting the room, walking through a hallway and stairs (opening four doors each way), then performed kicking ball and throwing ball tasks (ten times each). This was followed by one-minute sessions of cycling, running, lying down, and vacuuming. Participants then held two objects while standing, walked while carrying them, squatted, stood still, and finally sat quietly on a chair. The entire reversed sequence was repeated twice by each participant.

This protocol ensured that the collected dataset included a balanced mix of static, dynamic, and transitional activities performed in both forward and reversed order.

Procedure Details: In the throwing and kicking tasks, the ball was retrieved and returned to the participants by assistants. During door-opening actions, participants used their naturally preferred hand. For the cycling task, no restrictions on pedaling speed, but the resistance level was fixed across all trials.

4.5   Preprocessing

Figure 4 shows a portion of the synchronized sensor data from Sequence1 described in Sect. 4.4. Due to space limitations, only part of the activity sequence is illustrated, and Sequence 2 consists of the same set of activities performed in reverse order, and is not illustrated here due to space limitations. The five IMU sensors were worn so that their X axes were oriented vertically upward, and each sensor was placed in a consistent orientation and position across all participants.

Background colors are used to visually distinguish different activity segments. Note that similar colors do not imply identical activity labels; the color scheme is intended for visual clarity only.

4.6   Data Segmentation Experiment

In this study, we implemented the STM-based segmentation method using a window size of 200 samples (two seconds), a step size of 100 samples, and a 256-point FFT. The peak detection threshold for STM was set to the mean plus 0.5 times the standard deviation of the STM values. Unlike Murao et al. [3], who analyzed each axis independently, we simplified the computation by using the average resultant acceleration from five IMU sensors.

4.7   Activity Recognition Method

In this study, we performed activity recognition based on features extracted from segmented sensor data, using three different strategies for defining data segments:

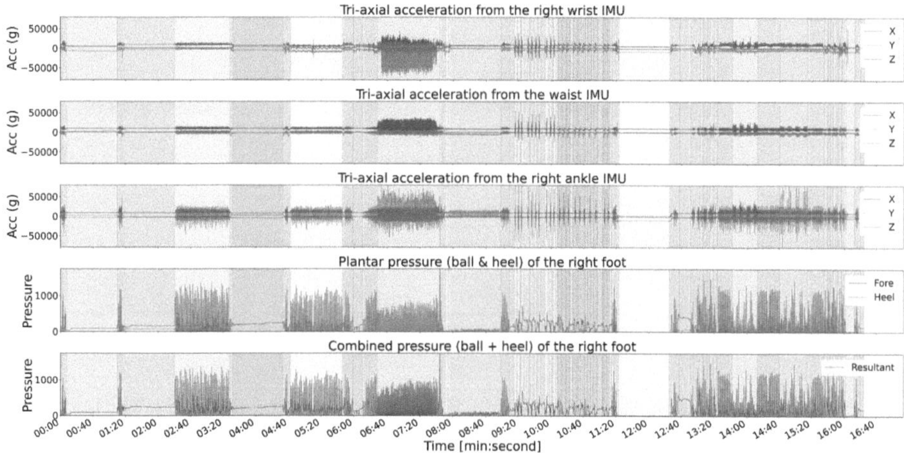

Fig. 4. Sensor data recorded during Sequence 1

- **Sliding-window (baseline):** While not a true segmentation method, this approach divides the entire time series into overlapping fixed-size windows and extracts feature vectors from each window, without considering actual activity boundaries.
  STM-based automatic segmentation: Segmentation points are determined automatically based on the mean magnitude of tri-axial acceleration signals from five IMUs placed on the wrists, waist, and ankles. This method detects points of high spectral transition to identify changes in activity.
- **Proposed plantar-pressure-based segmentation:** This method identifies activity boundaries using composite plantar pressure signals derived from two sensors positioned under the heel and the metatarsophalangeal joint of the right foot, as described in Sect. 3.

After segmentation, all resulting segments (as well as the raw sequence in the baseline method) were further divided into overlapping windows of 100 samples (approximately one second) with a 50-sample step size. From each window, we extracted six time-domain features: maximum, minimum, mean, standard deviation, root mean square, and absolute mean rate of change. Windows shorter than the defined size were also included to ensure full data utilization.

Feature extraction was performed using signals from five IMUs (each providing three-axis acceleration and angular velocity) and plantar pressure sensors located at the toe and heel of both feet, resulting in a 204-dimensional feature vector per window. All features were normalized using Min-Max scaling for consistency.

For classification, we employed a Random Forest model. To evaluate generalization ability, we used a leave-subject-out cross-validation scheme: models were trained on manually segmented data from ten subjects and tested separately on data segmented by the STM-based method, the proposed plantar-pressure-based

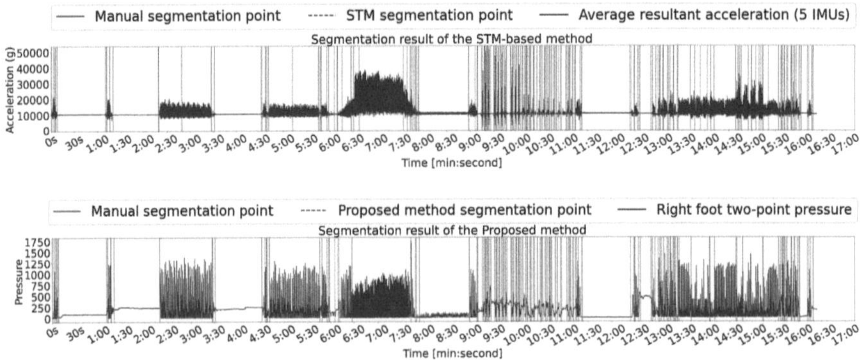

Fig. 5. Comparison of Segmentation Results from Two Automatic Methods

method, and the unsegmented baseline. This setup reflects practical scenarios where the training data are clean and annotated, while the test data are automatically segmented or raw.

To mitigate class imbalance in the training set, we applied the Synthetic Minority Oversampling Technique (SMOTE) for underrepresented activities, and randomly downsampled overrepresented classes (e.g., walking) to 200 instances per class. This ensured a balanced and representative dataset for training.

This experimental procedure allows for a fair comparison of the segmentation strategies and demonstrates the effectiveness of the proposed pressure-based method in improving recognition performance, especially around activity transitions.

Table 2. Comparison of Segmentation Accuracy

Method	Precision	Recall
STM-based Method	0.635	0.891
Proposed Method	0.589	0.496

Table 3. Activity recognition results (Inter-subject cross-validation)

Method	Precision	Recall
STM-based Method	0.943	0.910
Sliding-window Method	0.945	0.920
Proposed Method	0.943	0.912

5   Results and Discussion

5.1   Segmentation Result

As shown in Table 2, the STM-based method achieved slightly higher overall segmentation accuracy than the proposed method. Across 20 datasets with 1830 manually labeled segmentation points, it detected 2272 points, while the proposed method detected 1518.

To ensure a fair comparison, both methods were applied to the same data sequences. Figure 5 illustrates their respective segmentation results: blue curves represent the input signals (average IMU acceleration for STM, combined plantar pressure for the proposed method); green lines indicate ground-truth boundaries, and red dashed lines show automatically detected segmentation points.

Both methods effectively avoided producing redundant points during stationary periods, reflecting their ability to detect stable activities. However, the STM-based method produced more segmentation points overall, especially for brief, dynamic activities like *jumping* or *kicking the ball*, where rich acceleration signals allow for high sensitivity-but often result in over-segmentation.

In contrast, the proposed method, based on plantar pressure, was less responsive to such upper-body movements but exhibited higher consistency for continuous and repetitive activities such as *walking, running,* and *ascending or descending stairs*. These activities produce periodic signal patterns that STM-based segmentation often misinterprets as activity transitions. The proposed method, by detecting foot contact and evaluating segment similarity, avoids unnecessary segmentation within homogeneous activities, ensuring better temporal consistency and interpretability.

Overall, while less sensitive to brief transitions, the proposed method demonstrates better generalization in continuous-motion scenarios and complements the STM-based method when used together (Fig. 6).

Table 4. Activity recognition results (Within-subject cross-validation)

Method	Precision	Recall
STM-based Method	0.805	0.711
Sliding-window Method	0.807	0.713
Proposed Method	0.808	0.712

5.2   Activity Recognition Result

Tables 3 and 4 show the results of cross-subject and within-subject validations, respectively. The within-subject results are averaged across two datasets per subject.

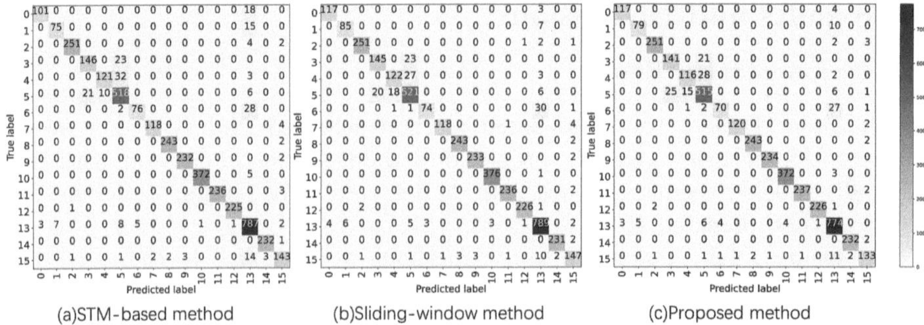

Fig. 6. The recognition results of the three methods and the ground-truth activity labels for Subject 6

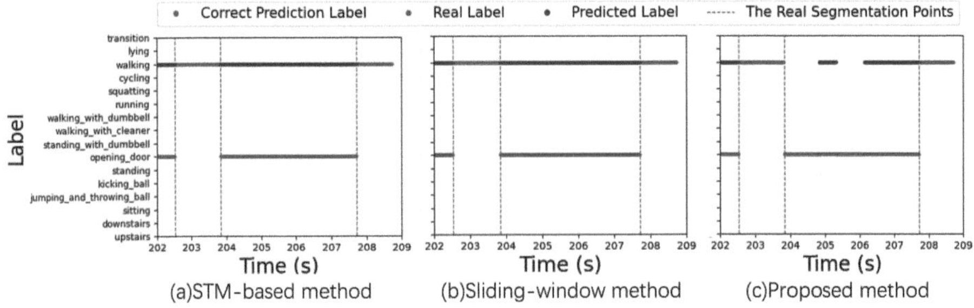

Fig. 7. Recognition results of activities at segmentation points by three different methods

Overall, the classification performance is similar across the three segmentation methods. Figure 6 presents the confusion matrices from cross-subject validation (leave-one-subject-out), where Subject 6's two datasets were used for testing and the others for training. The numeric labels 0–15 correspond to the activity IDs in Table 1. From the matrices, two groups of activities with frequent misclassifications are observed.

The first group (a) includes activities 5 (standing), 3 (jumping and throwing the ball), and 4 (kicking the ball). These errors stem from short pauses before and after activities 3 and 4, which often lead to impure features in brief windows. This is especially problematic for the fixed sliding-window method, which lacks segmentation and extracts features from windows that may contain multiple activities, resulting in misclassification.

The second group (b) includes activities 0 (upstairs), 6 (opening the door), 13 (walking), and 15 (transition), all of which involve similar lower-limb motions. For example, activities 0, 6, and 13 essentially consist of walking with minor pressure differences, and activity 15 includes various transitions (e.g., sitting, bending) that resemble walking in both acceleration and pressure patterns. As a result, they are frequently misclassified as walking.

Interestingly, activities 5 (standing) and 7 (standing with objects), despite being static, show high accuracy. Since acceleration and angular velocity are near zero in both, plantar pressure becomes the main distinguishing feature, highlighting the effectiveness of pressure sensors in recognizing static postures.

In terms of within-subject validation results (Table 4), the accuracy is slightly lower than that of cross-subject validation. This is due to the fact that the training and testing data proportions are nearly 1:1 within each subject, and the overall amount of data per subject is relatively small. These constraints limit the model's generalization ability and affect the recognition performance.

Figure 7 presents recognition results around activity transitions using three segmentation methods: (a) STM-based, (b) sliding-window, and (c) the proposed method. In the figure, green points represent the ground-truth activity sequence, blue points show predicted labels, and red points indicate correct predictions; these points are connected to form continuous traces. In addition, green dashed vertical lines mark the activity transition boundaries. The proposed method accurately detects activity transitions, especially when similar actions (e.g., walking and opening the door) alternate. As shown in Fig. 7, it performs notably well at the transition points, capturing precise changes from repetitive walking to the instantaneous action of opening a door. This capability makes the method suitable for applications requiring timely detection of activity onset.

In contrast, the STM-based method shows segmentation errors, leading to reduced accuracy around transitions. The sliding-window method also ignores activity boundaries and often spans multiple actions in a single window, causing delays or misclassifications.

Overall, the proposed method aligns more closely with true activity boundaries and enhances recognition performance, particularly in situations that demand timely detection of activity changes.

6   Conclusion

This study proposed an automatic segmentation method based solely on plantar pressure data from two sensors under the right foot. Although its overall segmentation performance was lower than that of the STM-based method using five IMUs, the proposed method showed superior consistency in repetitive activities such as *walking*, *running*, and *ascending/descending stairs*, where it effectively avoided redundant segmentation caused by minor fluctuations. In contrast, the STM-based method was more sensitive to abrupt changes, making it better suited for detecting instantaneous activities such as *jumping* or *kicking a ball*. However, this sensitivity often led to over-segmentation during steady movements. The two methods exhibit complementary strengths: combining them can improve segmentation accuracy by leveraging the STM method's responsiveness and the proposed method's stability. These findings highlight the potential of plantar pressure as a lightweight and practical modality for activity segmentation, particularly when integrated into multi-sensor systems.

Acknowledgments. This work was supported by JST SPRING, Grant Number JPMJSP2148.

References

1. Wang, G., Li, Q., Wang, L., Wang, W., Wu, M., Liu, T.: Impact of sliding window length in indoor human motion modes and pose pattern recognition based on smartphone sensors. Sensors **18**(6) (2018)
2. Huynh, T., Schiele, B.: Analyzing features for activity recognition. In: Proceedings of the 2005 Joint Conference on Smart Objects and Ambient Intelligence: Innovative Context-Aware Services, Usages and Technologies (sOc-EUSAI), pp. 159–163 (2005)
3. Murao, K., Terada, T.: Labeling method for acceleration data using an execution sequence of activities. In: Proceedings of the 1st International Workshop on Human Activity Sensing Corpus and its Application (HASCA 2013), pp. 611–622 (2013)
4. Lara, Ó.D., Pérez, A.J., Labrador, M.A., Posada, J.D.: Centinela: a human activity recognition system based on acceleration and vital sign data. Pervasive Mob. Comput. **8**(5), 717–729 (2012)
5. Bao, L., Intille, S.S.: Activity recognition from user-annotated acceleration data. In: Ferscha, A., Mattern, F. (eds.) Pervasive 2004. LNCS, vol. 3001, pp. 1–17. Springer, Heidelberg (2004). https://doi.org/10.1007/978-3-540-24646-6_1
6. Tsukamoto, A., Yoshida, N., Yonezawa, T., Mase, K., Enokibori, Y.: Where are the best positions of IMU sensors for HAR? Approach by a garment device with fine grained grid IMUs. In: Proceedings of the 2023 ACM International Joint Conference on Pervasive and Ubiquitous Computing & the 2023 ACM International Symposium on Wearable Computing (UbiComp/ISWC 23), pp. 445–450 (2023)
7. Sugimoto, C., Ozaki, K., Ezoe, R., Hosaka, H., Yamato, H.: Human activity recognition using foot pressure sensing shoes. J. Adv. Mech. Design Syst. Manufact. **4**(1), 206–213 (2010)
8. Fukahori, K., Sakamoto, D., Igarashi, T.: Exploring subtle foot plantar-based gestures with sock-placed pressure sensors. In: Proceedings of the 33rd Annual ACM Conference on Human Factors in Computing Systems (CHI '15), pp. 3019–3028 (2015)
9. Ohnishi, A., Terada, T., Tsukamoto, M.: A method for recognizing postures and gestures using foot pressure sensors. J. Inf. Process. **27**, 348–358 (2019)
10. Hegde, N., Bries, M., Swibas, T., Melanson, E., Sazonov, E.: Automatic recognition of activities of daily living utilizing insole-based and wrist-worn wearable sensors. IEEE J. Biomed. Health Inform. **22**(4), 979–988 (2018)
11. Furui, S.: On the role of spectral transition for speech perception. J. Acoust. Soc. Am. **80**(4), 1016–1025 (1986)
12. Dusan, S., Rabiner, L.: On the relation between maximum spectral transition positions and phone boundaries. Proc. Interspeech 1317–1323 (2006)
13. ATR-Promotion: http://www.atr-p.com/products/sensor.html. Accessed 28 May 2025
14. FlexiForce: https://www.tekscan.com/products-solutions/force-sensors/a201. Accessed 28 May 2025
15. Altima: https://www.atr-p.com/products/Altima.html. Accessed 28 May 2025

Security and Trust in Mobile Environments

Anti-ESIA: Analyzing and Mitigating Impacts of Electromagnetic Signal Injection Attacks on Image Sensing

Denglin Kang[1], Youqian Zhang[2]([✉]), Wai Cheong Tam[3], Xiapu Luo[2], and Eugene Yujun Fu[4]

[1] University of Southern California, Los Angeles, CA 90089, USA
denglin.kang@usc.edu
[2] The Hong Kong Polytechnic University, Hong Kong, China
you-qian.zhang@polyu.edu.hk, csxluo@comp.polyu.edu.hk
[3] National Institute of Standards and Technology, Gaithersburg, MD 20899, USA
waicheong.tam@nist.gov
[4] The Education University of Hong Kong, Hong Kong, China
eugenefu@eduhk.hk

Abstract. Image sensors are integral components of many critical intelligent systems. However, a growing threat, known as Electromagnetic Signal Injection Attacks (ESIA), poses a significant risk to these systems. ESIA enables attackers to remotely manipulate images captured by cameras which can potentially lead to malicious actions and catastrophic consequences. Despite the severity of this threat, the effects of ESIA remain poorly understood, and effective countermeasures are lacking. This paper aims to address these gaps by investigating ESIA from two distinct aspects: pixel loss and color strips. By analyzing these aspects separately on image classification tasks, we gain a deeper understanding of how ESIA can compromise intelligent systems. Additionally, we explore a lightweight solution to mitigate the effects of ESIA. Our findings provide valuable insights for future research and development in the field of camera security and intelligent systems.

Keywords: Image sensor · Image classification · Electromagnetic interference · Mitigation

1 Introduction

As intelligent systems become increasingly integrated into our daily life, they depend on sensors to perceive and act on the physical world. Image sensors from cameras are especially critical: they grant visual perception that lets machines "see" and "understand" scenes. Across mobile/edge platforms, robotics, health diagnostics, and surveillance, decisions with safety and security implications hinge on the integrity of camera-captured imagery. However, a new threat class, Electromagnetic Signal Injection Attacks (ESIA), jeopardizes this integrity [3,4,6,8,10,14–16]. Unlike traditional software-focused cyberattacks, ESIA acts at the physical layer, exploiting hardware imperfections to remotely inject adversarial EM signals into image-sensor circuitry, thereby disrupting and manipulating pixel transmission. Such remote manipulation can have grave consequences, misleading AI models in safety-critical deployments. Studies show ESIA can tamper with autonomous-vehicle image sensors [3,6,16], causing perception systems to miss obstacles and fatal collisions.

Despite its danger, documented incidents remain rare, giving a false sense of security. In reality, ESIA's novelty obscures its risk, leaving countless systems exposed. While prior work demonstrates ESIA's disruption of image sensing and AI accuracy, why these perturbations so strongly affect AI remains underexplored. Existing mitigations, such as adversarial training [14] incur substantial compute and degrade nominal performance, underscoring the need for lightweight defenses. This paper aims to address these gaps by making the following contributions:

(1) We identify pixel loss and color striping as the primary drivers of ESIA-induced errors in AI-based image sensing.
(2) We propose a lightweight framework that alleviates attack-induced distortions with modest overhead, enabling deployment under real-world resource constraints.

2   Background on Image Sensing

An image sensing system (Fig. 1) has an image sensor, an image-processing module, and a metallic wire connecting them. Modern image sensors integrate millions of photodiodes that transduce incident light into electrical voltages, producing electronic representations of a scene. A color filter array (CFA) (Fig. 1) overlays the photodiodes so each photodiode measures a single color. The most widely used CFA pattern, Bayer pattern [1], enforces red (R)/green (G)/blue (B) sampling. After photoelectric conversion, CFA samples are serialized (row-wise) and packetized for delivery to the processor. The processing module verifies

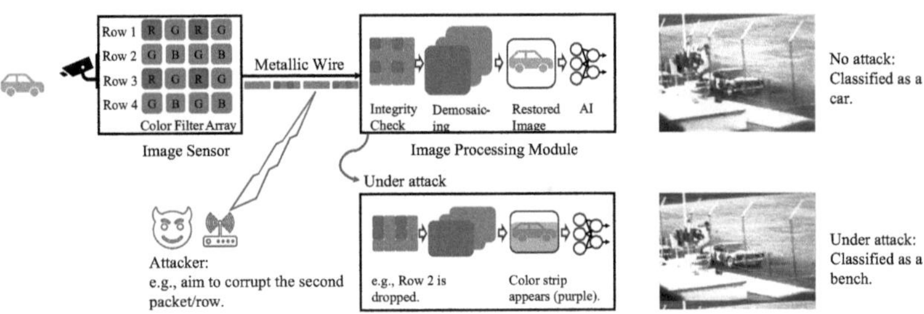

Fig. 1. Fundamentals of image sensing and impacts of electromagnetic signal injection attacks (ESIA).

packet integrity, discards corrupted data, and performs demosaicing. The resulting frames then feed downstream artificial intelligence (AI).

3 Analysis of ESIA

3.1 Attack Mechanism

Electromagnetic signal injection attacks exploit the physical characteristics of the metallic wiring that transmits data from the image sensor to the processing unit [3,14,16]. These wires behave as unintended antennas and pick up environmental electromagnetic (EM) waves [9,12]. An adversary can radiate EM waves with off-the-shelf radios (Fig. 1) remotely. Those EM waves are coupled into wires, inducing spurious voltages/currents that distort digital levels (1/0) [5,16], corrupting pixel data in the data packets. The receiving end then drops those packets that fail the integrity checks.

Commercial pipelines commonly replace missing rows with the next valid row [3]. For example, as shown in Fig. 1, assumes that Row 2 (GBGB) is attacked and dropped. The image processing module replaces it with Row 3 (RGRG). During demosaicing, the system still assumes that Row 2 follows the original Bayer pattern (i.e., it expects GBGB). However, since Row 2 has been replaced with RGRG, the reconstructed color mapping is incorrect, which will lead to mismatched color information during demosaicing. It manifests itself as a long-lasting purple color strip until the next corrupted row is encountered. Notably, if two consecutive rows are lost, the distorted color disappears because the Bayer pattern alignment effect is not impacted at all.

Prior work has shown the significant impact of such corruption on AI tasks: for instance, image classification systems produce incorrect labels [14], object detectors fail to detect critical objects [3,16], and segmentation algorithms generate faulty segmentation masks [6]. Please note that the attack mechanism has been extensively studied, and prior work [14] proposed and validated a synthetic method for generating attacked images. In the remainder of this work, we will utilize this synthetic method to create the attacked images for our analysis.

3.2 Two Factors

Upon analyzing the mechanism of ESIA, we identify two primary key contributing factors: pixel loss, and color strips. Let's define a strictly increasing tuple $R = (r_0, r_1, ..., r_{m-1})$, $m \in Z^+$, representing the dropped rows of pixels. A color strip is caused by a pair of dropped rows, i.e., r_i and r_{i+1}, where i is even. Note that if $(n-1)$ is an even number, it means the last strip will end at the bottom of the image. The overall degradation in model performance due to the attack can be expressed as $Degradation = f(R) + g(R)$, where $f(\cdot)$ is a function of the pixel loss, and $g(\cdot)$ is the function of the color strips (Note that we define $f(\cdot) \geq 0$, $g(\cdot) \geq 0$).

Next, we quantify the impacts of the identified factors. While there are various AI tasks that rely on image data, we focus on image classification, as it is one of the most fundamental tasks in computer vision. For this purpose, we utilize the ViT-B/32 model [2], Swin-V2-B model [7] and ResNeXt101-64X4D model [13], all of them are widely used and state-of-the-art architecture for image classification.

To perform our evaluation, we randomly selected 495 images from the validation set of the ImageNet Large Scale Visual Recognition Challenge dataset [11]. Using the previously described synthetic method, we generated two types of attacked images: **(1) Images with only pixel loss (no color strips)**, which were created by randomly dropping two consecutive rows of pixels; **(2) Images with both pixel loss and color strips**, which were generated by randomly dropping rows without restrictions, leading to the formation of color strips during image reconstruction. The number of dropped rows (n) was chosen as approximately 0%, 10%, 15%, 30%, 45%, and 50% of the total number of rows in the images. Image classification accuracy was used as the performance metric, and the results are summarized in Fig. 2.

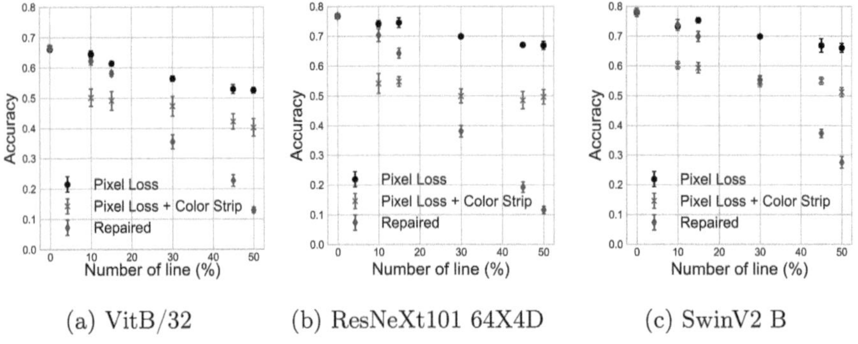

(a) VitB/32   (b) ResNeXt101 64X4D   (c) SwinV2 B

Fig. 2. Performance is degraded by ESIA with or without color strips, and performance can be recovered after applying our mitigation method.

When there is no color strip (pixel loss only), it shows that the accuracy drops from 66.1% to 52.5% (with a degradation of 13.6%), with increasing the number of dropped pixels. However, when pixel loss and color strips happen at the same, the accuracy declines from 66.5% to 40.2% (with a degradation of 26.3%). These results demonstrate that while pixel loss alone causes a noticeable but relatively moderate performance drop, the combination of pixel loss and color strips leads to a twice more severe degradation. This highlights the critical role of color strips together with pixel loss in amplifying the adverse impacts of the attacks.

4   Mitigation

To mitigate the effect of pixel loss, it is possible to use an imputation method using a median filter. However, it is essential to point out that imputation cannot simply solve the problem: as shown later, as the amount of pixel loss increases, this method can have adverse effects, further degrading the image quality. For mitigating color strips, our experiments revealed that when a single row of data is lost and is immediately followed by the loss of another row, the impact of the attack can be alleviated. The observation suggests that combining two solutions, i.e., as discussed above, imputation and drop more rows, can form a framework for managing color strips.

4.1 Framework

We propose a mitigation framework that operates between the integrity check and the demosaicing stages of the image processing pipeline (recalling the details in Sect. 2 together with Fig. 1. As shown in Fig. 3, the framework performs the following steps: **(1) Detection of pixel loss:** First, the image processing module determines whether any pixels have been lost, which is done by the integrity check. If no pixel loss is detected, the process proceeds directly to demosaicing. **(2) Mitigation strategy selection:** If pixel loss is detected, the framework evaluates the severity by measuring the number of dropped rows and comparing it against a predefined threshold, denoted as θ ($0 \leq \theta \leq 1$). If the number of lost rows is below the threshold, the framework applies the imputation method (e.g., median filter) to reconstruct the missing data. If the number of dropped rows exceeds the threshold, the framework opts for a drop-more-row strategy, where the affected rows and their following consecutive rows are removed entirely to avoid introducing further distortions like color strips. Then, the raw data is fed for demosasicing.

Specifically, regarding the mitigation strategy selection, we can convert the choice of threshold into an optimization problem, where the objective $J(\cdot)$ is given by:
$$J(R) = \begin{cases} f(R) + g(R), & \text{if } n < \theta, \\ f(R, R+1), & \text{otherwise.} \end{cases}$$
where $f(\cdot)$, $g(\cdot)$, R, and n have

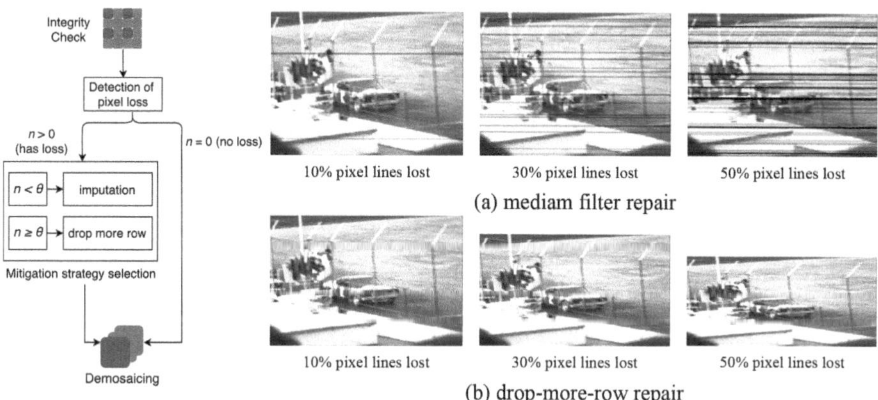

(a) mediam filter repair

(b) drop-more-row repair

Fig. 3. The proposed mitigation framework to reduce the impacts of the attacks.

been defined in Sect. 3.2, and we do not repeat them here; $R + 1$ represents adding 1 to each element in R. Lets define $z \in \{0, 1\}$ be a binary variable such that: $z = \begin{cases} 1, & \text{if } n < \theta, \\ 0, & \text{if otherwise.} \end{cases}$ This can be expressed using the binary variable z as: $J(R, \theta, z) = z\left[f(R) + g(R)\right] + (1 - z)\,f(R, R+1)$. The complete optimization problem is then given by: $\operatorname{argmin}_\theta\, z\left[f(R) + g(R)\right] + (1 - z)f(R, R + 1)$ subject to $0 \leq \theta \leq 1$ and $z \in \{0, 1\}$.

4.2 Experiments and Discussion

Imputation. As mentioned earlier, we use a median filter to repair missing pixels. Let's take ViT-B/32 model as an example for our analysis below. As shown in Fig. 2a, when the percentage of missing rows is below 15%, the imputation method is able to maintain the model's accuracy above 60%. However, when the percentage of missing rows exceeds 15%, the imputation method leads to a sharp decline in model accuracy. Upon further investigation, as shown in Fig. 3 (a), we observed that when a significant number of rows are missing, the imputation method not only fails to recover the lost pixel information but also introduces additional artifacts, such as more color strips, leading to incorrect predictions by the model.

Drop-More-Row. It is worth noting that the Drop-More-Row method mitigates the impact of color strips by sacrificing information. As shown in Fig. 2a, when the total number of missing rows reaches 50% of the image's total rows (with 25% caused by the attack and an additional 25% intentionally dropped by the Drop-More-Row method), the model's performance remains around 52%, which is about a 14% decrease compared to the baseline where no attack happens. We illustrate the visual results of this method in Fig. 3 (b). It can be observed that this approach effectively prevents the appearance of purple color strips, and we believe that by actually taking out the affected rows, it helps to model classify the image. However, as the number of dropped rows increases, the height of the image becomes visibly compressed.

Choice of Threshold and Overall Performance. Based on the quantitative data from Fig. 2a and the analysis above, we propose using 15% as the threshold for selecting the mitigation strategy. When only a small number of rows are dropped, the imputation strategy ensures that the image retains as much integrity as possible, maintaining the degradation within 4%. When more than 15% rows are dropped, the degradation impact of the attack on the model's performance can be limited to within 14%. The similar method and analysis also apply to the other two models, and we do not further discuss them here.

5   Conclusion

This paper has investigated the impact of Electromagnetic Signal Injection Attacks (ESIA) on image sensing. By analyzing the effects of ESIA, we have identified two primary factors contributing to model degradation: pixel loss and color strips. Our findings demonstrate that in the task of image classification, color distortion has a more significant impact on model performance than pixel loss. To mitigate the effects of ESIA, we explore a lightweight solution that can effectively address some instances of color distortion.

References

1. Bayer, B.: Color Imaging Array. United States Patent, no. 3971065 (1976)
2. Dosovitskiy, A.: An Image Is Worth 16×16 Words: Transformers for Image Recognition at Scale. arXiv preprint arXiv:2010.11929 (2020)
3. Jiang, Q., Ji, X., Yan, C., Xie, Z., Lou, H., Xu, W.: GlitchHiker: uncovering vulnerabilities of image signal transmission with IEMI. In: The 32nd USENIX Security Symposium (2023)
4. Köhler, S., Baker, R., Martinovic, I.: Signal injection attacks against CCD image sensors. In: Proceedings of the 2022 ACM on Asia Conference on Computer and Communications Security, pp. 294–308 (2022)
5. Kune, D.F., et al.: Ghost talk: mitigating EMI signal injection attacks against analog sensors. In: 2013 IEEE Symposium on Security and Privacy, pp. 145–159. IEEE (2013)
6. Liao, W., Yan, S., Zhang, Y., Zhai, X., Wang, Y., Fu, E.: Is your autonomous vehicle safe? Understanding the threat of electromagnetic signal injection attacks on traffic scene perception. In: Proceedings of the AAAI Conference on Artificial Intelligence. vol. 39, pp. 27464–27472 (2025)
7. Liu, Z., et al.: Swin transformer V2: Scaling up capacity and resolution. arXiv preprint arXiv:2111.09883 (2022). https://arxiv.org/abs/2111.09883
8. Liu, Z., Lin, F., Ba, Z., Lu, L., Ren, K.: MagShadow: physical adversarial example attacks via electromagnetic injection. IEEE Transactions on Dependable and Secure Computing (2025)
9. Paul, C.R., Scully, R.C., Steffka, M.A.: Introduction to Electromagnetic Compatibility. John Wiley & Sons (2022)
10. Ren, Y., Jiang, Q., Yan, C., Ji, X., Xu, W.: GhostShot: manipulating the image of CCD cameras with electromagnetic interference. In: NDSS (2025)
11. Russakovsky, O., et al.: ImageNet large scale visual recognition challenge. Int. J. Comput. Vision **115**(3), 211–252 (2015). https://doi.org/10.1007/s11263-015-0816-y
12. Wilson, P.F.: Radiation patterns of unintentional antennas: estimates, simulations, and measurements. In: 2010 Asia-Pacific International Symposium on Electromagnetic Compatibility, pp. 985–989. IEEE (2010)
13. Xie, S., Girshick, R., Dollár, P., Tu, Z., He, K.: Aggregated residual transformations for deep neural networks. arXiv preprint arXiv:1611.05431 (2017). https://arxiv.org/abs/1611.05431
14. Zhang, Y., et al.: Modeling Electromagnetic Signal Injection Attacks on Camera-based Smart Systems: Applications and Mitigation. arXiv preprint arXiv:2408.05124 (2024)

15. Zhang, Y., Ji, X., Wang, Z., Jiang, Q.: Rainbow artifacts from electromagnetic signal injection attacks on image sensors. In: 2025 IEEE International Workshop on Signal Processing Systems (2025)
16. Zhang, Y., et al.: Understanding impacts of electromagnetic signal injection attacks on object detection. In: IEEE International Conference on Multimedia and Expo. IEEE (2024)

User-to-PC Authentication Through Confirmation on Mobile Devices: On Usability and Performance

Andreas Pramendorfer[1,2]($\boxtimes$) and Rainhard Dieter Findling[1,3]($\boxtimes$)

[1] SAIL Department, University of Applied Sciences Upper Austria, Hagenberg, Austria
`s2310455004@fhooe.at`, `rainhard.findling@fh-hagenberg.at`
[2] x-tention Informationstechnologie GmbH, Hagenberg, Austria
[3] Google LLC, Hagenberg, Austria

Abstract. Protecting personal computers (PCs) from unauthorized access typically relies on password authentication, which is known to suffer from cognitive burden and weak credentials. As many users nowadays carry mobile devices with advanced security features throughout their day, there is an opportunity to leverage these devices to improve authentication to PCs. In this paper we empirically evaluate a token-based, passwordless approach in which users authenticate to their PC by confirming the authentication request on their smartphone or smartwatch. Upon a request to login to the PC, or to evaluate privileges, the PC issues an authentication request that users receive on their mobile devices, where users can confirm or deny the request. We evaluate button tap and biometric fingerprint verification as confirmation variants, and compare their authentication duration, success rate, and usability to traditional password-based authentication in a user study with 30 participants and a total of 1,200 authentication attempts. Smartwatch-based authentication outperformed password-based authentication and smartphone-based variants in authentication duration, while showing comparable success rates. Participants rated smartwatch-based authentication highest in usability, followed by password-based authentication and smartphone-based authentication.

Keywords: Computer authentication · Token-based authentication · Passwordless authentication · Multi device scenario · Mobile devices

1 Introduction

Personal computers (PCs) provide access to a noteworthy amount of sensitive data and services that need protection from unauthorized access. Users authenticating to those devices before they can use them, or before they can access sensitive data or services on those devices, is a key part of this protection. However, user authentication mechanisms can bring usability drawbacks [2]. PCs predominantly rely on passwords for user authentication, which are known to suffer

P. Delir Haghighi et al. (Eds.): MoMM 2025, LNCS 16329, pp. 93–107, 2026.
https://doi.org/10.1007/978-3-032-11768-7_8

from high cognitive load on users and bad scalability across accounts [1]. These drawbacks often cause users to reuse passwords or choose weak passwords [1]. Biometric authentication can offer improved usability over passwords, as users do not have to remember and cannot lose them. However, biometric authentication is unavailable on many desktop computers, and also on a noteworthy portion of consumer laptops.

Nowadays, many users carry one or more personal mobile devices on them throughout their day, such as a smartphone or smartwatch. Those mobile devices present an opportunity to enhance authentication to PCs – by incorporating the mobile devices into the authentication process. Modern smartphones are often equipped with advanced security features, including hardware-based secure enclaves for biometrics and cryptographic keys, making them well-suited as secure tokens [7,9]. As users already carry these mobile devices on them, they can be utilized as hardware authentication tokens for authentication to the user's PCs, without them having to carry any additional hardware. This could be utilized to improve the usability of authentication to the user's PC, while maintaining authentication security on the level of the security of their mobile devices.

In this paper, we evaluate an authentication approach for PCs that incorporates users' mobile devices to provide a user-friendly, secure, token-based authentication experience. When the user encounters a situation in which they have to authenticate to their PC (e.g. to login to the computer, or to elevate their privileges), the computer sends an authentication request to the user's mobile devices. Upon confirming the authentication on the mobile device through a button tap or biometric verification, the mobile device sends the confirmation back to the computer to complete the authentication. The user's mobile devices thereby act as authenticators for their PCs. To enroll a mobile device as an authenticator for a PC, the user registers the public key of a public/private key pair generated on the mobile device with the authentication service for the PC. On an authentication attempt, the PC notifies the mobile device with a cryptographic challenge. On user confirmation, the mobile device utilizes the private key to sign the cryptographic challenge and send the response back, which the PC verifies with the respective public key. This prevents replay attacks also for situations in which the connection between PC and mobile device would be insecure, and maintains authentication security on the level of the security of the mobile device.

To evaluate this approach, we implement it as a mobile device application for Android and Wear OS that communicates with a personal Linux computer over a REST API. We conduct a user study with 30 participants to answer the following research questions (RQ): RQ1: How does the authentication duration and success rate of this multi-device authentication approach compare to password-based authentication? RQ2: How do users perceive the usability of this multi-device authentication approach over password-based authentication?

2 Related Work

We review prior work on utilizing mobile devices as authenticators to unlock other devices or services, without the mobile devices being a second factor in multi-factor authentication. Most prior work in this area focuses on authentication approaches for the world wide web (web-based authentication). Some prior work covers other areas, such as continuous implicit authentication with mobile devices.

The FIDO2 standard provides an open authentication framework that allows users to authenticate through security keys, so-called passkeys, with the aim to make authentication passwordless. These passkeys can be stored on devices like smartphones, or dedicated authentication hardware tokens such as FIDO2 authenticator keys [4]. Microsoft Windows natively supports FIDO2 keys, and Linux provides support through extension modules. Both operating systems currently support only specific USB-based authenticator keys for system logons. The FIDO2 Web Authentication (WebAuthn) API enables web applications to utilize passwordless authentication, supporting platform authenticators as well as roaming authenticators [12]. Platform authenticators include built-in biometrics such as a fingerprint sensor built into a laptop. Roaming authenticators are portable hardware devices like USB security keys. Despite the many security benefits that FIDO2-like authentication protocols offer over password-based authentication, like resistance to phishing attacks or elimination of credential reuse, they still suffer from limitations. Lyastani et al. [6] investigated factors that could limit the future adoption of FIDO2. Their findings show that users consider FIDO2 passwordless authentication as more usable and acceptable than password-based authentication. However, the fact that the authenticator is yet another piece of hardware that users have to carry on them to allow them to authenticate in their everyday authentication situations, and the fear of losing those authenticators, which would result in the user losing access and the risks of non-authorized parties gaining access, are the main factors that potentially impede the adoption of FIDO2.

Symbolon [10] presents a multi-device authentication approach that requires at least t out of n authenticator devices to be present for the user to be able to perform an authentication. This addresses the risk of unauthorized access from loss or theft of one authenticator, as it is resilient to loss or theft of up to $t-1$ devices. They use threshold cryptography while staying compliant with the FIDO2 API. They have found Symbolon to be more secure than standard, single-factor FIDO2 while also allowing users to manage authenticators on their side without needing to do so on an account-by-account basis. Symbolon, utilizing the FIDO2 API for user authentication, inherits the standard FIDO2 limitation of primarily supporting USB-based authenticator keys for Windows and Linux system logons, due to operating system constraints.

Chaudhari et al. [3] provide a detailed survey of existing authentication systems, which they categorize into password-based, multi-factor, and passwordless methods. They evaluate the security, usability, and scalability of mechanisms such as two-factor authentication (2FA), token-based authentication, biometrics, magic links, and FIDO2 protocols. The paper highlights the vulnerabilities of traditional password systems, particularly their susceptibility to phishing and credential theft, and identifies biometric authentication as the most secure form of passwordless authentication. Based on this analysis, they propose a passwordless authentication framework that uses mobile notifications and biometric input on the mobile device for authentication on a web portal. However, implementation details of the proposed approach are omitted, and the system is not evaluated in a user study, limiting conclusions about its practical effectiveness and usability.

Hintze et al. [8] focus on continuous implicit authentication with multiple mobile devices, with the aim to improve the usability and security of mobile device authentication. Their approach continuously verifies the user's identity through different implicit modalities without requiring explicit authentication actions from the user. The authors implemented their approach as an Android authentication framework that uses transparent behavioral and physiological biometrics as authentication modalities, like gait, face, voice, and keystroke dynamics, to continuously evaluate the user's identity. In their evaluation, their approach was able to reduce the need for users to explicitly authenticate by up to 97%. However, they also find that for the framework to work in a production environment, support from the mobile device operating system vendors would be needed. The approach of this paper differs from this approach by users explicitly confirming authentication attempts on their mobile devices, instead of the approach continuously authenticating users through different modalities.

ShakeUnlock [5] proposes to transfer the authentication state from one mobile device to another through conjoint shaking. The approach leverages synchronized accelerometer data to determine if two devices, such as a smartwatch and smartphone, are being shaken together by the same user. Evaluation results indicate that conjoint shaking for 2 s yields a true match rate of 0.795 and a true non-match rate of 0.867, with a mean unlock time of about 2.5 s. ShakeUnlock shares similarities with our work, as it leverages mobile devices users carry on them throughout their day as authenticators for other devices, and as it deals with explicit authentication through user gestures. Key differences to our work include shaking as authentication modality and the resulting limitation to users authenticating to mobile devices – conjoint shaking cannot be applied with PCs, hence is not applicable for user-to-PC authentication.

In summary, prior research has investigated how utilizing multiple mobile devices can help improve usability and security in authentication scenarios. FIDO2-based approaches use authentication tokens and APIs such as WebAuthn to replace password-based with passwordless authentication [4,10]. These approaches predominantly focus on web-based authentication and face usability challenges from users having to carry additional hardware authentication tokens, and from the risk of loss or theft of those tokens [6]. Symbolon [10] addresses the fear of imminent unauthorized access following token loss by using threshold cryptography to enhance security, improve recovery processes, and manage authenticators across devices. However, it inherits the FIDO2 limitation of primarily supporting USB-based authenticator keys for Windows and Linux system logons. Implicit authentication with behavioral and physiological biometrics shows promise for user-friendly authentication, but challenges remain in terms of system integration, device support, and user adoption [8]. Additionally, prior research on implicit authentication mainly targets continuous rather than explicit authentication, hence addresses a related but different challenge. Shake-Unlock [5] proposes a form of explicit authentication by transferring authentication states from one mobile device to another by conjoint shaking, which is not applicable for user-to-PC authentication. Users authenticating to PCs via mobile devices they already carry on them remains under-examined, especially regarding the resulting authentication success rate, authentication duration, and usability, in comparison to password-based authentication that most PCs use as of today.

3 Approach

The approach allows users to authenticate to their PCs through a button tap or biometric verification on their mobile devices that they already carry on them throughout their day.

To enroll a mobile device such as a smartphone or smartwatch as an authenticator for a PC, the smartphone first generates a public/private key pair. The user registers the public key with the authentication service for the PC, so that the mobile device with the matching private key can later confirm the authentication request for this computer. This ensures that only authorized mobile devices can confirm authentication requests for a PC, and prevents replay attacks even in case the connection between PC and mobile device would be insecure. Device enrollment, particularly the exchange of public keys between devices and services, is a well-established process in modern authentication systems. Solutions such as the WebAuthn API [12] or the U2F registration process [11] exemplify device enrollment with public keys. Furthermore, this enrollment needs to be done only once per PC and mobile device – and hence does not impact the duration, success rate, or usability of authentication attempts that are conducted after enrollment. For this reason, we declare details of the enrollment process to be out of scope of this paper – in the remaining paper, we focus on authentication attempts that are conducted after enrollment.

In authentication scenarios the approach is utilized as follows (Fig. 1): when the user encounters a situation in which they have to authenticate to their PC (e.g. to login to the computer, or to elevate their privileges) they are informed that they can confirm the authentication request on their mobile device, together with a randomly chosen 3 digit comparison code. In the background, the PC sends an authentication request to the authentication service, which creates a cryptographic challenge and sends it to the user's smartphone. On their smartphone, the user is notified of the incoming authentication request via an operating system notification. A tap on this notification opens the authenticator application, where they can confirm or deny the request. There they also see the

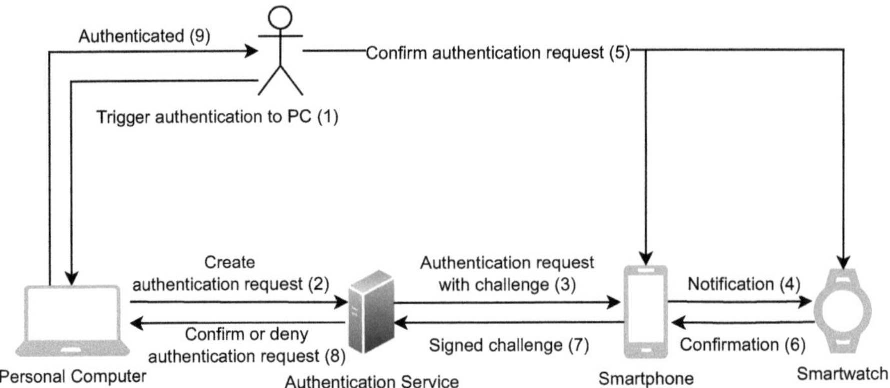

Fig. 1. Overview of the authentication process.

same randomly chosen 3-digit comparison code, which reassures them they are about to confirm the correct authentication request. We provide and compare different variants for users to confirm their authentication requests on their mobile devices. Those include: to tap an on-screen button on their smartphone or their smartwatch, and to do a biometric fingerprint verification on their smartphone or their smartwatch. Upon user confirmation, the authenticator application signs the cryptographic challenge and sends it back to the authentication service. The authentication service verifies the signature with the public key for the mobile device, and if correct, confirms the authentication attempt.

3.1   Computer Authentication Module

The authentication module is integrated with the PC's operating system authentication system. When users attempt to log in to the PC, or to elevate their privileges on the PC, then the operating system authentication system triggers this authentication module as one way to conduct the authentication. The module informs users that they can confirm the authentication on their mobile device, and creates the authentication requests at the authentication service of the approach. The module then waits for the response from the authentication service to accept or deny the authentication attempt. If the response does not arrive within a specific time, the module will deny the authentication attempt. For our evaluation we implement this module as a PAM (Pluggable Authentication Module). This allows the module to be integrated with the PAM framework, and thereby to authenticate to computers and operating systems that support the PAM framework, such as Linux, without requiring further modifications to the computer, operating system, or any further installed applications.

3.2   Authentication Service

The authentication service handles the communication between the authentication module and the mobile device through which users can confirm authentication requests. On an authentication request from the authentication module, it generates a unique challenge and sends it to the mobile device. On receiving the response, it verifies it with the mobile device public key, and notifies the authentication module to accept or deny the authentication request accordingly. For our evaluation, we implement this authentication service as a REST-API that the mobile applications communicate with, utilizing the .NET Core framework and its built-in cryptographic features.

3.3   Mobile Applications

The mobile applications run on users' mobile devices and enable those devices to act as authenticators for the PC. On the first start, the smartphone application generates a public/private key pair and stores the private key in the secure storage of the phone. When the application receives an authentication request, it prompts the user to confirm or deny the authentication. On confirmation it signs the authentication request challenge with the private key and sends the signature back to the authentication service. Different confirmation variants are possible: users can confirm either on their smartphone or smartwatch, either via a button tap or a biometric fingerprint verification. We compare those variants in our evaluation. The communication between smartwatch and smartphone is based on the connection between those devices that results from them being paired to each other. For our evaluation we implement those mobile applications as Android and Wear OS applications.

4   Evaluation

We implement the approach in a prototype[1] and evaluate it in a user study with 30 participants and compare its authentication duration, success rate, and usability to password-based authentication.

4.1   Evaluation Procedure

The evaluation was conducted in a controlled environment. Participants were seated in an empty room where only the supervisor and the participant were present. A supervisor provided instructions and monitored the session. In the setup phase of the study, participants filled out a pre-study questionnaire that assessed their technical expertise. The questionnaire result allowed the supervisor to assign the participant to either the technically versed or less technically versed group of participants, which had slightly different study procedures (Sect. 4.2). Then, participants were instructed to choose a password for the PC

---

[1] https://github.com/apramendorfer/mobile-linux-auth.

of the complexity they would typically use for PC authentication, and to not reuse a password they used outside the study. This password was set as the password for the PC. Participants then configured fingerprint authentication on the smartphone, locked it, and stored it as they would when they carry it throughout their day (e.g. in their trousers' pocket). They were then instructed to store the smartphone the same way after every authentication they conducted during the study. They then attached the smartwatch, which was already paired with the smartphone, to their preferred wrist. Participants were instructed to unlock the smartwatch and to keep it on their wrist for the remaining study, so that it would not lock from being removed from the wrist. This setup simulates how users typically carry their devices throughout the day: the smartphone locked and stored away, the smartwatch unlocked and worn on their wrist.

After the setup phase, participants engaged in a series of tasks, such as browsing the web or copying text, during which they had to authenticate 8 times to the PC (Table 1). Participants repeated this series of tasks 5 times, utilizing a different authentication mechanism for each series: (1) password authentication on the PC, (2) confirmation via button tap on the smartphone, (3) confirmation via biometric verification on the smartphone, (4) confirmation via button tap on the smartwatch, (5) confirmation via biometric verification on the smartwatch. For every participant the first series utilized password authentication, which represents the baseline to compare to. The order of the remaining authentication mechanisms series was chosen randomly for every participant, to avoid potential bias effects from an authentication mechanism coming earlier or later in the study. After completing the 5 series of tasks, participants filled out a usability questionnaire.

4.2   Questionnaires and Measurements

In the pre-study questionnaire that participants filled out before the study, they stated their age (numeric), gender (male/female/other), if they currently work in a job that falls into a technical area like IT, engineering, or software development (from "fully disagree" to 'fully agree"), if and how often they use a smartphone, smartwatch, Linux, git, or a command line (5 separate questions, "never" to "very often"), as well as their self-assessed level of knowledge in areas such as two-factor authentication, biometric authentication, or token-based authentication (1 question, "no knowledge/no experience" to "expert knowledge/frequent use"). Based on their questionnaire answers, they were assigned to the technically versed or the less technically versed group of participants. Participants that fulfill all of the following were assigned to the technically versed group: they agree or fully agree to work in a technical field, have basic knowledge of authentication methods like two-factor authentication, biometrics, or token-based authentication, and have executed sudo commands on Linux at least rarely.

For authentications that participants performed during the study, we measure the duration that it took participants to conduct the authentication attempt and if the authentication attempt was successful. For unlocking the PC we measure the authentication duration as the time in between participants triggering

Table 1. Series of tasks for the less technically versed and technically versed participant groups. Every task that includes login to the PC or execution of a sudo command required authentication.

Less technically versed	Technically versed
1. Login to the PC	1. Login to the PC
2. Open a web browser	2. Open a web browser
3. Logout+login to the PC	3. Logout+login to the PC
4. Navigate to a search engine in the web browser	4. Navigate to a search engine in the web browser
5. Logout+login to the PC	5. Logout+login to the PC
6. Search for an encyclopedia website and open it	6. Search for an encyclopedia website and open it
7. Logout+login to the PC	7. Logout+login to the PC
8. Search for "Austria" on the encyclopedia website	8. Open a terminal emulator
9. Logout+login to the PC	9. Execute `sudo apt update` in the terminal emulator
10. Scroll down to the "Sports" section	10. Close and reopen terminal emulator
11. Logout+login to the PC	11. Execute `sudo apt install git` in the terminal emulator
12. Open a notepad application	12. Close and reopen terminal emulator
13. Logout+login to the PC	13. Execute `sudo apt remove git` in the terminal emulator
14. Copy a paragraph from the "Sports" section opened earlier into the notepad application	14. Close and reopen terminal emulator
15. Logout+login to the PC	15. Execute `sudo apt autoremove` in the terminal emulator
16. Save the notebook application content into a file on the file system	

the PC login screen, which triggers the authentication attempt, and the authentication attempt being confirmed, which unlocks the PC. For sudo commands we measure the authentication duration as the time in between participants submitting the sudo command, which triggers the authentication attempt, and the authentication attempt being confirmed, which executes the sudo command. We also assess the password complexity of passwords that participants chose for the study via the zxcvbn password strength estimator [13]. This yields a score $[0, 4]$ per password, from 0 for very weak passwords, to 4 for very strong passwords.

The usability questionnaire that participants filled out after the study contained a total of 22 5-point Likert-scale questions: 2 questions for password-based authentication, to assess participants' perception of ease of use (from "very difficult" to "very easy") and speed (from "very slow" to "very fast"), as the baseline to compare to. And 5 questions for each of the 4 variants of the approach (authentication confirmation via button tap or biometric verification, on smartphone or smartwatch), to assess participants' perception of ease of use and speed (same possible answers as for password-based questions), and also for ease of adaptation (from "very hard" to "very easy"), reliability (from "very unreliable" to "very reliable"), and the likelihood of switching from password-based authentication to the proposed approach if it were available today (from "very unlikely" to "very likely").

4.3   Participants, Hardware, and Recorded Data

Participants were recruited for our evaluation study through word of mouth among students of the University of Applied Sciences Upper Austria and their relatives, friends, and colleagues. Most participants received compensation for their participation in form of a beverage. 30 participants (mean age 34.1 years, age standard deviation 12.3; 17 male, 13 female, 0 other) completed the study. 18 participants were assessed to belong to the technically versed group of participants, 12 to the less technically versed group. While nearly all participants (28) were regular smartphone users, only 10 participants stated that they regularly use a smartwatch. All of the 30 participants completed the series of tasks for each of the 5 authentication variants, which each consist of 8 authentications. This results in 40 authentications per participant, 240 authentications per authentication variant, and 1200 authentications in total.

All participants used a Google Pixel 6, a Samsung Galaxy Watch4, and a Lenovo Yoga Creator 7 Laptop to complete the evaluation. The Google Pixel 6 comes with an under-display biometric fingerprint sensor which we use for the biometric confirmation. The Galaxy Watch4 does not have a biometric fingerprint sensor. Instead, the mobile application for the evaluation on the smartwatch mocks a biometric fingerprint sensor as follows: it imitates the UI for under-display fingerprint sensors found on Android smartphones by displaying a round button with a fingerprint icon. When pressed, the button triggers a ripple effect, and after being pressed for 400 ms, the application confirms the authentication. If pressed less than 400 ms the authentication fails. Participants were informed that the fingerprint sensor on the smartwatch is simulated.

5   Results and Discussions

Table 2 shows the duration required to perform the authentication and the authentication success rate for all variants of the approach. Authentication variants with confirmation on the smartwatch were the fastest, with a mean authentication duration of 4.5 s (button tap) and 4.6 s (biometric verification). Password-based authentication to the PC ranked second, with a mean duration of 4.6 s. In contrast, smartphone-based authentication confirmation was noticeably slower with a mean duration of 7.0 s. One factor that causes confirmations to take noticeably longer on the smartphone than on the smartwatch is that users first

Table 2. Mean authentication duration (standard deviation) and mean authentication success rate, per variant and group of participants.

Variant	All		Technical		Less Technical	
	Duration	Success	Duration	Success	Duration	Success
Password	4.6 s (1.8 s)	97%	3.5 s (0.9 s)	97%	6.4 s (1.4 s)	97%
Phone (Button)	6.6 s (2.3 s)	100%	6.5 s (1.7 s)	100%	6.7 s (3.0 s)	100%
Phone (Biometric)	7.4 s (2.0 s)	98%	6.9 s (1.8 s)	100%	8.1 s (2.3 s)	96%
Watch (Button)	4.5 s (2.0 s)	96%	4.4 s (1.8 s)	96%	4.6 s (2.4 s)	96%
Watch (Biometric)	4.6 s (1.5 s)	98%	5.0 s (1.8 s)	97%	3.9 s (1.2 s)	99%

Table 3. Mean results of the usability questionnaire, for all participants (All), technically versed participants (T), and less technically versed participants (LT). Answers reflect users' perception of ease of use (Q1), speed (Q2), ease of adoption (Q3), reliability (Q4), and likelihood of utilizing the approach if it were available today (Q5).

Variant	Q1			Q2			Q3			Q4			Q5		
	All	T	LT	All	T	LT	All	T	LT	All	T	LT	All	T	LT
Password	4.5	4.7	4.3	3.4	3.5	3.3	n/a	n/a	n/a	n/a	n/a	n/a	n/a	n/a	n/a
Phone (Button)	3.9	3.7	4.3	3.7	3.5	4.0	4.1	4.0	4.3	4.1	3.8	4.5	3.2	3.3	3.0
Phone (Biometric)	4.1	4.0	4.3	3.9	3.8	4.0	3.9	3.8	4.0	4.0	3.8	4.3	3.2	3.7	2.5
Watch (Button)	4.7	4.5	4.9	4.6	4.5	4.8	4.6	4.5	4.8	4.2	4.0	4.5	3.8	4.2	3.3
Watch (Biometric)	4.6	4.5	4.8	4.5	4.5	4.4	4.7	4.7	4.8	4.4	4.3	4.5	4.1	4.5	3.5

have to authenticate to the smartphone to unlock it, before they can confirm the authentication request. In contrast, the smartwatch remains unlocked on their wrist, which allows to confirm the authentication request without having to at first unlock the smartwatch. On both the smartphone and smartwatch, confirming via biometric verification was slower, which aligns with biometric verification taking longer than tapping a confirmation button on a device.

Almost all participants (27) chose a strong or very strong password. As a result, the authentication time measurements for password-based authentication are primarily based on strong and very strong passwords. Due to the small number of weaker passwords in the study, we refrain from drawing conclusions about the relationship between weaker passwords and study results. Furthermore, all authentication approaches had a high success rate. Password-based authentication achieved a 97% success rate, and the mean success rate for the approach was 98%, ranging from 96–100%. The differences between the confirmation variants were minor (Table 2).

Participants generally found the approach easy to use (Table 3), with smartwatch-based authentication receiving the highest rating (mean 4.7), followed by password-based authentication (mean 4.5), and smartphone-based authentication (mean 4.0). The inclusion of biometric verification did not notice-ably impact how participants perceived ease of use.

When asked if they would use the approach instead of password-based authentication if it were available today, participants expressed stronger interest in the smartwatch-based variants (mean 4.0) compared to smartphone-based variants (mean 3.2). Inclusion of biometric verification had no noticeable impact on users' interest to use the approach over password-based authentication. This indicates that the choice of device, which in turn impacts the duration it takes to perform an authentication, likely is a stronger decision factor than the choice between button tap or biometric verification as authentication confirmation method.

In between the technically versed and less technically versed groups of participants we observed a noticeable difference in authentication duration for password-based authentication (Table 2). Password-based authentication took noticeably less time for participants in the technically versed group (mean 3.5 s) over the less technically versed group (mean 6.4 s). In contrast, for the smartphone- and smartwatch-based approach, this gap in authentication duration was noticeably smaller between the two groups (mean difference of 0.7 s for both approaches). This indicates that the authentication duration of the approach is less affected by the users' technical expertise than password-based authentication. No noticeably relevant difference in success rates was found between the two groups.

Usability results also varied between the technically versed and the less technically versed group of participants. When asked how likely they would use the approach over password-based authentication if it were available today, technically versed users rated the smartwatch variant with biometric confirmation with a mean of 4.5, while less technically versed users rated it with a mean of 3.5. This difference could indicate that greater familiarity with the technology and the respective mobile devices increases the likelihood of users adopting the approach.

Limitations of the approach and its evaluation include that the security of the approach inherently depends on the security of the mobile devices used as authenticators. If a mobile device used as authenticator gets compromised, then this also compromises the approach and allows attackers to confirm an authentication attempt to the PC. However, this also requires attackers to obtain access to the mobile device that serves as authenticator device – either in an already unlocked state, or with the additional effort of also obtaining the means to unlock the mobile device. Concretely, if a smartphone used as authenticator is protected by a weak authentication mechanism (e.g. a weak PIN), if attackers obtain physical access to it, then they might be able to unlock and compromise it. In contrast, smartwatches typically stay unlocked while attached to the user's wrist and lock when being taken off the wrist. For this reason attackers could create a malicious authentication request in a moment where the user does not observe the notification on their smartwatch, e.g. because they are distracted. Then the attackers could try to confirm the authentication attempt on the unlocked smartwatch attached to the user's wrist, without the user noticing, e.g. because they are in a crowded space. We leave it to future work to investigate how likely users are to notice such attacks.

Furthermore, password-based authentication to the PC will still need to be available as a fallback authentication for situations in which confirming authentication attempts via a mobile device is not possible. As a result, the security of the PC is still inherently dependent on the strength of its authentication password. However, as users would not need to enter or remember their fallback authentication password on a regular basis, they could choose a significantly stronger password that they look up in the rare cases when they need it. We leave it to future work to investigate the impact that regularly confirming authentication attempts on mobile devices instead of entering a password has on the strength of the password that users would choose for fallback authentication.

6   Conclusion

In this paper we investigated how authentication duration, success rate, and usability of users confirming authentication requests to their PCs on mobile devices they possess and already carry throughout their day compare to users authenticating to their PCs via entering a password. For the former, we evaluated a multi-device authentication approach that allows users to trigger an authentication on their PCs, e.g. to unlock it or to elevate their privileges, and then to confirm or deny the authentication request on a mobile device, e.g. a smartphone or smartwatch. We investigated different variants for how users can confirm this on their mobile devices: via a button tap or a biometric fingerprint verification, on their smartphone or their smartwatch.

To answer the research questions (RQ) posed in this paper we conducted a user study with 30 participants that evaluates and compares the different confirmation variants with traditional password-based authentication. With regards to RQ1, our results indicate that confirmation on the smartwatch is the fastest variant, followed by password-based authentication and confirmation on the smartphone (4.6 s, 4.6 s, and 7.0 s mean duration to authenticate, respectively). Success rates for confirmation on mobile devices are comparable to password-based authentication (98% and 97% mean authentication success rates). With regards to RQ2, participants rated the usability of confirmation on the smartwatch the highest, followed by password-based authentication and confirmation on the smartphone (4.7, 4.5, and 4.0 on a 5-point Likert-scale, respectively). Participants also indicated a stronger interest to switch their PC authentication to confirming on a smartwatch than on a smartphone, if the approach were available today (4.0 and 3.2 on a 5-point Likert-scale).

While our findings highlight the potential to improve user authentication to PCs through confirmation on mobile devices users already carry throughout their day, we acknowledge several limitations of our evaluation. The setup process, including device pairing and key exchange, was not part of the evaluation. These steps could impact user adoption and satisfaction in real-world scenarios. Also, the evaluation does not investigate how easy it would be for attackers to confirm an authentication request on the user's smartwatch while its attached to the user's wrist, without the user noticing. Furthermore, the impact of confirmation fatigue, where users are overwhelmed by the number of confirmations they have to do, and susceptibility to confirmation fatigue attacks, where attackers exploit that users have developed a habit of approving authentication requests on their mobile devices without verifying their legitimacy, have not been assessed.

Future research could investigate how strongly this setup process impacts usability, and how easy it would be for attackers to conduct those attacks. Furthermore, future research could investigate alternative methods of users confirming an authentication request on their mobile device, such as user gestures sensed by smartwatch sensors. It could also investigate user-friendly recovery mechanisms as an alternative to password-based authentication fallback for when the mobile device as the primary authenticator fails or is unavailable, e.g. through approaches like secure token syncing or threshold cryptography.

References

1. Bonneau, J., Herley, C., Oorschot, P.C.V., Stajano, F.: The quest to replace passwords: a framework for comparative evaluation of web authentication schemes. In: 2012 IEEE Symposium on Security and Privacy, pp. 553–567 (2012). https://doi.org/10.1109/SP.2012.44
2. Braz, C., Robert, J.M.: Security and usability: the case of the user authentication methods. In: Proceedings of the 18th Conference on l'Interaction Homme-Machine. p. 199–203. IHM '06, Association for Computing Machinery, New York, NY, USA (2006). https://doi.org/10.1145/1132736.1132768
3. Chaudhari, A., Pawar, A., Pawar, A., Pawar, A., Pawar, G.: A comprehensive study on authentication systems. In: 2023 7th International Conference On Computing, Communication, Control And Automation (ICCUBEA), pp. 1–5 (2023)
4. FIDO Alliance: FIDO2, Accessed 13 July 2024
5. Findling, R.D., Muaaz, M., Hintze, D., Mayrhofer, R.: ShakeUnlock: securely unlock mobile devices by shaking them together. In: Proceedings of the 12th International Conference on Advances in Mobile Computing and Multimedia, pp. 165–174 (2014)
6. Ghorbani Lyastani, S., Schilling, M., Neumayr, M., Backes, M., Bugiel, S.: Is FIDO2 the kingslayer of user authentication? a comparative usability study of FIDO2 passwordless authentication. In: 2020 IEEE Symposium on Security and Privacy (SP), pp. 268–285 (2020). https://doi.org/10.1109/SP40000.2020.00047
7. Google: android Keystore system. https://developer.android.com/privacy-and-security/keystore, Accessed 13 Dec 2024
8. Hintze, D., et al.: CORMORANT: on implementing risk-aware multi-modal biometric cross-device authentication for Android. In: Proceedings of the 17th International Conference on Advances in Mobile Computing & Multimedia, pp. 117–126. MoMM2019, ACM, New York, NY, USA (2020). https://doi.org/10.1145/3365921.3365923
9. Inc., A.: Protecting keys with the secure enclave (2024), https://developer.apple.com/documentation/security/protecting-keys-with-the-secure-enclave, Accessed 10 Dec 2024

10. Laing, T., Marin, E., Ryan, M.D., Schiffman, J., Wattiau, G.: Symbolon: enabling flexible multi-device-based user authentication. In: 2022 IEEE Conference on Dependable and Secure Computing (DSC), pp. 1–12 (2022). https://doi.org/10.1109/DSC54232.2022.9888854
11. Srinivas, S., Balfanz, D., Tiffany, E., Czeskis, A., Alliance, F.: Universal 2nd factor (u2f) overview. FIDO Alliance Proposed Standard **15**, 1–5 (2015)
12. W3C: Web Authentication: An API for accessing Public Key Credentials Level 2. https://www.w3.org/TR/webauthn-2/, Accessed 13 Dec 2024
13. Wheeler, D.L.: zxcvbn: low-budget password strength estimation. In: 25th USENIX Security Symposium (USENIX Security 16), pp. 157–173. USENIX Association, Austin, TX, August 2016, https://www.usenix.org/conference/usenixsecurity16/technical-sessions/presentation/wheeler

Silent Speech Recognition Using Ear Canal Pressure Changes

Yasufumi Hoji, Hiroki Watanabe[✉], and Yoshinari Takegawa

Future University Hakodate, 116-2 Kamedanakano-cho, Hakodate, Hokkaido
041-8655, Japan
{g2124042,hwata,yoshi}@fun.ac.jp

Abstract. Hearables, wearable earphone-type devices, are often operated via voice commands. However, voice control faces limitations such as sensitivity to environmental noise, difficulty in silent environments, and privacy concerns. Silent speech interaction (SSI) has been proposed to address these issues, with methods using IMUs and ultrasound showing promise. Yet, SSI using ear canal pressure remains underexplored. In this study, we propose a novel SSI method that recognizes silent speech by analyzing pressure changes in the ear canal, measured by a built-in barometric sensor. These signals are classified using machine learning techniques such as SVM, DTW, and kNN. Experiments were conducted with seven participants using five predefined commands related to music control. The proposed method achieved an average recognition accuracy of 72.0%. This low-power approach could be integrated with existing SSI methods, enabling adaptive switching depending on context while improving usability in diverse environments.

Keywords: SSI · Ear canal pressure · Hearable · Earable · Wearable computing

1 Introduction

Recent wireless earbuds offer a variety of features, including music playback, phone calls, activity tracking, noise cancelation, and ambient sound capture through transparency mode. These multifunctional devices are commonly referred to as "hearables" or "earables" [3,11]. Hearables are projected to account for over 60% of all wearable device shipments by 2025, a trend that is expected to continue [7]. Consequently, the number of hearable users is anticipated to increase further in the coming years.

Most methods of operating hearables involve linking them to a smartphone and operating them from the smartphone, or by touching itself. However, using a smartphone to operate hearables is not intuitive, and operating hearables by touching itself is not desirable in a wearable environment where hands-free operation is required. Voice control of devices is commonly used as a method to enable

P. Delir Haghighi et al. (Eds.): MoMM 2025, LNCS 16329, pp. 108–121, 2026.
https://doi.org/10.1007/978-3-032-11768-7_9

hands-free operation. However, voice control has some issues, such as being easily affected by environmental noise, being difficult to use in quiet spaces, and the possibility of information leakage when inputting information.

As a method to solve these problems, the silent speech interaction (SSI) has been attracting attention. SSI methods include transmitting ultrasound into the ear canal and obtaining the change in ear canal shape during speech from reflected waves to perform SSI [4,14,15], using an inertial measurement unit (IMU) and an electromyography sensor on the skin surface [13], and using magnetic implants [5]. Meanwhile, sensing methods using air pressure sensors installed in hearables have also been attracting attention in recent years [6,9]. However, to our knowledge, there has been no research investigating SSI using a barometric pressure sensor. If SSI using ear canal pressure could be realized, it could be used in conjunction with existing IMU or ultrasound-based methods, or adaptively switched between them, expanding SSI methods in hearables.

Therefore, the purpose of this study is to explore the performance of an SSI method using ear canal air pressure. Specifically, the change in air pressure caused by deformation of the ear canal during silent speech (SS) is measured by an air pressure sensor installed inside the hearable, and the content of the SS is estimated from the air pressure change.

We conducted experiments to evaluate the performance of the proposed method. An average recognition rate of 72.0% was obtained for five subjects and seven commands.

The contributions of this study are as follows:

- We propose SSI method using ear canal pressure changes measured by a barometric pressure sensor embedded in a hearable device.
- The proposed method operates at a low sampling rate (30 Hz), enabling significantly lower power consumption compared to ultrasound-based or IMU-based SSI methods, which makes it well-suited for practical deployment in wearable environments.
- We conducted a user study with seven participants and achieved an average F1-score of 72.0% across five silent speech commands, demonstrating that SSI is feasible using a simple sensor configuration.

2   Related Work

2.1   SSI Methods

There has been many researches into SSI using various methods. Dong used ultrasonic sensing of the ear canal to obtain SS [4]. Ultrasonic sensing in hearables devices is a method in which an ultrasonic signal emitted from an earphone speaker is reflected by the shape of the ear canal, and the reflected wave is obtained by a microphone facing the ear canal [4]. The accuracy rate was 89.3% for a vocabulary of 100 words and 73.3% for a vocabulary of 1000 words. Srivastava placed the IMU and the Electrode (ExG) signals on headphones and VR goggles to obtain SS [13]. In this system, the IMU sensor captures the movement of the jaw and facial muscles, and the ExG sensor detects low-amplitude muscle activity related to speech production. In the experiment, participants were wearing both headphones and VR goggles. The accuracy rate was 94.2% for 12 types of commands. Gilbert used a magnetic implant and a magnetic sensor to obtain SS [5]. In this study, permanent magnets are attached to the tongue and lips, and changes in the magnetic field caused by their movement are detected by an external magnetic sensor. The obtained sensor data is classified using DTW. The accuracy rate was over 90% for 57 words. In comparison with these studies, this study proposes a method of SSI, which is rarely used for ear canal pressure. This is a method that can reduce power consumption compared to ultrasonic sensing.

Dong et al. used ultrasonic signals in the frequency band of 17.5–23 kHz, and although the sampling frequency was not specified, a sampling rate of 46 kHz or more is required according to the Nyquist theorem [10]. In this study, a method with low power consumption is proposed by setting the sampling frequency to 30 Hz. It is difficult to attach a large battery to a small device such as hearables. In addition, it is important to reduce power consumption in terms of popularizing it in general devices. Furthermore, by combining it with a sensor such as an IMU, it is expected that the accuracy will be improved in the future. In addition, compared to studies using ExG sensors and magnetic sensors, the ear canal pressure sensor used in this study can be worn in the ear like an everyday earphone without touching the skin, which reduces the discomfort caused to the subject.

2.2   Sensing Research Using Air Pressure Sensors Installed in Hearables

There are studies that use pressure sensors installed in hearables for sensing. Iguma et al. proposed gesture recognition for hearables [9]. They implemented a device that measures the pressure in the ear canal by installing a pressure sensor in hearables, and recognized eight types of operation methods from the pattern of pressure change in the ear canal caused by contact input, such as pressing and releasing hearables with a finger, and the pattern of pressure change caused by non-contact input, such as covering the auricle with a hand and applying pressure. For accuracy, they tried each gesture 50 times for eight subjects, and the maximum average F-measure was 0.93. Hossain is also detecting food intake [6]. They created hearables equipped with an accelerometer and a pressure sensor to detect food intake and count the number of chews. In terms of accuracy of food intake detection, for 10 subjects who wore the device for an hour and ate, the average F-score was 87.6% when classification was done using only the pressure sensor, and 88.6% when using features from both the pressure sensor and the accelerometer. In terms of accuracy of counting the number of chews, for 10 subjects, classification using only the pressure sensor was 95.5%.

In comparison to these studies, this study performs SSI. There are no examples of SSI recognition methods that incorporate a pressure sensor in hearables, and its potential has not been fully explored.

3   Proposed Method

When a person speaks, they move their jaw and tongue to produce speech. These movements also cause changes in the pressure within the ear canal. As shown in Fig. 1, such pressure changes occur due to alterations in the shape of the ear canal, which result from the positional relationship between the mandibular condyle and the ear canal [2]. Based on this, we propose a method for recognizing SS by capturing pressure variations in the ear canal caused by jaw and tongue movements during speech. Figure 2 shows the proposed method. The user wears a hearable with a built-in air pressure sensor. When the user speaks silently, characteristic changes appear on the air pressure sensor. These changes are identified using machine learning, and the content of the silent speech is obtained.

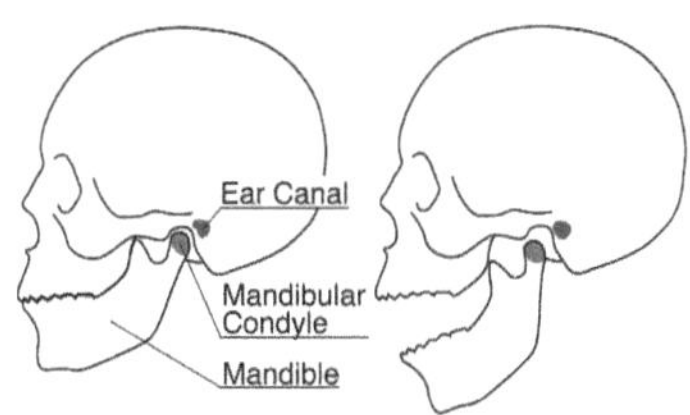

Fig. 1. How pressure in the ear canal changes

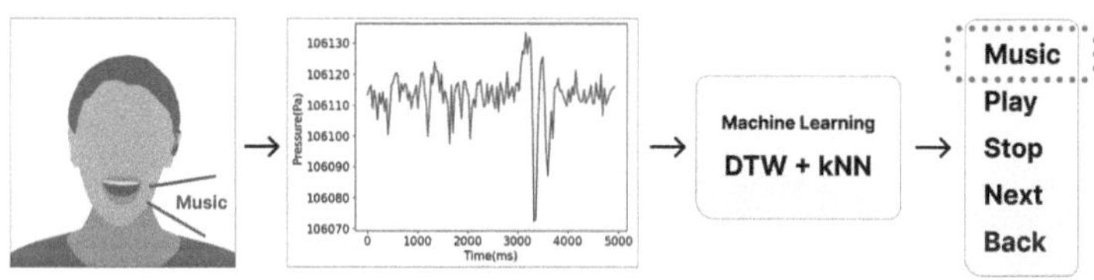

Fig. 2. Overview of the proposed method

3.1   Data Acquisition Environment

We used the OpenEarable v1.3 to capture pressure changes in the ear canal [12]. As shown in Fig. 3, OpenEarable is an earbud-shaped smart device equipped with an IMU sensor, an ear canal pressure sensor, and a temperature sensor.

For the ear tips, we used canal-type earpieces that provide high sealing and excellent sound isolation. The material of the ear tips was a soft polyurethane memory foam. The OpenEarable device is operated using the dedicated web application OpenEarable Dashboard, which communicates via WebBLE to acquire data. The sampling rate was set to 30 Hz.

In this study, data were collected in 5,000 ms segments corresponding to each utterance. The acquired data were saved in CSV format and processed using Python.

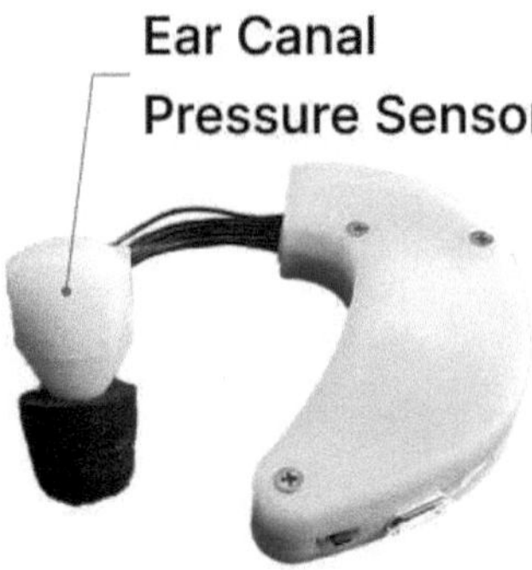

Fig. 3. OpenEarable

3.2   Preprocessing

The following preprocessing is performed on the data obtained for each participant. The preprocessing is shown in Fig. 4:

1. The raw data (Fig. 4(a)) contain high-frequency noise unrelated to SS. Therefore, a Butterworth low-pass filter was applied to attenuate frequencies above 4 Hz (Fig. 4(b)).
2. The initial pressure values from the built-in sensor may vary depending on the altitude at the time of acquisition and the fit of the device. To correct for this, baseline correction was performed. Specifically, the average value of the first 3,000 ms of each signal was calculated and subtracted from the entire signal to normalize the baseline to zero (Fig. 4(c)).
3. Although 5,000 ms of data were recorded per utterance, no distinctive patterns were observed near the start and end. Therefore, only the segment between 2,500 ms and 4,500 ms—where more prominent features were found—was extracted (Fig. 4(d)).
4. Due to instability in the silent speech gestures and variability in the device fit among individuals, some signals exhibited insufficient variation. To address this, outlier removal based on peak-to-peak values and the interquartile range (IQR) was performed. Specifically, the peak-to-peak values of all recordings were computed, and any samples with values above the third quartile + 1.5×IQR or below the first quartile - 1.5×IQR were considered outliers and

excluded from further processing. The average number of outliers per participant was approximately 9 out of 1050 (150 samples × 7 participants) (Fig. 4(e)).

An example of the data after the above preprocessing steps is shown in Fig. 5. This figure illustrates silent speech utterances of five different commands, spoken in the participant's native language, assuming use in a music application. As shown in the figure, each utterance produces a waveform with distinct characteristics. These differences suggest that silent speech can be classified based on these signal features.

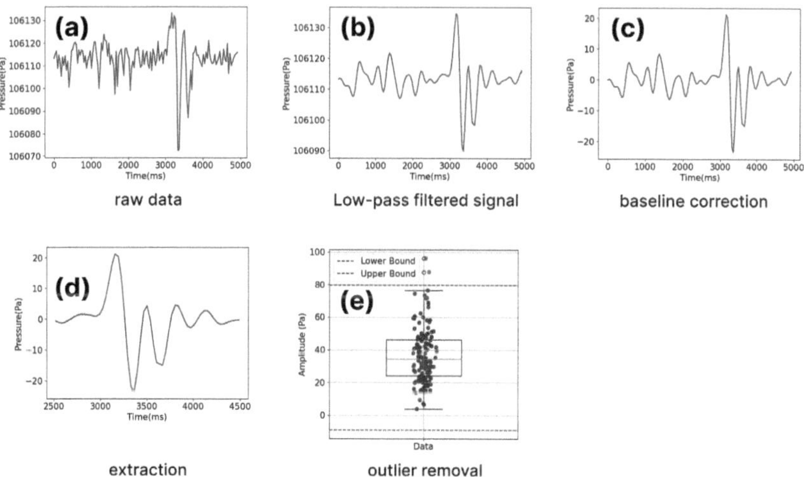

Fig. 4. Preprocessing: (a) raw data, (b) Low-pass filtered signal, (c) baseline correction, (d) extraction, and (e) outlier removal

3.3   Feature Extraction & Classification

In this study, we implemented two classification approaches: DTW + kNN, which classifies based on waveform shape, and SVM, which classifies based on features extracted from the waveform. DTW is a method for measuring similarity by expanding and contracting the time axis. Since the time axis of ear canal pressure data expands and contracts depending on the speed and strength of speech, we thought that DTW would be useful.

DTW + kNN: As shown in Fig. 5, each spoken command produces a distinct time-series waveform, enabling recognition using Dynamic Time Warping (DTW). The classification procedure is as follows:

1. The dataset is split into 20% test data (5 commands × 6 utterances) and 80% training data (5 commands × 24 utterances).

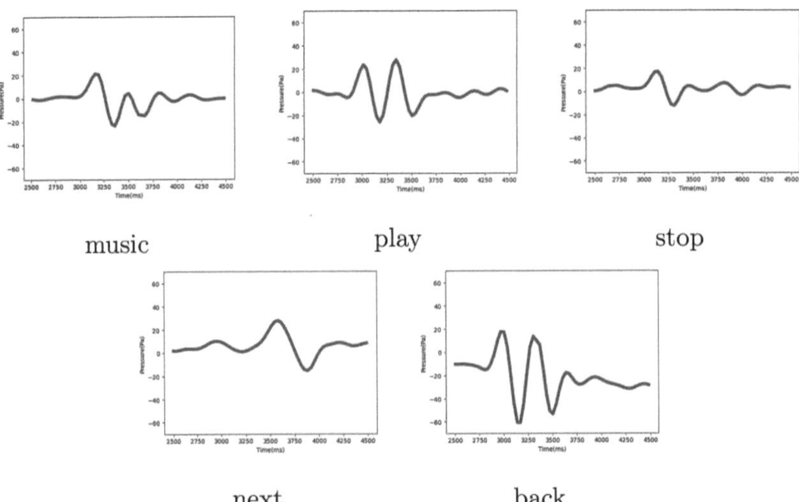

music   play   stop

next   back

Fig. 5. Waveform data for five voice commands

2. The DTW distance between each test sample and all training samples is computed.
3. Using the k-Nearest Neighbor (kNN) algorithm, the k training samples with the smallest DTW distances to the test sample are selected. The label of the test sample is determined based on the majority label among the selected samples. Based on results from an informal pre-test, k was set to 5.

SVM: Features were extracted from the waveform data obtained in the previous section. Effective features were selected from the 16 features using a feature selection method. Mutual information was used as the feature selection method. The top five features were obtained based on the correlation between the features and the objective variable. As a result, the following five features were used: standard deviation (sd), variance (var), kurtosis, meanMin10, and energy.

4   Evaluation

4.1   Procedure

In the evaluation experiment, we evaluated the recognition accuracy of the proposed method for five different silent speech commands. A total of seven participants (five male, two female; mean age = 27.14 ± 12.32 SD) took part in the experiment. Among these participants, there was one who was over 40 years old. However, the age-related hearing loss of this participant is not due to deformation of the ear canal, so it is thought that this will not affect the method.

Participants were asked to silently articulate five commands—"music," "stop," "play," "next," and "back"—in their native language, assuming operation of a music player. These commands were adopted from a previous study by Igarashi et al. [8], and prior research has shown that approximately five commands are sufficient for simple hands-free input scenarios [1].

Participants were instructed to move their mouths just enough to produce noticeable changes in the waveform. In addition, the waveform was visualized in real time using the OpenEarable Dashboard, allowing participants to verify the degree of movement required to generate such changes themselves.

Silent speech was performed in response to pre-recorded audio prompts. Each prompt counted down three seconds, played a chime on the fourth second, and then provided a two-second window for articulation. This process was repeated ten times for each command, with the same command repeated in each set. The commands were obtained in the following order: music, play, stop, next, and back. For each participant, a total of 150 samples were collected (5 commands × 10 repetitions × 3 sets). Participants did not remove or put on the device at any time during data collection.

Notably, we observed individual differences in ear canal pressure changes; therefore, we developed only person-dependent models in this study. The models were evaluated using 5-fold cross-validation.

4.2   Result

Table 1 presents the results for each participant. The average F1-score for DTW + kNN was 72.0% (minimum: 55.2%, maximum: 81.2%), while that for SVM was 54.1% (minimum: 33.5%, maximum: 75.0%).

Figure 6 shows the confusion matrix for the DTW + kNN method, and Fig. 7 shows the confusion matrix for the SVM method. Note that the values in each confusion matrix are normalized per row. In the case of DTW + kNN, the best-performing command was "next" with 76.5% accuracy, while the worst-performing command was "back" with 64.8%, which tended to be confused with "music." In the case of SVM, the best-performing command was "play" with 66.0% accuracy, while the worst-performing command was "back" with 50.0%, which tended to be confused with "music."

5   Discussion

As shown in Table 1, the proposed method achieved an average F-measure of 72.0% using DTW + kNN. This performance is lower compared to methods based on IMU and the electrode (ExG) signals (94.2%) [13] and ultrasound-based methods (89.3%) [4]. However, ultrasound-based methods require actively emitting acoustic signals and typically operate at a high sampling rate, such as 48 kHz. In contrast, the proposed method operates at a much lower sampling rate of 30 Hz, which implies significantly lower power consumption. In wearable environments, the limited device size restricts battery capacity, making high-power-consumption methods undesirable. Therefore, the proposed method contributes by enabling silent speech recognition with moderate performance while keeping power consumption low. In the future, there is potential to develop hybrid

Table 1. Recognition results for each participant (R: recall, P: precision, F: F-measure)

	DTW + kNN			SVM		
	P (%)	R (%)	F (%)	P (%)	R (%)	F (%)
P1	81.0	80.7	80.7	75.7	75.3	75.0
P2	74.1	71.8	71.4	58.4	57.1	55.8
P3	70.1	69.3	69.2	34.0	34.7	33.5
P4	66.8	64.7	64.9	60.5	57.3	57.9
P5	83.7	81.1	81.2	60.7	62.2	60.3
P6	56.8	55.2	55.2	44.7	43.8	43.5
P7	82.8	82.0	81.3	54.7	54.7	53.0
Ave.	73.6	72.1	72.0	55.6	55.0	54.1

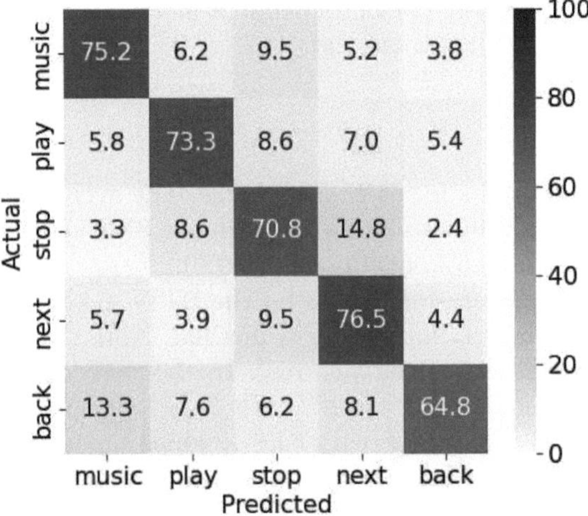

Fig. 6. Confusion matrix of DTW + kNN

systems that adaptively combine high-accuracy but power-intensive methods, such as ultrasound, with lower-power but moderate-accuracy approaches like the proposed method. This could lead to systems that better balance recognition accuracy and energy efficiency.

In this study, we compared two classification methods: DTW + kNN and SVM. DTW + kNN yielded better performance. One possible reason for this is that, as shown in Fig. 5, the characteristics of silent speech tend to appear in the overall shape of the waveform. Since the pressure changes caused by silent speech typically manifest as oscillations around the baseline, the feature differences may not have been sufficiently captured by the statistical features used in this study (e.g., standard deviation and variance).

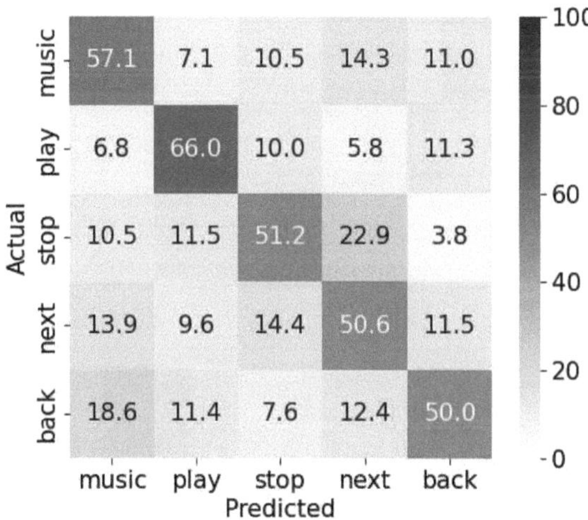

Fig. 7. Confusion matrix of SVM

As shown in Fig. 6, many misclassifications occurred between the commands "music" and "back." This may be attributed to the vowels used in the language employed in this study. The language includes five vowels: "a," "i," "u," "e," and "o." The commands used here and the correspondence between the vowels contained in them are shown in Table 2. The confusion matrix from a preliminary experiment on vowel recognition is shown in Fig. 8. From this preliminary experiment, it was found that the vowels that cause the most pressure changes in the ear canal are "a" and "o." Of the five commands used in this study, "stop" and "next" did not contain these vowels. However, the accuracy of "stop" was low at 70.8%, while the accuracy of "next" was high at 76.5%. The reason why only "next" was high in accuracy is thought to be because there were no consecutive vowels included in the command. "stop" contains the vowel "eii" and "next" contains the vowel "uie." Here, "stop" contains the consecutive vowel "i," while "next" does not. The reason why the accuracy of "back" was low is also related to consecutive vowels. The commands "music," "play," and "back" all contain the vowels "a" and "o," but the accuracy of "back" is low at 64.8%. From this, it can be inferred that "back" contains the vowel "oou," and the consecutive vowel "o" reduces the accuracy. Therefore, it can be seen that the presence or absence of consecutive vowels has a greater effect on accuracy than the presence of the vowels "a" and "o."

Also, the reason for the confusion in classification of the commands "music" and "back" is thought to be that the commands contain similar vowels, such as "oau" in "music" and "oou" in "back."

Figure 9 shows the confusion matrix for the participant with the highest F1-score using DTW + kNN, while Fig. 10 shows the confusion matrix for the participant with the lowest F1-score. These results indicate that there is considerable individual variation among participants. One possible cause is the fit of

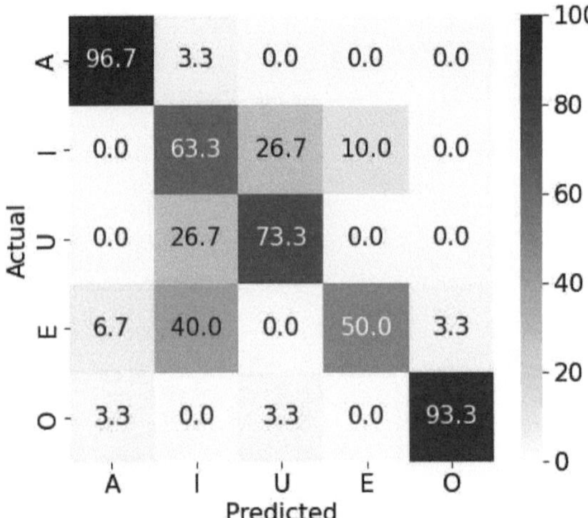

Fig. 8. Confusion matrix of vowel recognition

Table 2. Command and vowel correspondence

Command types	Spoken commands	Vowel
music	ongaku	oau
play	saisei	aiei
stop	teishi	eii
next	tsugihe	uie
back	modoru	oou

the earpieces used during the experiment. It is speculated that using earpieces that better match the shape of each individual's ear canal could improve performance. In fact, for the participant with the highest accuracy, over 90% recognition accuracy was achieved for the commands "music," "play," and "stop."

5.1   Limitation

In this study, we focused on investigating whether SS recognition is feasible using ear canal pressure changes, and did not explore the detection of SS onset. However, to make the system practical for real-world use, it is essential to detect when SS occurs, in order to prevent unintended activation of the system due to other actions. Possible approaches include training a model to distinguish between pressure changes caused by SS and those caused by other movements, or using a trigger signal that rarely occurs in daily life, such as jaw clenching sounds, to activate the system. This remains a subject for future work, and multiple approaches should be investigated to address this issue.

   In this study, we employed methods such as DTW and SVM; however, neural network–based approaches, such as 1D-CNN, have the potential to achieve

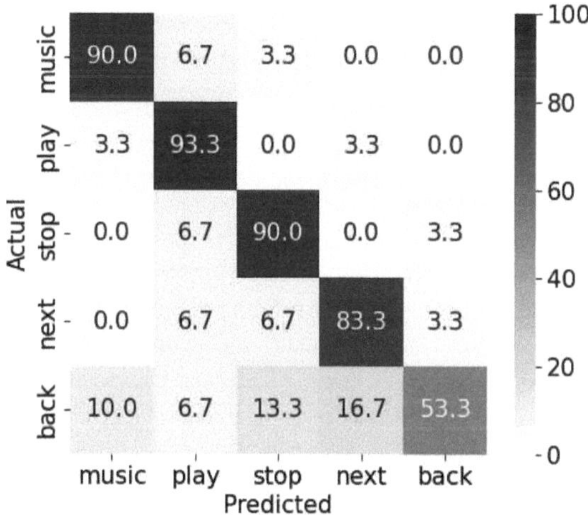

Fig. 9. Confusion matrix of participants with the most accurate DTW + kNN

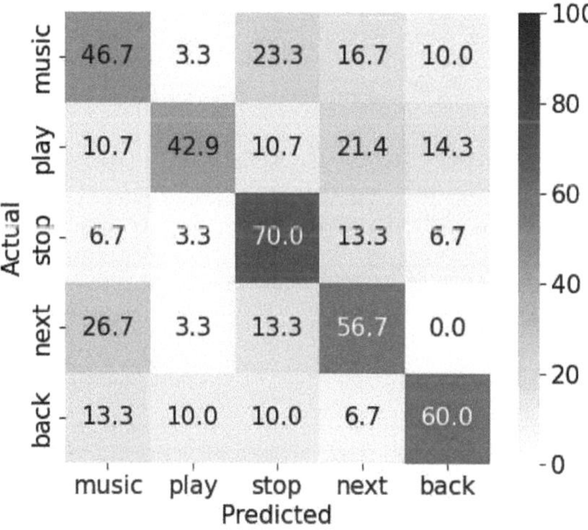

Fig. 10. Confusion matrix of participants with the least accuracy in DTW + kNN

higher recognition accuracy. Due to the limited amount of data available, preliminary experiments with these neural network models did not yield satisfactory recognition performance, and thus they were not used in this study. However, if a larger dataset can be constructed in the future, it is expected that neural network–based approaches will enable more accurate recognition.

In this study, evaluation was conducted using user-dependent models. However, for practical use, it is desirable to develop models that are user-independent or require only minimal additional training for each individual. As future work, it is necessary to investigate user-independent learning models and to determine the amount of additional user-specific training required for effective use.

6   Conclusion

To address the challenges associated with voice input methods for hearable devices—namely, their susceptibility to environmental noise, difficulty of use in silent environments, and the risk of personal information leakage—we proposed a silent speech recognition method based on ear canal pressure changes. The evaluation experiment demonstrated an average F-measure of 72.0% for five-command classification, indicating that the proposed method can realize silent speech input with a simple sensor configuration. Furthermore, since the proposed approach operates with lower power consumption compared to conventional methods, it holds promise for achieving higher recognition accuracy when combined with other techniques such as IMU or ultrasound.

Acknowledgments. This work was supported by JSPS KAKENHI Grant Numbers JP21K11973, JP24K02988

References

1. Amesaka, T., Watanabe, H., Sugimoto, M.: Facial expression recognition using ear canal transfer function. In: Proceedings of the 2019 ACM International Symposium on Wearable Computers, ISWC 2019, pp. 1–9. ACM, New York, NY, USA (2019). https://doi.org/10.1145/3341163.3347747
2. Ando, T., Kubo, Y., Shizuki, B., Takahashi, S.: Canalsense: face-related movement recognition system based on sensing air pressure in ear canals. In: Proceedings of the 30th Annual ACM Symposium on User Interface Software and Technology, UIST 2017, pp. 679–689. ACM, New York, NY, USA (2017). https://doi.org/10.1145/3126594.3126649
3. Crum, P.: Hearables: here come the: technology tucked inside your ears will augment your daily life. IEEE Spectrum **56**(5), 38–43 (2019)
4. Dong, X., et al.: Rehearsse: recognizing hidden-in-the-ear silently spelled expressions. In: Proceedings of the 2024 CHI Conference on Human Factors in Computing Systems. CHI 2024, ACM, New York, NY, USA (2024). https://doi.org/10.1145/3613904.3642095
5. Gilbert, J., et al.: Isolated word recognition of silent speech using magnetic implants and sensors. Med. Eng. Phys. **32**(10), 1189–1197 (2010)
6. Hossain, D., Ghosh, T., Haider Imtiaz, M., Sazonov, E.: Ear canal pressure sensor for food intake detection. Front. Electron. **4** (2023). https://doi.org/10.3389/felec.2023.1173607
7. IDC: Wearable devices market insights (2025), https://www.idc.com/promo/wearablevendor
8. Igarashi, Y., Futami, K., Murao, K.: Silent speech eyewear interface: Silent speech recognition method using eyewear with infrared distance sensors. In: Proceedings of the 2022 ACM International Symposium on Wearable Computers, ISWC 2022, pp. 33–38. ACM, New York, NY, USA (2022). https://doi.org/10.1145/3544794.3558458

9. Iguma, K., Murao, K., Watanabe, H.: Input interface with touch and non-touch interactions using atmospheric pressure for hearable devices. In: Proceedings of the 2023 ACM International Symposium on Wearable Computers, ISWC 2023, pp. 1–5. ACM, New York, NY, USA (2023). https://doi.org/10.1145/3594738.3611354

10. Nyquist, S.C.: Measurement of telegraph distortion. A.I.E.E.Jl. **46**, 231 (1927)

11. Röddiger, T., et al.: Sensing with earables: a systematic literature review and taxonomy of phenomena. Proc. ACM Interact. Mob. Wearable Ubiquitous Technol. **6**(3), 1–57 (2022)

12. Röddiger, T., King, T., Roodt, D.R., Clarke, C., Beigl, M.: Openearable: open hardware earable sensing platform. In: Proceedings of the 1st International Workshop on Earable Computing, EarComp 2022, pp. 29–34. ACM, New York, NY, USA (2023). https://doi.org/10.1145/3544793.3563415

13. Srivastava, T., Winters, R.M., Gable, T., Wang, Y.T., LaScala, T., Tashev, I.J.: Whispering wearables: multimodal approach to silent speech recognition with head-worn devices. In: Proceedings of the 26th International Conference on Multimodal Interaction, ICMI 2024, pp. 214–223. ACM, New York, NY, USA (2024). https://doi.org/10.1145/3678957.3685720

14. Yincheng, J., et al.: Earcommand: "hearing" your silent speech commands in ear. vol. 6. ACM, New York, NY, USA, July 2022. https://doi.org/10.1145/3534613

15. Zhang, R., et al.: Hpspeech: silent speech interface for commodity headphones. In: Proceedings of the 2023 ACM International Symposium on Wearable Computers, ISWC 2023, pp. 60–65. ACM, New York, NY, USA (2023). https://doi.org/10.1145/3594738.3611365

Dependency-Based Evolution Planning of a Multi-version Microservice RAN Application

Emma Witt and Simin Nadjm-Tehrani[✉]

Linköping University, Linköping, Sweden
`simin.nadjm-tehrani@liu.se`

Abstract. Future communication systems are complex infrastructures with virtualized software services that are updated regularly as requirements evolve. This paper addresses the adaptation of microservices under dependency and efficiency constraints. We formalize the evolution of microservices as a combination of two subproblems, the Microservice Dependency Problem and the Evolution Planning Problem, both of which are difficult to solve optimally. We then propose a method based on the Binate Covering Problem (BCP) with branch-and-bound, and introduce a novel algorithm that finds the deployment steps towards a desired new configuration. Our proposed method, DEP-DS, is then compared with two heuristics on three sample datasets from historical radio access network update records run on Kubernetes. We further show that BCP with greedy search is faster but finds fewer solutions to the evolution plan. Overall, DEP-DS is able to find solutions to all samples, generates deployment plans within an average time of 1–2 s, and the plans are similar to other heuristics in terms of CPU usage.

Keywords: Microservices · Evolution plans · RAN virtualization

1 Introduction

A Radio Access Network (RAN) manages wireless communication between user devices and the core network. As RAN software grows in complexity, microservice architectures have been adopted to split systems into independently executable components. Despite low coupling, microservices often require integration to deliver full functionality, resulting in complex and hard-to-manage dependencies in large systems. The version dependency problem arises from the independent deployment of microservices. When a microservice is upgraded to a newer version, its communication endpoints may change, and other microservices and external systems that previously interacted with it will no longer be

---

E. Witt—The work was carried out when the first author **was at** Ericsson AB, Linköping. The work does **not relate** to the first author's current position at Amazon Web Services.

P. Delir Haghighi et al. (Eds.): MoMM 2025, LNCS 16329, pp. 122–136, 2026.
https://doi.org/10.1007/978-3-032-11768-7_10

able to do so. To ensure smooth transitions, multiple versions often coexist. A multi-versioning strategy [8] or dependency-based orchestration [1] helps manage these deployments. The goal is to deploy and maintain compatible versions without service disruption or resource waste. Replacing a needed microservice as a result of an update can make other service chains non-operational. Maintaining multiple versions in parallel to preserve all existing dependencies intact will inevitably waste resources. Manual deployment is error-prone, especially in complex systems like RAN where there may exist 10 or more distinct microservices and multiple versions of them at any point in time, making automation critical. However, algorithms to perform the above task autonomously have a large state space (of all service chains, all possible versions, and endpoints) to deal with. They still need to perform updates with reasonable latency and strike a balance between (CPU) resource utilization and service continuity.

This paper addresses this challenging problem by subdividing it into two orthogonal problems for each update cycle. The first problem is to create a representation of current dependencies that need to be maintained after a revision of a bunch of microservices, the Microservice Dependency Problem (MDP). The second is to construct a deployment plan for desired updates across all microservice chains, the Evolution Planning Problem (EPP). Our study of the existing literature reveals that solutions to the first problem exist; however, to our knowledge, the second problem has not been characterized or solved in the context of dependency-constrained settings, nor does an existing approach appear to address both problems jointly. An ambitious solution to the problem would be to optimize the solution for multiple requirements, e.g., maximizing the number of performed updates at each cycle, minimizing the use of CPU (thereby energy) after the updates, minimizing the number of versions for each microservice, adding constraints as to how fast an update round should be, and so on. However, solving the multi-objective optimization problem would have an infeasible overhead in RANs due to the combinatorial problems mentioned before.

This paper is a first attempt at finding a combined solution to the above two problems through heuristics that can be studied in an experimental setting using realistic data. Our method leverages solutions to two algorithms, namely the Binate Covering Problem (BCP) solved using Branch and Bound (BB) resolution to achieve the combined goal, together with a tree-based algorithm to find the path to the desired deployment from the current deployment. The approach uses BCP as the vehicle to find the desired post-deployment state via the Branch and Bound algorithm. The practical applicability of the approach is then evaluated with historical data from a real RAN system. The contributions of this paper are as follows:

- Formally defining the microservice dependency problem, MDP, and a heuristic for the evolution planning problem, EPP, in RAN applications.
- Proposing a Dependency-based Evolution Planning and Deployment Solver (DEP-DS) method using BCP, BB, combined with a novel algorithm, and implementing it in a Kubernetes environment, where Kubernetes is a well-known platform for virtualized deployments.

- Extracting representative samples based on historical data from real RAN application updates to use as a basis for evaluation of our method, and make them available to other researchers.
- Evaluating DEP-DS in terms of finding an evolution plan for the extracted samples, average time to compute, and CPU usage in planned evolutions compared to two baselines.

The structure of the paper is as follows. Section 2 describes the required background and the relation to previous work. Section 3 presents the problem formalization and assumptions that capture our system model. Section 4 presents the algorithms that make up the DEP-DS method for constructing evolution plans, and Sect. 5 evaluates it. The paper is concluded in Sect. 6.

2   Background and Earlier Work

This section reviews previous research on microservices orchestration and relates it to our problem area and approach. We first review the works that address the main goal, namely, the evolution planning strategy. Then we relate the problem of constructing the dependency graph for microservice updates to known graph construction and manipulation problems. Finally, we describe the necessary background on BCP and BB.

2.1   Earlier Work

Although the problem of updating multiple nodes in a distributed system with consistency requirements is an old problem in computer science, the deployment of virtualized services in networks makes the problem more complex [10]. Researchers have recognized that careful analysis of update algorithms is critical to preventing failures in systems with high availability requirements [11]. The problem is multi-faceted in the sense that high-availability systems need to have several versions of each service running in parallel, meaning that a snapshot of the system does not have a fixed number of nodes as in the classical problem.

Moreover, in addition to the functional correctness of individual updates, the overall update process has other dimensions: the practical interoperability of services in multiple programming languages [12], the amount of resources used before and after updates, and the efficiency of the update process itself [13], or the traceability of updates and return to a pre-update state [14].

Works that focus on evolution planning with some resource constraints typically end up with scalability problems as optimization within large state spaces is not feasible in continuous evolution [13], for example, evaluate a greedy method on 6 worker nodes and 11 containers. In this paper, we focus on the process of creating evolution plans with heuristics to manage the run-time scalability issue and do not aim at finding optimum solutions.

He et al. [2] proposed a greedy-based algorithm to generate an evolution plan that minimizes average response time while adhering to resource constraints.

This approach prioritizes immediate gains, similar to the dependency-based orchestration algorithms explored in this thesis, which consider the sequence of resource utilization and deployment operations. Such algorithms require a thorough search across potential configurations to identify optimal solutions, particularly for complex microservice interactions that suffer from the combinatorial explosion.

The microservice dependency problem parallels well-known problems in software package management, where the objective is to assign specific package versions that satisfy dependency constraints without conflicts [7]. Unlike traditional package managers, microservice architecture allows multiple versions to be concurrently active, which adds complexity to dependency resolution.

The Minimum Set Cover Problem (MSCP) is a special case of the package management problem, which is solved using various heuristic approaches, such as the Hill Climbing algorithm proposed by Akhter [3]. MSCP is based on a predefined universe of constraints, and solving it involves finding a minimum number of sets that cover all elements in it. In contrast, in our case, it is unclear which microservices should be included in the deployment, making the universe of constraints unnecessarily large and the solution thus likely to be suboptimal.

The package management problem can be modeled as a Boolean satisfiability (SAT) problem, where packages are represented as Boolean variables and constraints (dependencies/conflicts) are described as clauses, which together form a Boolean formula in Conjunctive Normal Form (CNF). Once encoded, SAT solvers can be used to determine whether a feasible set of packages exists that satisfies each clause in the CNF [5]. While the SAT focuses purely on feasibility, the Binate Covering Problem (described below) extends this by introducing a cost minimization objective (e.g., minimizing the number of selected variables or weighted variables). The SAT problem is NP-complete, and BCP is known to be at least as hard as SAT because any instance of SAT can be reduced to an equivalent instance of BCP.

2.2   Background

The binate covering problem (BCP) is a combinatorial optimization problem that seeks to choose a minimum-cost assignment of truth values (0/1) to Boolean variables, or *literals*, that satisfies a collection of clauses. Clauses can contain complemented and uncomplemented literals. BCP is usually represented by a binate matrix $\mathcal{A} \in \{-, 0, 1\}^{m \times n}$, with m rows representing clauses (constraints) and n columns representing Boolean variables, and each entry A_{ij} is defined as:

$$A_{ij} = \begin{cases} 1, & \text{if} \quad \text{variable } c_j \text{ appears in clause } r_i \\ 0, & \text{if} \quad \text{variable } c_j \text{ appears in in complemented form in clause } r_i \\ -, & \text{otherwise} \end{cases}$$

$$(1)$$

A variable assignment means choosing a truth value for each variable: $x_j = 1$ if the variable c_j is selected (set to true) or $x_j = 0$ if variable c_j is not selected (set to false). An assignment x_j covers clause r_i if it satisfies the clause according to the matrix, i.e., $x_j = 1$ when $A_{ij} = 1$ or $x_j = 0$ when $A_{ij} = 0$. Given that each variable c_j is associated with a cost w_j, the objective of the BCP is to find a variable assignment x such that all rows are covered and the total cost is minimized: $\min \sum_{j=1}^{n} w_j x_j$ [4].

Solving the BCP typically starts with a preprocessing (reduction) phase before the actual search. If a row i can only be covered by one variable c_j, then that variable is considered essential and must be assigned A_{ij} in all feasible solutions. Furthermore, a row r_k is dominated by another row r_l if every variable in r_l is also present in r_k, with the same sign, i.e., satisfying r_l automatically satisfies r_k. Removing dominated rows and all rows covered by essential variables simplifies the matrix without losing potential solutions. Iterative approaches of such reductions, for example, Gimpel's reduction, produce a reduced covering matrix. If the reduced matrix ends up empty, a minimal and immediate solution can be obtained from the essential variables identified.

Suppose such a minimal and immediate solution cannot be obtained. In that case, Branch and Bound (BB) resolution can be applied, where the problem is partitioned into subproblems (branches), each of which is attempted to be solved recursively to the optimal level [6]. For each subproblem, we approximate a lower bound L on the objective value. If the current best solution is greater than or equal to L, we conclude that this branch cannot improve upon the current best solution and prune it. Finding the exact lower bound is as difficult as solving the BCP itself and typically requires heuristic methods. Coudert [4] utilizes the concept of a Maximal Independent Set (MIS), which is the largest subset of rows such that no two rows cover the same column; it is maximal because no additional rows can be included without violating this independence. The greedy procedure to obtain the MIS is as follows: First, all rows with negated variables are moved. Then, the shortest row is iteratively added to MIS (the row length is given by $|r_i| = \sum_{j=1}^{n} \mathbf{1}_{\{A_{i,j} \in \{0,1\}\}}$, i.e., the sum of all non-empty entries in that row), is iteratively added to MIS. This process is repeated until all rows have been removed. Finally, the lower bound is given by the sum of the weights of each row $r_i \in MIS$, that is, the cost of the least costly variable in MIS:

$$L = \sum_{r_i \in MIS} \text{weight}(r_i) = \sum_{r_i \in MIS} \min_{j \in \{j \mid A_{ij}=1\}} w_j \tag{2}$$

The heuristic for selecting variable c_j^* in branching considers columns covering many rows and is less costly compared to the weights of these rows, according to Eq. 3. Short rows have fewer available columns, making decisions around them more impactful. Columns intersecting many short rows are thus favored to prioritize solving the most constrained of the problem first [4].

$$c_j^* = \arg\max_{j \in 1,\ldots,n} \left(\frac{1}{w_j} \sum_{r_i \in \{j \mid A_{ij}=1\}} \frac{\text{weight}(r_i)}{|r_i|} \right) \tag{3}$$

3   System Model and Problem Definition

We now formally define our problem and present the assumed model. The microservice version dependency problem can be formulated as a binary optimization problem over a set of versioned microservices and versioned interfaces. The dependencies between microservices are captured by their provided (and consumed) interfaces to (provided by) other microservices.

Definition 1. Microservice Dependency Problem. Let $S = \{S_1, S_2, \ldots, S_m\}$ be the set of distinct microservices and $V_j = \{S_j^{(1)}, S_j^{(2)}, \ldots, S_j^{(k_j)}\}$ the set of available versions of S_j, where $S_j^{(i)}$ denotes version i of microservice S_j. The universe of deployable microservice versions can thus be defined as:

$$M = \bigcup_{j=1}^{m} V_j = \left\{ S_j^{(i)} \mid 1 \leq j \leq m,\ 1 \leq i \leq k_j \right\}.$$

Each versioned microservice $S_j^{(i)} \in M$ is associated with a set of provided interfaces $I_p(S_j^{(i)}) \subseteq I$, a set of consumed interfaces $I_c(S_j^{(i)}) \subseteq I$, and a CPU requirement $\mathrm{cpu}(S_j^{(i)}) \in \mathbb{R}^+$, where I denotes the universe of versioned interfaces.

We define the final deployment set as:

$$D_f = \{S_j^{(i)} \in M \mid x_j^{(i)} = 1\}, \tag{4}$$

$$\text{where} \quad x_j^{(i)} = \begin{cases} 1, & \text{if microservice version } S_j^{(i)} \text{ is deployed.} \\ 0, & \text{otherwise.} \end{cases} \tag{5}$$

Constraints. Each deployment set must satisfy the following constraints:

$$\sum_{S_j^{(i)} \in M : v \in I_p(S_j^{(i)})} x_j^{(i)} \geq 1, \qquad \forall v \in \mathcal{E}_{\mathrm{req}} \tag{C1}$$

Given a set of required external interfaces $\mathcal{E}_{\mathrm{req}}$, *the external interface constraint* (C1) ensues that each $v \in \mathcal{E}_{\mathrm{req}}$ is provided by at least one deployed microservice.

$$x_j^{(i)} \leq \sum_{S_{j'}^{(i')} \in M : v \in I_p(S_{j'}^{(i')})} x_{j'}^{(i')}, \quad \forall S_j^{(i)} \in \mathcal{M},\ \forall v \in I_c(S_j^{(i)}) \tag{C2}$$

The internal interface dependency constraint (C2) ensures a microservice S_j^i can only be deployed if each interface it consumes is provided by at least one deployed microservice.

$$\mathrm{CPU}_{\mathrm{total}} = \sum_{S_j^{(i)} \in \mathcal{D}_f} x_j^{(i)} \cdot \mathrm{cpu}(S_j^{(i)}) \leq \mathrm{CPU}_{\mathrm{max}} \tag{C3}$$

The resource constraint (C3) ensures the deployment stays below a resource quota CPU_{max}.

Definition 2. Evolution Planning Problem. The evolution planning problem involves transitioning a microservice-based system from an initial deployment state $D_0 \subseteq M$ to a target deployment state D_f. This transition is governed by an Evolution Plan EP, formally represented as:

$$EP = \langle DS_1, \ldots, DS_f \rangle, \tag{6}$$

where each deployment step DS_k is a sequence of operations: $\qquad$ (7)

$$DS_k = \{o_{k_1}, \ldots, o_{k_K}\}, \quad \text{and each operation is either} \tag{8}$$

$$o_k = \begin{cases} \text{Deploy}(S_j^{(i)} & \text{deploying microservice version } S_j^{(i)}. \\ \text{Remove}(S_j^{(i)}), & \text{removing an existing microservice version } S_j^i \end{cases} \tag{9}$$

Applying all operations in DS_k updates the system incrementally:

$$D_k = (D_{k-1} \cup \text{deploys}(DS_k)) \setminus \text{removes}(DS_k), \quad \text{where} \tag{10}$$

$$\text{deploys}(DS_k) = \{S_j^{(i)} | o_k = \text{Deploy}(S_j^{(i)}, o_k \in DS_k\} \tag{11}$$

$$\text{removes}(DS_k) = \{S_j^{(i)} | o_k = \text{Remove}(S_j^{(i)}), o_k \in DS_k\} \tag{12}$$

Each state of the system D_k represents a valid subset of microservice versions deployed that satisfies predefined constraints: $D_k \vDash C1, C2, C3,$

Objective. The deployment set D_f is not necessarily unique - multiple allowed deployment sets may exist, as well as numerous EPs may exist between D_0 and the same final state D_f. The objective is to determine our preferred final deployment state D_f and compute EP from our current deployment state to D_0 to D_f so that the total usage of CPU resources is minimized, reflecting the goal: $\min(CPU_{total})$.

4 Our Proposed Approach: DEP-DS

This section describes the main contribution of this work. The Dependency-based Evolution Planning and Deployment Solver, DEP-DS, aims to solve the microservice dependency problem and the evolution planning problem in two stages:

- Solving the Microservices Dependency Problem: Given a universal set of deployable microservices M, a current deployment set D_0, find a final deployment set D_f such that all external interface requirements $\mathcal{E}_{req}$, internal dependencies are satisfied while the overall system remains below a resource quota CPU_{max}. The objective is to minimize the CPU usage of D_f, given that each microservice is associated with a $\text{cpu}(S_j^{(i)})$. MDP is modeled as a BCP and solved by utilizing branch and bound.

– Solving the Evolution Planning Problem: Given the calculated output D_f, find the Evolution Plan EP consisting of a sequence of deployment steps (deployments and removals) to transition from the current state to D_f.

4.1 Solving the Microservice Dependency Problem

The microservice version dependency problem is addressed by first modeling it as a Binate Covering Problem (BCP) and solving it using Branch and Bound resolution. Each microservice version $S_j^{(i)} \in M$ corresponds to a Boolean variable $x_j^{(i)}$, representing the inclusion of a microservice version, which is associated with a column in the covering matrix. Furthermore, each microservice version $S_j^{(i)}$ is associated with a cost $= c_j^{(i)}$ (e.g., CPU resource usage). Internal and external interface constraints are expressed as Boolean clauses over these variables and thereby define clauses in the covering matrix. External interface constraints (C1) yield positive clauses 13 and internal interface requirements yield implications. Internal interface dependencies (C2) imply a relationship between selected microservices and the requirement that at least one provider for each consumed interface must be chosen. Applying the conversion rule: $P \implies Q \leftrightarrow \neg P \vee Q$, this translates into a Boolean clause with one negated literal and at least one positive literal 14 [9].

$$\bigvee_{S_j^{(i)} \in M : v \in I_p(S_j^{(i)})} x_j^{(i)} \quad \text{for all} \quad v \in \mathcal{E}_{\text{req}} \tag{13}$$

$$\neg x_j^{(i)} \vee \left(\bigvee_{S_{j'}^{(i')} \in M : v \in I_p(S_{j'}^{(i')})} x_{j'}^{(i')} \right), \forall S_j^{(i)} \in \mathcal{M}, \ \forall v \in I_c(S_j^{(i)}) \tag{14}$$

We calculate the lower bound L as the sum of the costs of all variables covering a row in the Maximal Independent Set (MIS): $L = \sum_{r_k \in MIS} \sum_{S_j^{(i)} \in R_{r_k}} c_j^{(i)}$, where $R_{r_k} = \{S_j^{(i)} \in M | A_{k, S_j^{(i)}} = 1\}$. This differs slightly from Eq. 2, where only the least costly variables of each row in the MIS were added to the lower bound. Since no complemented rows, i.e., internal dependencies, are included in MIS, we are likely to get a lower bound far from the actual lower bound using Eq. 2. Thus, this decision leads to faster convergence. We adapt the heuristic selection for case splitting as explained by Coudert [4] (Eq. 3) to select microservice $S_{j*}^{(i^*)}$ to branch on. Redefining the variables to represent our system's resources and dependency relationships gives the following:

$$S_{j*}^{(i^*)} = \underset{S_j^{(i)} \in M}{\arg \max} \left(\frac{1}{c_j^{(i)}} \sum_{r_k \in R_{S_j^{(i)}}} \frac{\text{weight}(r_k)}{|r_k|} \right), \tag{15}$$

where

$$R_{S_j^{(i)}} = \{r_k \subset M | A_{k, S_j^{(i)}}\}$$

4.2 Solving the Evolution Planning Problem

Algorithm 1 computes a valid Evolution Plan EP for transitioning a microservice from a current deployment state D_0 to a target deployment state D_f, where each deployment state $D_t \in \{D_0, D_1, \ldots, D_{f-1}, D_f\}$ is reached by applying a sequence of deployment operations according to Eq. 6. This process begins by identifying the required changes, specifically the microservices *to_add* and *to_remove* by comparing D_{curr} with D_f. This is preceded by identifying the allowed Add and Remove operations to transition from D_{curr} to D_{next}. The algorithm is recursively applied until $D_{curr} = D_f$, and finally outputs a correct EP that the Kubernetes operator can follow to reach the desired system configuration.

FindSafeToRemove. A microservice $S_j^{(i)} \in D_{curr}$ is considered safe to remove if it has no future or current dependencies, meaning that none of the interfaces it provides are required as external interfaces or consumed by any microservices in D_{curr} or D_f. Formally, this holds if.

$$S_{j'}^{(i')}) \cap I_p(S_j^{(i)}) = \emptyset \text{ and } I_p(S_j^{(i)}) \cap \mathcal{E}_{\text{req}} = \emptyset \text{ for all } S_{j'}^{(i')} \in to\_add \quad \cup D_{curr}.$$

$S_j^{(i)} \in D_{curr}$ is also safe to be removed if, for each $v \in I_p(S_j^{(i)}) = \emptyset$, it must be provided by another microservice in the deployment or only consumed by microservices that are themselves redundant.

Suppose that the above conditions are not met *individually*. Then a set of microservices $R \subset D_{curr}$ might still be jointly removable if they form a dependency cycle and collectively satisfy the constraints, as shown by Algorithm 2.

FindSafeToDeploy. A microservice $S_j^{(i)} \in D_{curr}$ is considered safe to deploy if, for each $v \in I_c(S_j^{(i)})$, it must be provided by another microservice in D_{curr}, and the system remains within the CPU quota CPU_{max}. Similarly to finding safe microservices to remove, there might exist cycles of microservices that can be deployed jointly, as described by Algorithm 3.

5 Experimental Evaluation

The experimental setup was based on a conceptual architecture that splits an existing multi-version RAN application into 14 microservices, each available in different versions, collectively supporting 48 interfaces designed by Ericsson AB for Cloud Deployment and managed by Kubernetes. A local Kubernetes cluster served as the test environment for the evaluation, with each microservice represented as a Kubernetes Deployment and interfaces as Kubernetes Services. A Custom Resource Definition (CRD) of the kind deployment update was established and outlined in a manifest file, specifying the universe of deployable microservices M, their supported interface versions, and the external interface

---

Algorithm 1. FindEvolutionPlan

Require: D_0, D_f, M, $\text{CPU}_{\max}$, $EP \leftarrow [\ ]$
Ensure: EP deployment plan from D_0 to D_f
 1: $D_{\text{curr}} \leftarrow D_0$
 2: $to\_add \leftarrow D_f \setminus D_{\text{curr}}$ $\qquad\qquad\qquad\qquad$ $\triangleright$ Identifying required changes
 3: $to\_remove \leftarrow D_{\text{curr}} \setminus D_f$
 4: $removable \leftarrow \text{FINDSAFETOREMOVE}(to\_remove, D_{\text{curr}})$
 5: **for all** $S_{j'}^{(i')}$ **do**
 6: $\qquad DS = DS \cup Remove(S_{j'}^{(i')})$
 7: $\qquad D_{\text{curr}} \leftarrow D_{\text{curr}} \setminus S_{j'}^{(i')}$
 8: $\qquad to\_remove \leftarrow to\_remove \setminus S_{j'}^{(i')}$
 9: **end for**
10: $deployable \leftarrow \text{FINDSAFETODEPLOY}(to\_add, D_{\text{curr}}, \text{CPU}_{\max})$
11: **for all** $S_{j'}^{(i')}$ in $deployable$ **do**
12: $\qquad \text{CPU}_{proj} \leftarrow \sum_{S \in D_{curr}} \text{cpu}(S) + \text{cpu}(S_j^{(i)})$
13: $\qquad$ **if** $\text{CPU}_{proj} \leq \text{CPU}_{\max}$ **then**
14: $\qquad\qquad DS = DS \cup Deploy(S_{j'}^{(i')})$
15: $\qquad\qquad D_{\text{curr}} \leftarrow D_{\text{curr}} \cup S_{j'}^{(i')}$
16: $\qquad\qquad to\_add \leftarrow to\_add \setminus S_{j'}^{(i')}$
17: $\qquad$ **else**
18: $\qquad\qquad removable \leftarrow \text{FINDSAFETOREMOVE}(to\_remove, D_{\text{curr}})$
19: $\qquad\qquad$ **for all** $S_{j'}^{(i')}$ **do**
20: $\qquad\qquad\qquad DS = DS \cup Remove(S_{j'}^{(i')})$
21: $\qquad\qquad\qquad D_{\text{curr}} \leftarrow D_{\text{curr}} \setminus S_{j'}^{(i')}$
22: $\qquad\qquad\qquad to\_remove \leftarrow to\_remove \setminus S_{j'}^{(i')}$
23: $\qquad\qquad$ **end for**
24: $\qquad$ **end if**
25: **end for**
26: $EP.\text{append}(DS)$
27: **if** $D_{\text{curr}} = D_f$ **then return** EP
28: **end if**
29: $\text{FINDEVOLUTIONPLAN}(D_0, D_f, M, \text{CPU}_{\max}, EP)$

---

requirements $\mathcal{E}_{req}$. The CRD enabled the implementation of the operator pattern, a software extension to Kubernetes that listens to custom resource modifications and updates the environment. The data provided includes the amount of resources (CPU and memory) that every microservice consumes, measured beforehand in internal laboratories. Based on that, suitable requests and limits are set for each microservice to use at runtime. These values are always specified in advance and not adjusted during run-time. Kubernetes uses these requests and limits to allocate resources to each container accordingly.

Algorithm 2. FindSafeToRemove

Require: to_remove, D_{curr}
Ensure: Set of removable microservices
1: $removable \leftarrow \emptyset$
2: **for all** $S_j^{(i)} \in to\_remove$ **do**
3:      **if** No $S_{j'}^{(i')}$ in $D_{curr} \cup D_f$ depends on any $v \in I_p(S_j^{(i)})$ **and** $v \notin \mathcal{E}_{req}$ **then**
4:          $removable \leftarrow removable \cup \{S_j^{(i)}\}$
5:      **else if** All $v \in I_p(S_j^{(i)})$ are either provided by others or only used by redundant services **then**
6:          $removable \leftarrow removable \cup \{S_j^{(i)}\}$
7:      **end if**
8: **end forreturn** $removable$

Algorithm 3. FindSafeToDeploy

Require: to_add, D_{curr}, $\text{CPU}_{\max}$
Ensure: Set of deployable microservices
1: $deployable \leftarrow \emptyset$
2: **for all** $S_j^{(i)} \in to\_add$ **do**
3:      **if** All $v \in I_c(S_j^{(i)})$ are provided by some $S_{j'}^{(i')} \in D_{curr}$ **then**
4:          $\text{CPU}_{proj} \leftarrow \sum_{S \in D_{curr}} \text{cpu}(S) + \text{cpu}(S_j^{(i)})$
5:          $deployable \leftarrow deployable \cup \{S_j^{(i)}\}$
6:      **end if**
7: **end forreturn** $deployable$

5.1   Generation of Problem Instances

Interface samples for problem instances were selected based on historical system data, which contained a total of 4261 time-stamped interface updates over eight years. Problem instances are created based on the assumption that updates to the external interfaces typically drive a system upgrade. The samples were generated by organizing the data into weekly and daily samples, capturing each update to the external interface. A total of 67 interface samples were generated: 51 weekly samples from 2022, as this year represents the highest update frequency with 40 (out of 48) distinct interface updates; 16 daily samples from February 2024, as this month contains the most samples with external interface updates. Furthermore, the microservices supporting the newly upgraded interfaces were sampled in three ways, with varying levels of complexity, as follows.

- **Large:** This sample presents the largest and most complex search space, where all providers and consumers of interfaces that are subject to an upgrade are upgraded to support the new version. This implies that the minimal solution typically involves one version of each microservice,
- **Medium:** All providers are upgraded. Among consumers, half are randomly selected to be upgraded to support the new version.

– **Small:** All providers are upgraded. For each updated interface, exactly one consumer is randomly selected to be upgraded. If a microservice consumes multiple updated interfaces, it is upgraded to support only the selected one.

Our intuition is that while medium and smaller problem instances are easier to solve due to the smaller search space, their final solution will likely be less resource-efficient. Since not all microservices are upgraded, multiple versions usually need to coexist in the final deployment to satisfy dependencies, resulting in a solution that consumes more CPU than a solution to the large sample.

Each sample $s \in \mathcal{S}$ thus generates three problem instances, giving a total of $3 \cdot 67 = 201$ instances. Each problem instance serves as an input to the algorithm, where the initial deployment state D_0 consists of one version of each microservice, the set of required interfaces $\mathcal{E}_{req}$ is extended to include the updated interfaces in the corresponding interface sample. For each sample, the universe of deployable microservices M is then extended to include the microservice versions selected by the sampling scheme.

The interface sample that constitutes the Large problem instances is available for sharing with the research community and can be found in Appendix C, Table C.1 of the author's previous work, which forms the basis of this paper [15].

5.2   Baselines and Evaluation Metrics

In addition to DEP-DS, two baseline algorithms, Ideal Dependency Resolver and Scheduler (IDRS), and Dependency Resolver and Scheduler with Stratified Pruning (DRS-SP), were implemented for the evaluation:

1. Ideal Dependency Resolver and Scheduler (IDRS): A tree-based algorithm to find all EPs from D_0 to any valid deployment state D_k, which then chooses the EP that minimizes the total system resource usage (CPU request).
2. Dependency Resolver and Scheduler with Stratified Pruning (DRS-SP): A modification of IDRS that utilizes a stratified sampling technique to sample child nodes based on their size. Each node represents one or more deployment stage, and the size is denoted by the number of microservices to be deployed in that stage. If the size exceeds 30, this approach partitions and chooses the 10 largest, 10 in the middle, and 10 smallest child nodes.

The following metrics were used for evaluation and calculated for all three samples in each algorithm setting:

1. Success Rate. The ratio of the successfully solved problem instances.
2. Resource Efficiency (CPU_{avg}): The average CPU request, that is, the sum of the CPU requests for microservices in each of the problem instances that the algorithm successfully solved, divided by the number of solved ones.
3. Average Response Time (T_{avg}): Average time taken to produce an evolution plan (for the problem instances that the algorithm successfully solved).

5.3   Evaluation Outomes

Table 1 shows a comparative evaluation of the three algorithms with the data created using the three sampling strategies (Large, Medium, Small), and in total for the three samples.

Table 1. Evaluation outcomes

	Large	Medium	Small	Total
Success Rate				
IDRS	84%	95.6 %	97%	92.5%
DRS-SP	97%	97%	97%	97.0%
DEP-DS	**100%**	**100%**	**100%**	**100%**
T_{avg} (s)				
IDRS	15.10	11.90	0.35	9.11
DRS-SP	0.92	0.95	1.15	1.00
DEP-DS	2.46	0.69	0.2	1.15
CPU_{avg} (mCPU)				
IDRS	480.80	530.00	532.58	512.20
DRS-SP	480.69	533.77	532.58	515.59
DEP-DS	480.00	530.23	534.23	514.47

Based on the success rate, T_{avg} and CPU_{avg}, the main findings are that while the algorithms have similar performance in terms of CPU_{avg}, DEP-DS is the only algorithm capable of resolving all problem instances (success rate 100% for all samples), and with a shorter response time compared to IDRS and DRS-SP.

Overall, as seen in the CPU_{avg} section of the table, IDRS can explore larger search spaces and identify solutions with lower CPU consumption in smaller problem instances. However, it faces scalability issues as problem complexity increases, as evidenced by a decreased success rate for instances in the Large sample.

In addition, we tried to see if DEP-DS could be made even faster by adopting a greedy resolution instead of branch and bound. It turned out that it would be faster to resolve all three instances, but at the cost of a lower success rate (86%, 95%, and 86% for Large, Medium, and Small, respectively) compared to the third row in the table (100% for all instances).

Moreover, DEP-DS running with greedy search gave a CPU_{avg} that grew substantially for all three samples (624.52, 613.57, and 615.56 for Large, Medium, and Small, respectively). This suggests that a greedy approach is ideal when fast evolution plan generation is prioritized, although it may come with higher resource usage. Given that our objective was to minimize the CPU usage, DEP-DS outperforms the greedy approach given that the response time, row 6 of Table 1 is acceptable even for the large sample.

6 Conclusions and Future Works

This research shows that DEP-DS is a promising method for solving the Microservice Dependency Problem and the Evolution Planning Problem, evidenced by its perfect success rate and good resource efficiency during evaluation. DEP-DS effectively balances solution quality, making it more suitable for larger, more intricate instances.

When solving MDP and EPP, our first priority was to find something workable, leaving room for improvement when it comes to optimizing the branch and bound algorithm (through a lower bound calculation and heuristic selection), and even other heuristics to replace branch and bound.

We found that obtaining relevant data to base the evaluation on was in itself a major challenge. To obtain historical data for prototypes evaluated by researchers is not an easy task, and we were able to solicit authentic data to illustrate that the solutions would be workable in a real context. The samples that were selected according to the criteria in Sect. 5 are shared with the research community, and we welcome new approaches that use the same data and novel algorithms to further this work.

The problem instances were generated from calendar days with external interface updates and selected based on predicted difficulty. They are therefore to be seen as an approximation to the worst-case scenarios based on historical data. Studying scenarios based on other samples that would be more representative of an average day would be another problem to look at. This could be done, for example, by choosing days at random, which would be another direction for future work. Further studies on real-world conditions, such as failures, latency, and dynamic resource changes are needed.

Acknowledgements. The Second author was supported by ELLIIT, Excellence Center at Linköping- Lund on Information Technology. The authors wish to thank Erik Malmberg, Klas Strömberg, and Elisabeth Sjöstrand at Ericsson AB for discussions on our work and for providing the historical data for experimental evaluations. The authors also wish to thank Soheil Samii at the Department of Computer Science (IDA) for supporting the research.

References

1. Merkouche, S., Haroun, T., Bouanaka, C., Smaali, M.: TERA-scheduler for a dependency-based orchestration of microservices. In: International Conference on Advanced Aspects of Software Engineering (ICAASE), pp. 1–8. IEEE (2022). https://doi.org/10.1109/ICAASE56196.2022.9931568
2. He, X., Tu, Z., Liu, L., Xu, X., Wang, Z.: Optimal evolution planning and execution for multi-version coexisting microservice systems. In: Kafeza, E., Benatallah, B., Martinelli, F., Hacid, H., Bouguettaya, A., Motahari, H. (eds.) ICSOC 2020. LNCS, vol. 12571, pp. 3–18. Springer, Cham (2020). https://doi.org/10.1007/978-3-030-65310-1_1

3. Akhter, F.: A heuristic approach for minimum set cover problem. In: International Journal of Advanced Research in Artificial Intelligence, pp. 40–45. Citeseer (2015). https://doi.org/10.14569/IJARAI.2015.040607

4. Coudert, O.: On solving covering problems [logic synthesis]. In: 33rd Design Automation Conference Proceedings, pp. 197–202. IEEE (1996). https://doi.org/10.1109/DAC.1996.545572

5. Le Berre, D., Parrain, A.: On SAT technologies for dependency management and beyond. In: First Workshop on Software Product Lines (ASPL2008), vol. 2, pp. 197–200 (2008)

6. Edelkamp, S., Schrödl, S.: Heuristic Search: Theory and Applications. Academic Press (2012), ISBN: 978-0-12-372512-7

7. Florisson, M., Mycroft, A.: Towards a theory of packages. ACM SIGPLAN Notices (2017). https://doi.org/10.1145/800225.806833

8. Gholami, S., Goli, A., Bezemer, C., Khazaei, H: A framework for satisfying the performance requirements of containerized software systems through multi-versioning. ICPE 2020 (2020). https://doi.org/10.1145/3358960.3379125

9. Nilsson, U., Maluszynski, J.: Logic, Programming and Prolog (2ED). Wiley (1995), ISBN: 9780471959960

10. Chait-Roth, D., Namjoshi, K.S., Wies, T.: Consistent updates for scalable microservices. CoRR abs/2508.04829 (2025). https://doi.org/10.48550/ARXIV.2508.04829

11. Zhang, Y., et al.: Understanding and detecting software upgrade failures in distributed systems. In: SOSP 2021: ACM SIGOPS 28th Symposium on Operating Systems Principles (2021), pp. 116–131. ACM. https://doi.org/10.1145/3477132.3483577

12. Shi, Q., Xie, X., Fu, X., Di, P., Li, H., Zhou, A., Fan, G.: Datalog-based language-agnostic change impact analysis for microservices. In: 47th IEEE/ACM International Conference on Software Engineering (ICSE), pp. 78–89. IEEE (2025). https://doi.org/10.1109/ICSE55347.2025.00115

13. Pham, M.C., Truc, M.T., Hoang, X.T., Nguyen, K-K.: Energy-efficient update of microservices applications in kubernetes clusters. In: 16th International Conference on Knowledge and System Engineering (KSE), pp. 167–172. IEEE (2024). https://doi.org/10.1109/KSE63888.2024.11063630

14. Wang, Y., Conan, D., Chabridon, S., Bojnourdi, K., Ma, J.: Runtime models and evolution graphs for the version management of microservice architectures. In: 28th Asia-Pacific Software Engineering Conference (APSEC), IEEE (2021). https://doi.org/10.1109/APSEC53868.2021.00064

15. Witt, E.: Dependency-based orchestration of a multi-version microservice RAN application. Master's thesis, Linköping University (2024), https://liu.diva-portal.org/smash/record.jsf?pid=diva2%3A1906848&dswid=8369

Immersive and Context-Aware Computing

Napping in the Virtual World: Exploring the Effects of VR Audiovisual Relaxation on Napping

Masahiro Kawarai$^{(\boxtimes)}$ and Tatsuo Nakajima

Waseda University, Tokyo, Japan
{m.kawarai,tatsuo}@dcl.cs.waseda.ac.jp

Abstract. Napping is known to have many benefits for cognitive and psychological health, specifically improving alertness and mood and reducing stress. Relaxation prior to napping can enhance its effectiveness, and while auditory relaxation is commonly used, Virtual Reality (VR) offers an immersive environment that integrates visual and auditory senses, potentially producing greater relaxation effects. However, studies measuring the effects of VR-based audiovisual relaxation on napping remain limited. In our experiment, 12 participants experienced a nap with VR-based audiovisual relaxation and a nap with auditory relaxation. The results showed that napping with VR-based audiovisual relaxation significantly increased HRV scores, an objective indicator of stress, compared to napping with auditory relaxation, while no significant differences were found in alertness and mood. These findings suggest that VR-based relaxation may further enhance stress reduction during naps, warranting further research into its applications across various settings.

Keywords: Virtual Reality · Napping · Audiovisual Relaxation

1 Introduction

Short sleep during the day is called napping, and the practice is becoming more widespread [28]. Napping is becoming increasingly popular because of its many benefits to cognitive and psychological health [12,22]. Specifically, it has been reported to improve alertness, mood, and reduce stress [12,14,20–22]. In today's society, the lack of sleep in the workplace and at school is causing a decline in alertness and productivity, and napping is an important strategy to address this issue [10].

Improving the quality of sleep, including naps, can be effectively achieved through relaxation prior to sleep, which has been shown to promote sleep and enhance the quality of naps [19,31]. Among the various sleep-promoting methods, auditory relaxation using music or natural sounds is a popular way [23]. This approach is considered safe and effective, with no side effects [6,7].

Moreover, it has been reported that combining visual relaxation with auditory relaxation can further enhance the relaxation effect [25]. In recent years,

P. Delir Haghighi et al. (Eds.): MoMM 2025, LNCS 16329, pp. 139–152, 2026.
https://doi.org/10.1007/978-3-032-11768-7_11

Virtual Reality (VR) has been increasingly explored as a promising tool for relaxation. VR provides an immersive environment that integrates visual and auditory stimulation, and it has been reported to provide greater relaxation effects compared to auditory relaxation alone [25]. Therefore, the VR-based relaxation method is expected to be more effective as a pre-nap relaxation strategy. Indeed, Pai et al. reported that VR-based audiovisual relaxation significantly reduced sleep onset time [26]. However, this finding does not necessarily demonstrate improved nap quality. Furthermore, the effects of VR-based relaxation applied to napping remain unclear. Interestingly, Yin et al. reported that some users use VR during sleep, motivated by surrealistic sensations and the desire to escape reality [34]. This growing social use further highlights the importance of investigating the effects of VR on napping. This study aims to address this gap by investigating the effects of VR-based audiovisual relaxation on napping.

The research question of this study is to investigate how napping with VR-based audiovisual relaxation impacts the effectiveness of naps compared to napping with traditional auditory relaxation. Specifically, the study focuses on the following three aspects of the effects of napping: 1) improvement in alertness, 2) improvement in mood, 3) reduction in stress. This study contributes to providing empirical evidence to expand our understanding of the effect of VR-based audiovisual relaxation on napping. Furthermore, beyond advancing knowledge in sleep research, our study identifies future challenges, aiming to facilitate practical applications in workplaces, educational settings, and the medical field.

2   Related Work

This section summarizes the role and benefits of napping, highlights the importance of pre-sleep relaxation, and introduces auditory relaxation as a common method. It then discusses the benefits of VR-based audiovisual relaxation and presents examples of its application to nighttime sleep and napping.

2.1   Benefits of Napping and the Importance of Pre-Sleep Relaxation

In today's society, short naps are considered an important method of maintaining alertness [10]. Short naps, often referred to as "power naps", have been reported to be effective in improving alertness [12, 22]. Additionally, napping is known to improve mood [14, 21, 22] and reduce stress [12, 20]. In addition, napping for as short as 20 min is known to reduce sleep inertia and is effective in situations such as at work, where the individual is likely to resume activities immediately [9, 10].

Pre-sleep relaxation is important for napping or improving sleep quality [19, 31]. Relaxation prior to sleep has been noted to facilitate sleep and improve sleep quality [19], which is also true for short naps [31].

Auditory relaxation using music or nature sounds is a popular method of sleep promotion [23]. Music, which is expected to have a sedative effect, has been reported to relax the body and bring better quality sleep [6, 7]. Moreover, auditory relaxation has no side effects and is likely to have a consistent effect [6,7].

Moreover, audiovisual relaxation, which combines audio and visual content, has been explored in recent years. In particular, VR provides a highly immersive environment that integrates visual and auditory perception. Audiovisual relaxation has been reported to have a more relaxing effect than auditory relaxation [25]. Furthermore, VR has characteristics that can effectively block noise and light stimuli from the external environment, creating a sense of detachment from reality [2]. These characteristics lead to the potential use of VR as a new method of sleep promotion, especially in environments with a lot of external influences, e.g., office spaces. However, research on the use of VR-based audiovisual relaxation during naps remains limited, and the present study aims to address this gap.

2.2 Characteristics of VR Relaxation and Its Application to Sleep

Audiovisual relaxation using VR has been increasingly studied as a novel method of relaxation. Neaf et al. found that audiovisual relaxation with VR significantly lowered heart rate and significantly increased subjective relaxation compared to visual-only and auditory-only relaxation [25].

Recent studies have explored the application of audiovisual relaxation, including VR, for sleep. Zambotti et al. reported that the introduction of audiovisual relaxation during sleep improved the quality of sleep [36]. Based on this result, Zambotti et al. pointed out that VR may be effective as a sleep-promoting tool [35]. Indeed, several examples exist of VR being used as a sleep promotion tool. For instance, Lee et al. found that using VR as a pre-sleep meditation tool significantly improved subjective sleep quality and efficiency compared to a group that did not use VR meditation before sleep [17]. Also, Pai et al. demonstrated that using VR during napping significantly decreased sleep onset time compared to those who did not use VR devices [26]. However, these studies did not compare auditory relaxation to the use of audiovisual relaxation as a sleep-promoting method, and it remains unclear whether auditory or audiovisual relaxation is more effective for sleep.

While it is unclear whether audiovisual relaxation using VR is effective in promoting sleep, there are users who actually use VR during sleep. Yin et al. conducted semi-structured interviews with users who actually use VR during sleep and found that there are experiential motivations, consisting of the desire for surrealistic sensations and reality escape, and social motivations, consisting of the desire for reduced loneliness and intimate connection with others [34].

While VR is gaining social attention as a novel method of sleep promotion, its effectiveness remains unclear, and the present study aims to address this gap. Specifically, we measure quantitatively and qualitatively the changes in participants' alertness, mood, and stress, which are indicators of nap quality before and after napping, comparing VR-based relaxation with traditional auditory relaxation.

3   Method

Based on the research question, this section outlines the methodology of our experiment, which investigated the effects of VR-based audiovisual relaxation on alertness, mood, and stress, compared with auditory relaxation during naps.

Beach

Forest

Indoor on a rainy day

Fig. 1. VR environments: Beach, Forest, Indoor on a rainy day.

3.1   Participants

The study included 12 participants (10 males and 2 females; mean age = 22.5 years, SD = 1.45). Among them, 3 had less than 5 h of VR experience, while 9 had prior experience. None had a diagnosed sleep disorder. Napping habits included 1 participant who napped daily, 7 who napped several times a week, and 4 who rarely took naps. No one had ever slept in a VR space. Participation in the experiment was voluntary, and informed consent was obtained from all participants.

3.2   Material

Three VR environments were prepared for this study: "Beach," "Forest," and "Indoor on a rainy day" as shown in Fig. 1. These environments were created

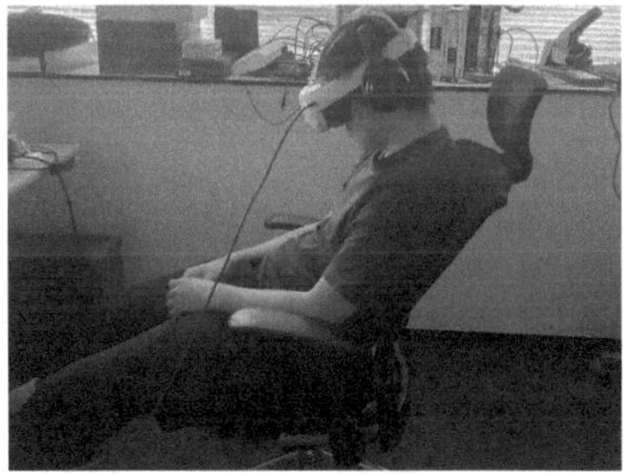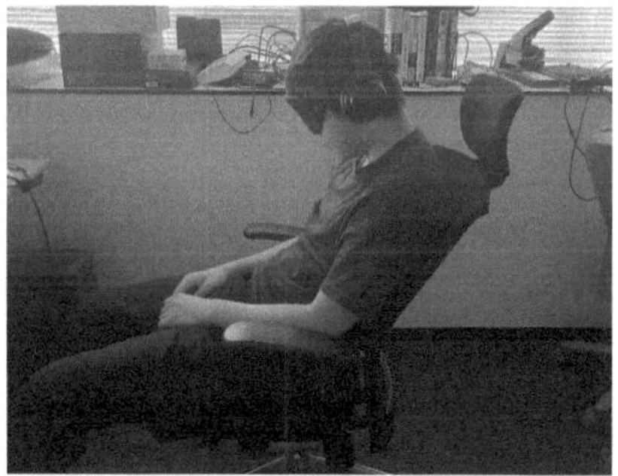

VR condition   Audio condition

Fig. 2. Experimental conditions: VR condition, Audio condition.

using Unreal Engine 5.3.2. In a related study that utilized VR for napping, natural environments such as a beach and a lodge by the woods, as well as indoor spaces like hotel rooms and participants' own rooms, were popular as ideal sleeping environments based on their survey [26]. Following these findings, we designed three VR environments: a serene beach, a forest with a cozy tent and river, and an indoor room furnished with a bed. For the auditory component of the environments, natural sounds, known for their relaxation effects [1], were used. Each environment was accompanied by corresponding natural sounds— ocean waves, river flow and birdsong, and rainfall[1]—with spatial audio effects enhancing the sense of immersion [29]. Participants listened to these natural sounds using noise-canceling headphones[2]. To further improve immersion, interactive objects were placed within the spaces [33]. Additionally, time and lighting within the environments were made adjustable, allowing participants to nap comfortably. The environments were displayed on a Meta Quest 3 connected to a computer[3] with its blue light filter enabled to reduce short-wavelength light, which can disrupt sleep [11]. Navigation and interaction were performed using Meta Quest 3 controllers. Heart rate variability (HRV) was measured using HRV4Training[4] on an iPhone SE (Gen2), which also ran the NASA Psychomotor Vigilance Test (NASA PVT+)[5] to measure alertness.

3.3   Study Design

This study employed an experimental design to compare two conditions: the VR condition and the Audio condition. A within-subject experimental design

---

[1] Natural sounds: Beach (https://youtu.be/bn9F19Hi1Lk), River flow and birdsong (https://youtu.be/eKFTSSKCzWA), Rainfall (https://youtu.be/mPZkdNFkNps).

[2] Soundcore Life Q30: https://www.ankerjapan.com/products/a3028.

[3] NEXTGEAR   J6-A7G60GN-A: https://www.mouse-jp.co.jp/store/g/gngear-j6a7g60gnadcw102dec/.

[4] HRV4Training: https://www.hrv4training.com/

[5] NASA PVT+: https://apps.apple.com/us/app/nasa-pvt/id1146834402.

was employed and counterbalanced to prevent order effects between conditions. The experiment was conducted over two separate days, ensuring that participants did not experience both conditions on the same day. In the VR condition, participants used Meta Quest 3 and took a nap within an audiovisual relaxation environment. In the Audio condition, participants napped while listening to relaxation sounds only. Before the experiment, participants chose their preferred theme from three options: beach, forest, or indoor on a rainy day. Among 12 participants, 7 chose beach, 3 forest, and 2 indoor on a rainy day (analyses were not conducted separately by theme due to the small sample size). Each participant experienced both conditions with the same selected theme on both days, and the sounds used within the theme were consistent. The nap duration was standardized to 20 min for both conditions, and naps were scheduled to take place between 1 p.m., and 5 p.m. This time setting is because it is known that naps of 20 min are less likely to produce sleep inertia [9, 10]. In addition, 1 to 5 p.m. is the time of day when drowsiness reemerges [24], and taking a nap during this time has been shown to have no negative effect on nighttime sleep [5].

3.4   Procedure

Participants were instructed to refrain from consuming alcohol and excessive caffeine on the day of the experiment, and to avoid heavy meals, smoking, and hard exercise within two hours prior to the experiment. These guidelines were based on a related study measuring HRV [27] and were designed to eliminate factors that could affect the experimental results. Furthermore, we confirmed in person that participants were not sleep deprived the previous day. For safety reasons, the experiment was conducted with participants maintained in a seated posture in a reclining chair fixed at approximately a 60° angle. During the nap and HRV measurement, the room was darkened and kept quiet, the temperature was maintained at 24 °C throughout the experiment.

The experiment began with a questionnaire that measured the participant's subjective alertness, mood, and stress prior to napping. Next, the PVT was conducted for 5 min to quantitatively measure alertness. This was followed by a 5-min rest period to reduce test-induced fatigue. After rest, HRV4Training was used to measure HRV and was taken. Participants were then assigned to either the VR condition or the Audio condition, and Fig. 2 illustrates these experimental conditions. In the VR condition, participants wore Meta Quest 3 and headphones with noise cancellation turned on, and practiced basic operations such as moving, changing direction, and manipulating objects in the VR space. They then conducted 3 min of free exploration to familiarize themselves with the environment. The participants then took a nap for 20 min after adjusting the time and brightness in the environment. In the Audio condition, participants wore noise-canceling headphones and napped for 20 min while listening to natural sounds. Participants in this condition could wear an eye mask if desired. After the nap, HRV was measured again. Participants then completed another set of questionnaires regarding their subjective alertness, mood, and stress. Finally, the PVT was conducted once more to measure changes in alertness quantitatively.

3.5 Measures

Subjective alertness was measured using the Japanese version of the Karolinska Sleepiness Scale (KSS-J) [13]. The KSS-J is a validated measure for alertness and uses a 9-point Likert scale from 1 (very alert) to 9 (very sleepy). For quantitative measurement of alertness, the validated NASA PVT+ was used [3], and reaction time (RT) was recorded. The psychomotor vigilance task included in the NASA PVT+ is quite sensitive to sleep deprivation [18] and has also been found to be correlated with KSS-J results [13]. Also, mood was measured using the Japanese version of the Positive and Negative Affect Schedule (PANAS), whose validity has been confirmed [30]. The Japanese version of PANAS evaluates 8 items of positive affect (PA) and negative affect (NA) using a 6-point Likert scale (1 = not at all, 6 = very much). The order of the questions was randomized following suggested instructions [30]. Moreover, subjective stress levels were measured using a 10-point Likert scale (1 = very stressed, 10 = not stressed at all). HRV was measured using HRV4Training. HRV is known to change in response to stress level [15], and HRV4Training has been verified as a highly reliable measurement tool by third parties [32].

3.6 Statistical Analysis

The normality of the data was evaluated using the Shapiro-Wilk test. If normality was confirmed, the paired t-test was conducted. If not, the Wilcoxon signed-rank test was used. The significance level for all statistical tests was set at $\alpha -$ 0.05. Furthermore, the amount of change (Δ) was calculated by subtracting the pre-nap score from the post-nap score. Outliers were excluded from statistical analyses using the Interquartile Range method (IQR) method, while the figures show the distribution of the full dataset, including outliers, to illustrate overall trends.

4 Result

This section presents the experimental results. The analysis focused on three main endpoints: alertness, mood, and stress, which indicate the quality of napping. These results are summarized in Fig. 3.

4.1 Alertness

The KSS-J was used as a subjective indicator of alertness. The normality of the changes (ΔKSS-J) was evaluated using the Shapiro–Wilk test, which revealed that normality could not be confirmed. Therefore, the data were analyzed with the Wilcoxon signed-rank test. The results showed no significant difference between the VR and Audio conditions ($W = 26.0, p = 0.918$). Although improvements in alertness and negative ΔKSS-J values were expected, both increases and decreases in scores were observed among participants after napping.

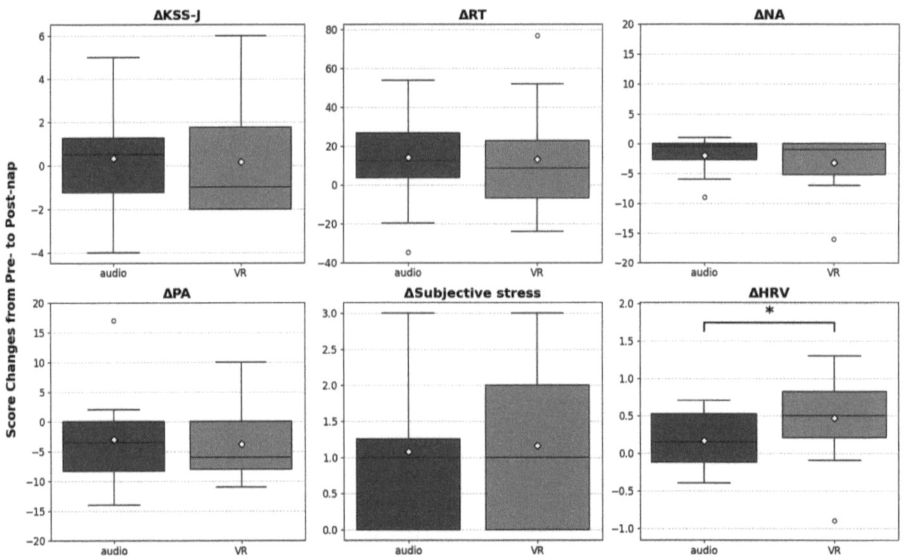

Fig. 3. Changes in alertness, mood, and stress measures. * indicates significant difference ($p < 0.05$). For ΔKSS-J, ΔRT, and ΔNA, lower scores represent favorable changes; for others, higher scores do.

The NASA PVT+ was used as an objective measure of alertness. The changes in reaction time (ΔRT) were analyzed with the paired t-test because the normality of the data was confirmed. The results showed no significant difference between the VR and Audio conditions ($t(11) = 0.104$, $p = 0.919$). Although improvements in alertness and negative ΔRT values were expected, both increases and decreases in scores were observed among participants after napping.

4.2   Mood

The Japanese version of the PANAS was used to assess mood, with scores analyzed separately for negative affect and positive affect.

The Wilcoxon signed-rank test was applied because the normality of the change in NA (ΔNA) was not confirmed. The results showed no significant difference between the VR and Audio conditions ($W = 3.50$, $p = 0.341$). However, ΔNA decreased after napping in both conditions, suggesting that napping contributed to the reduction of negative affect.

Similarly, the Wilcoxon signed-rank test was applied for PA because the normality of the change (ΔPA) was not confirmed. The results showed no significant difference between the VR and Audio conditions ($W = 16.5$, $p = 0.888$). In both conditions, ΔPA decreased after napping, indicating a tendency toward lower positive affect.

4.3   Stress

Subjective stress levels were analyzed using the Wilcoxon signed-rank test because the Shapiro–Wilk test did not confirm normality of the change (ΔSubjective stress). The results showed no significant difference between the VR and Audio conditions ($W = 9.0$, $p = 0.824$). However, a general tendency for subjective stress levels to decrease after napping was observed in both conditions.

HRV was used as an objective measure of stress. Because the normality was confirmed for the change (ΔHRV), the data were analyzed with the paired t-test. The results showed that ΔHRV was significantly greater in the VR condition than in the Audio condition ($t(11) = -2.50$, $p = 0.0315$), suggesting that the VR condition may be more effective in reducing stress.

5   Discussion

In this section, we discuss the experimental results by comparing the VR and Audio conditions, focusing on their effects on alertness, mood, and stress, which are indicators of nap quality. This discussion aims to provide deeper insights into the research question.

5.1   Alertness

Regarding alertness, subjective measures were obtained using the KSS-J and objective measures using the PVT. Neither measure revealed significant differences between the VR and Audio conditions. Some participants showed improved alertness after napping, while others showed a decline, which may be related to individual napping habits.

It has been reported that individuals who regularly nap tend to have better quality naps than those who do not take naps [8], and that people who do not are more likely to have stronger sleep inertia [22]. Thus, those who regularly take naps are more likely to improve their alertness after a nap. A correlation analysis between changes in alertness measured by the KSS-J and participants' napping habits revealed small negative correlations in both conditions (Audio: $r = -0.316$; VR: $r = -0.140$), suggesting that habitual nappers tended to show greater improvements in alertness.

In addition, in this experiment, participants napped while seated in a chair, although none reported typically napping in this position (6 usually nap in a bed, 5 lying elsewhere, and 1 on a desk). This unfamiliar posture may also have influenced the results.

Considering these factors, further research is needed to clarify the effects of VR-based audiovisual relaxation on alertness during napping.

5.2   Mood

With regard to mood, changes in NA and PA scores were assessed using the Japanese version of the PANAS. Neither factor showed significant differences between the VR and Audio conditions. NA scores decreased after napping in both conditions, indicating that napping was effective in reducing negative affect. In contrast, PA scores also tended to decrease, suggesting a reduction in positive affect. This outcome may be influenced by cultural factors.

Of the participants, 11 were Japanese and 1 was Chinese. Previous studies have reported that positive and negative affect are positively correlated among Japanese and Chinese individuals [4,30]. Therefore, the observed decrease in positive affect is likely to have been influenced by the simultaneous decrease in negative affect.

Nevertheless, as no significant differences were found between the VR and Audio conditions, further research is needed to clarify the potential effects of VR-based audiovisual relaxation on mood.

5.3 Stress

Stress was measured subjectively using a questionnaire and objectively using HRV4Training. In both measurements, stress reduction was confirmed after napping in both VR and Audio conditions. Although no significant differences were found between conditions in subjective stress, the VR condition showed a significantly greater change in HRV scores than the Audio condition ($t(11) = -2.50$, $p = 0.0315$). Because higher HRV scores indicate reduced stress [15], this finding suggests that the VR condition may be more effective for stress reduction. One possible reason for the absence of significant differences in subjective stress levels may be differences in relaxation methods used in this experiment.

Kim et al. reported that while relaxation using VR significantly increased HRV score compared to relaxation using biofeedback, but did not significantly reduce subjective stress, concluding that the relaxation methods themselves may have influenced the results [16]. Their findings are consistent with the present study, suggesting that methodological differences in stress reduction approaches across conditions may account for the lack of significant differences in subjective stress.

Overall, a reduction in subjective stress and a significant increase in HRV, reflecting decreased objective stress, were observed during VR-based naps. These findings suggest that VR-based naps are effective and may be more effective than naps with auditory relaxation in reducing stress.

6   Limitaions and Future Works

Several limitations of this study should be noted. First, differences in participants' usual napping postures and nap frequency may have influenced the results. Second, many participants reported discomfort from the head-mounted display (HMD), which was applied only in the VR condition in this prototype experiment; thus, the independent effect of wearing the device could not be isolated. Future studies should investigate the impact of improved, more comfortable hardware and consider applying the HMD in both VR and Audio conditions to clarify the role of visual input. Third, the small sample size limited the ability to conduct theme-specific analyses. Moreover, both the small and relatively homogeneous sample, with most participants falling within a narrow age range, restricted the generalizability of the findings. Finally, the study did not assess long-term effects of repeated VR-based naps.

Future research should address these limitations by optimizing VR nap conditions (e.g., body posture and VR content), developing more comfortable devices for use during napping, including larger and more diverse participant samples, and conducting long-term trials to confirm and extend the present findings.

7   Conclusion

In this study, the effects of VR-based napping with audiovisual relaxation were compared with those of napping with auditory relaxation. The results showed a significant increase in HRV scores in the VR condition, indicating a significant reduction in objective stress. In contrast, no significant differences were observed between conditions in mood and alertness. Taken together, these findings suggest that VR-based napping may be more effective than auditory relaxation in reducing stress, although its effects on mood and alertness remain inconclusive.

Overall, VR-based napping appears to be a promising approach for sleep promotion, but further research is needed to address current limitations and optimize its application.

A   System Description

As an appendix, we introduce the system created for this study. This system was designed to allow users to adjust time and brightness within a VR environment,

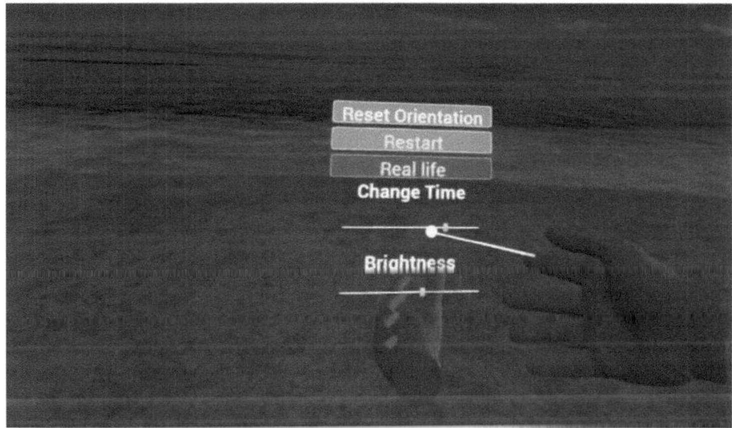

Fig. 4. Created User Interface.

providing a comfortable napping experience. The interface was developed to ensure intuitive controls for participants during the experiment.

As shown in Fig. 4, participants controlled time and brightness using a slider function operated with Meta Quest 3 controllers.

Beach in the night

Forest in the night

Indoor room in the night

Fig. 5. VR environments during the night: Beach, Forest, Indoor.

Additionally, Fig. 5 illustrates environments where the time of day has been adjusted to nighttime. In contrast, Fig. 1 shows the same environments during the daytime.

Using this time and brightness adjustment system, some participants reported that setting the time to night and reducing the brightness made them feel as if it were currently nighttime, which induced drowsiness.

References

1. Alvarsson, J.J., Wiens, S., Nilsson, M.E.: Stress recovery during exposure to nature sound and environmental noise. Int. J. Environ. Res. Public Health **7**(3), 1036–1046 (2010)
2. Anderson, A.P., Mayer, M.D., Fellows, A.M., Cowan, D.R., Hegel, M.T., Buckey, J.C.: Relaxation with immersive natural scenes presented using virtual reality. Aerosp. Med. Hum. Perform. **88**(6), 520–526 (2017)

3. Arsintescu, L., Kato, K.H., Cravalho, P.F., Feick, N.H., Stone, L.S., Flynn-Evans, E.E.: Validation of a touchscreen psychomotor vigilance task. Accid. Anal. Prev. **126**, 173–176 (2019)
4. Bagozzi, R.P., Wong, N., Yi, Y.: The role of culture and gender in the relationship between positive and negative affect. Cogn. Emot. **13**(6), 641–672 (1999)
5. Campbell, S.S., Murphy, P.J., Stauble, T.N.: Effects of a nap on nighttime sleep and waking function in older subjects. J. Am. Geriatr. Soc. **53**(1), 48–53 (2005)
6. Cordi, M.J., Ackermann, S., Rasch, B.: Effects of relaxing music on healthy sleep. Sci. Rep. **9**(1), 9079 (2019)
7. De Niet, G., Tiemens, B., Lendemeijer, B., Hutschemaekers, G.: Music-assisted relaxation to improve sleep quality: meta-analysis. J. Adv. Nurs. **65**(7), 1356–1364 (2009)
8. Dinges, D.F., et al.: Cumulative sleepiness, mood disturbance, and psychomotor vigilance performance decrements during a week of sleep restricted to 4–5 hours per night. Sleep **20**(4), 267–277 (1997)
9. Dutheil, F., et al.: Effects of a short daytime nap on the cognitive performance: a systematic review and meta-analysis. Int. J. Environ. Res. Public Health **18**(19), 10212 (2021)
10. Faraut, B., Andrillon, T., Vecchierini, M.F., Leger, D.: Napping: a public health issue. from epidemiological to laboratory studies. Sleep Med. Rev. **35**, 85–100 (2017)
11. Green, A., Cohen-Zion, M., Haim, A., Dagan, Y.: Evening light exposure to computer screens disrupts human sleep, biological rhythms, and attention abilities. Chronobiol. Int. **34**(7), 855–865 (2017)
12. Hsouna, H., et al.: Effect of different nap opportunity durations on short-term maximal performance, attention, feelings, muscle soreness, fatigue, stress and sleep. Physiol. Behav. **211**, 112673 (2019)
13. Kaida, K., et al.: Validation of the karolinska sleepiness scale against performance and EEG variables. Clin. Neurophysiol. **117**(7), 1574–1581 (2006)
14. Kaida, K., Takahashi, M., Otsuka, Y.: A short nap and natural bright light exposure improve positive mood status. Ind. Health **45**(2), 301–308 (2007)
15. Kim, H.G., Cheon, E.J., Bai, D.S., Lee, Y.H., Koo, B.H.: Stress and heart rate variability: a meta-analysis and review of the literature. Psychiatry Investig. **15**(3), 235 (2018)
16. Kim, H., et al.: Effect of virtual reality on stress reduction and change of physiological parameters including heart rate variability in people with high stress: an open randomized crossover trial. Front. Psych. **12**, 614539 (2021)
17. Lee, S.Y., Kang, J.: Effect of virtual reality meditation on sleep quality of intensive care unit patients: a randomised controlled trial. Intensive Crit. Care Nurs. **59**, 102849 (2020)
18. Lim, J., Dinges, D.F.: Sleep deprivation and vigilant attention. Ann. N. Y. Acad. Sci. **1129**(1), 305–322 (2008)
19. Liu, K., Chen, Y., Wu, D., Lin, R., Wang, Z., Pan, L.: Effects of progressive muscle relaxation on anxiety and sleep quality in patients with covid-19. Complement. Ther. Clin. Pract. **39**, 101132 (2020)
20. Lou, S., et al.: Benefits of napping habits in healthy adults: maintaining alerting performance and cortisol levels change within 90 min of habitual napping time. Sleep Med. **119**, 214–221 (2024)
21. Luo, Z., Inoué, S.: A short daytime nap modulates levels of emotions objectively evaluated by the emotion spectrum analysis method. Psychiatry Clin. Neurosci. **54**(2), 207–212 (2000)

22. Milner, C.E., Cote, K.A.: Benefits of napping in healthy adults: impact of nap length, time of day, age, and experience with napping. J. Sleep Res. **18**(2), 272–281 (2009)
23. Morin, C.M., LeBlanc, M., Daley, M., Gregoire, J., Merette, C.: Epidemiology of insomnia: prevalence, self-help treatments, consultations, and determinants of help-seeking behaviors. Sleep Med. **7**(2), 123–130 (2006)
24. Mullens, È.: Apprendre à faire la sieste. Josette Lyon (2017). https://www.editions-tredaniel.com/apprendre-faire-la-sieste-p-3338.html
25. Naef, A.C., et al.: Investigating the role of auditory and visual sensory inputs for inducing relaxation during virtual reality stimulation. Sci. Rep. **12**(1), 17073 (2022)
26. Pai, Y.S., et al.: Napwell: an EOG-based sleep assistant exploring the effects of virtual reality on sleep onset. Virtual Reality **26**(2), 437–451 (2022)
27. Park, B.J., Tsunetsugu, Y., Kasetani, T., Kagawa, T., Miyazaki, Y.: The physiological effects of shinrin-yoku (taking in the forest atmosphere or forest bathing): evidence from field experiments in 24 forests across japan. Environ. Health Prev. Med. **15**, 18–26 (2010)
28. Pilcher, J.J., Michalowski, K.R., Carrigan, R.D.: The prevalence of daytime napping and its relationship to nighttime sleep. Behav. Med. **27**(2), 71–76 (2001)
29. Poeschl, S., Wall, K., Doering, N.: Integration of spatial sound in immersive virtual environments an experimental study on effects of spatial sound on presence. In: 2013 IEEE Virtual Reality (VR), pp. 129–130. IEEE (2013)
30. Sato, A., Yasuda, A.: Nihongoban panas no sakusei. Seikaku Shinrigaku Kenkyu **9**(2), 138–139 (2001)
31. Simon, K.C., McDevitt, E.A., Ragano, R., Mednick, S.C.: Progressive muscle relaxation increases slow-wave sleep during a daytime nap. J. Sleep Res. **31**(5), e13574 (2022)
32. Stone, J.D., et al.: Assessing the accuracy of popular commercial technologies that measure resting heart rate and heart rate variability. Front. Sports Active Living **3**, 585870 (2021)
33. Yeo, N.L., et al.: What is the best way of delivering virtual nature for improving mood? An experimental comparison of high definition TV, 360 video, and computer generated virtual reality. J. Environ. Psychol. **72**, 101500 (2020)
34. Yin, M., Xiao, R.: Drifting off in paradise: why people sleep in virtual reality. In: Proceedings of the 2023 CHI Conference on Human Factors in Computing Systems, pp. 1–13 (2023)
35. de Zambotti, M., Barresi, G., Colrain, I.M., Baker, F.C.: When sleep goes virtual: the potential of using virtual reality at bedtime to facilitate sleep. Sleep **43**(12), zsaa178 (2020)
36. de Zambotti, M., Sizintsev, M., Claudatos, S., Barresi, G., Colrain, I.M., Baker, F.C.: Reducing bedtime physiological arousal levels using immersive audio-visual respiratory bio-feedback: a pilot study in women with insomnia symptoms. J. Behav. Med. **42**(5), 973–983 (2019). https://doi.org/10.1007/s10865-019-00020-9

A Method for Reducing Cognitive Load by Virtually Relocating the Visual Position of Distracting Sound Sources Away from the Task Direction

Kyosuke Yamamoto[1], Kyosuke Futami[1,2]($\boxtimes$) (iD), and Kazuya Murao[1] (iD)

[1] Ritsumeikan University, Osaka, Japan
kyosuke.yamamoto@iis.ise.ritsumei.ac.jp, murao@cs.ritsumei.ac.jp
[2] Digital Spirit Tech, Tokyo, Japan
futami@fc.ritsumei.ac.jp

Abstract. When a sound source that can interfere with concentration exists in the same direction as a user's focused task, it can lead to problems such as reduced ease of work and increased workload. This study addresses situations where a distracting sound source is present in the same direction as the user's focused task and proposes a method to improve the ease of performing the task. The proposed method uses AR technology to virtually move only the visual information of the distracting sound source (e.g., the appearance of people conversing) to a direction different from the user's focused task. This aims to make the user perceive the distracting sound source as being at that virtual location, thereby improving the ease of task performance. The results of an evaluation experiment confirmed that the proposed method has the effect of significantly reducing the workload of a cognitive task. These findings aid the design of AR-based task concentration support systems.

Keywords: AR · Cognitive science · Improving task performance

1 Introduction

Providing an environment where people can easily concentrate on their work to reduce their workload is important from the perspective of maintaining labor productivity and safety. However, in the real world, there are situations where a sound-emitting entity that can interfere with concentration is located in the direction of a user's focused task. For example, when performing a task in front (e.g., desk work, manual labor), distracting sounds (e.g., conversation, environmental noise) may be heard from people or objects also located in the front. In many cases, it is not possible for the user to physically move these entities.

On the other hand, findings in cognitive science show that when two senses, such as vision and hearing, receive information from different events and one must be ignored, it is most difficult to do so when both events occur in the same direction [1]. The reason for this is that, due to the characteristics of the cerebral cortex, a person's attention is allocated not to a specific object, but to the physical space or direction where it exists [1,2]. Based on this knowledge, in the aforementioned situations, since the task the user should concentrate on and the distracting sound source are located in the same direction, a portion of the concentration that should be allocated to the task may be unintentionally diverted to the distracting sound source, potentially leading to reduced ease of task performance and increased workload. Therefore, a technology that can easily create an environment where the distracting sound source is removed from the direction of the user's focused task would be beneficial.

Therefore, this study targets situations where a distracting sound source exists in the same direction as a user's focused task and proposes a method to improve the ease of performing that task. The proposed method uses AR technology to virtually move only the visual information of the distracting sound source (e.g., the appearance of people conversing) to a direction different from the user's focused task (e.g., to the rear if the user is performing a forward-facing task). This makes the user perceive that the distracting sound source exists at that virtual location, consequently improving the ease of performing the task. Considering the principle of the ventriloquism effect, a cross-modal perceptual phenomenon between vision and hearing, the perception of a sound source's location is more strongly influenced by visual information than by auditory information. Therefore, we hypothesize that by simply moving the visual information of the distracting sound source virtually, we can make the user feel that the source is not in the direction they are concentrating on.

2 Proposed Method

In the experiment to verify the effectiveness of this method, the following two conditions are set.

In the **Control Condition**, the task the user should concentrate on and the distracting sound source are in the same direction. For example, this is a situation where people are conversing in front of the user while they are performing a forward-facing task. When the user performs the task, a portion of their concentration may be diverted to the distracting sound from the same direction, potentially making the task harder to perform.

On the other hand, in the **Proposed Method Condition**, the visual information of the distracting sound source is concealed by a mask (e.g., blended with the background). Then, the visual information of the sound source (e.g., an AR video of the speakers) is presented via AR at a location different from the task's direction (e.g., behind the user). This makes the user feel that the distracting sound source is behind them, making it easier to concentrate on the forward task (as forward-directed attention is less likely to be diverted to the distracting sound source).

A top-down schematic diagram of the control and proposed method conditions is shown in Fig. 1. When performing a task on a PC screen in front, the distracting person located in front is masked to blend with the background, and appears in the rear as an AR object.

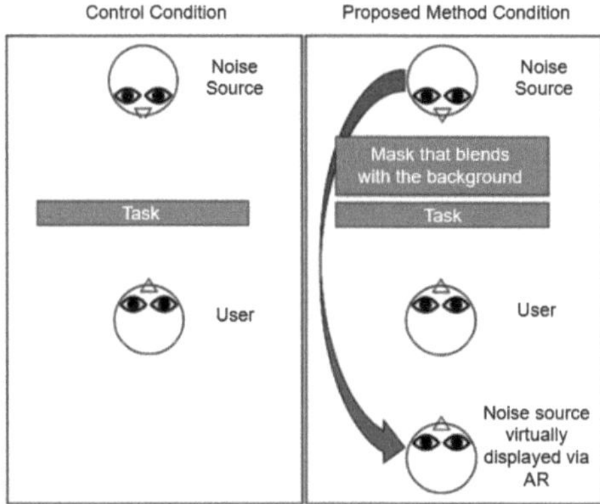

Fig. 1. Schematic diagram of the proposed method condition.

Application Implementation: An application for the experiment was implemented. The entire system consisted of a PC (Lenovo Legion 5-15ITH6H), an HMD (Meta Quest 3), and a speaker (JBL Flip 5). The Meta Quest 3, equipped with a full-color passthrough function, was adopted as the HMD, allowing the user to see the external environment and perform tasks even while wearing it. As the distracting sound source, a video of two speakers conversing was displayed within the HMD. In the control condition, this video was displayed in front of the user, and in the proposed method condition, it was displayed behind the user. The conversation audio of these speakers, serving as the distracting sound, was played from a speaker physically placed in front of the user in both the control and proposed method conditions. An AR image that blended with the background (the lab wall) was presented in front of the speaker from the user's perspective, visually masking the speaker itself. The application was developed using Unity. The positional relationship between the speaker and the user during the experiment was the same as the relationship between the distracting source and the user in Fig. 1, with the speaker placed 3 m in front of the user.

3   Evaluation

We evaluated whether the proposed method improves the ease of performing a task (i.e., reduces workload). Seventeen Japanese participants (16 male, 1 female; mean age 22.6, range 21–28) took part in the study.

Experimental Task. In this experiment, a Stroop task was assigned to the participants as a visual task. In this task, an arrow shape and a character, indicating one of the four directions (up, down, left, or right), were presented in the center of the participant's forward view. Simultaneously with the shape and character, an instruction "Answer by character" or "Answer by shape" was presented. Participants were asked to respond with the correct direction as quickly and accurately as possible using a controller's joystick. A new question was presented 3 s after a response, and this continued for 3 min (the experimental results showed an average of 55.32 responses (MIN 43, MAX 65)). The Stroop task screen was displayed in front of the participant. During this task, as a distracting sound source, a video of two speakers conversing was played, and their audio was presented from a speaker located in front of the user. The speakers were a Japanese comedy duo (Sandwichman), and a video of their manzai, a form of conversational comedy, was used. Since the duo has a history of winning a Japanese manzai contest, it can be assumed that they are performing a conversation that is generally perceived as humorous in Japan.

Experimental Conditions. Figure 2 shows the participant's field of view for each condition. Two conditions were tested: Control, where distractor visuals were in the same forward direction as the task, and Proposed Method, where distractor visuals were positioned behind the participant. In both conditions, participants performed the front-facing task, with the distracting speaker positioned physically in front.

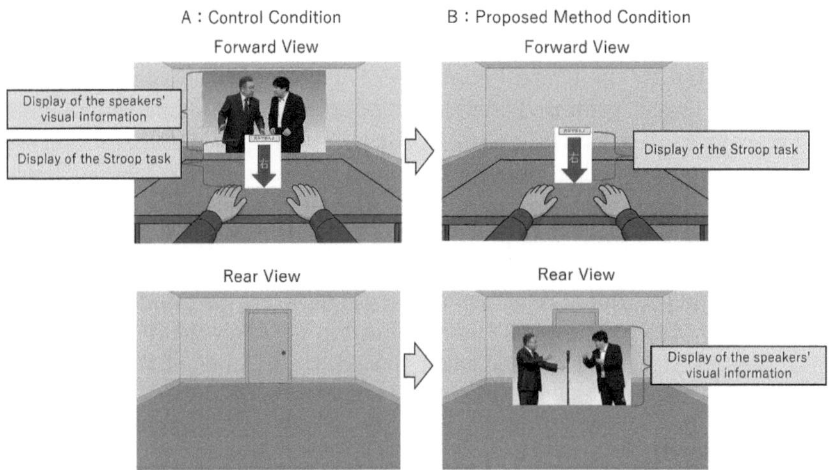

Fig. 2. Appearance of the field of view for each condition in the experiment.

Experimental Procedure. The experiment consisted of a pre-explanation phase, a practice phase, a control condition phase, a break phase, and a proposed method condition phase. The order of the control and proposed method conditions was counterbalanced among the participants.

1. Pre-explanation Phase: First, after obtaining informed consent, the task (Stroop task) and the presentation of distracting sounds were explained. Participants were instructed to perform the task as quickly and accurately as possible, and it was announced that top performers would receive a prize in addition to their compensation. This was intended to increase the participants' motivation for the experiment.
2. Practice Phase: Before the measurement for each condition began, participants practiced the Stroop task alone for about 1 min. During this phase, no distracting sound information was presented. The purpose was to allow participants to get used to the task operation.
3. Control Condition Phase (or Proposed Method Condition Phase): The order in which participants undertook the control or proposed method condition was counterbalanced. The following describes an example where the control condition was performed first. Before the start of the experimental task, the position of the distracting speakers was confirmed for about 60 s while their video was playing. In the control condition, the speakers were located in the front. After that, the experimental task screen was displayed in front, and the task was performed for 3 min. After the task, a NASA-TLX questionnaire was administered for subjective workload evaluation.
4. Break Phase: Participants took a 3-minute break.
5. Proposed Method Condition Phase (or Control Condition Phase): Participants performed the experimental condition that was different from the one before the break. Before the task, the position of the speakers was confirmed for about 60 s while their video was playing. In the proposed method condition phase, the speakers were located in the rear. Afterward, the task was performed for 3 min, followed by a workload questionnaire.

Evaluation Metrics. (1) The ease of task performance (subjective workload) was measured using the NASA-TLX. (2) As a secondary metric, we measured whether the task results also changed as the ease of performing the task changed. The task results were twofold. The first was the task response speed. This was the time from when the Stroop task symbol was displayed until a response was made. The second was the task accuracy rate. This was the percentage of correct answers in the Stroop task.

Results. The results of NASA-TLX were as follows. The average values of the subscales of the questionnaire are shown in Fig. 3. The error bars indicate the standard error. A test was conducted on the total scores, and a significant difference was found between the conditions ($p = 0.005 < 0.05$). This result means that our method reduced the subjective workload. However, no significant difference was found between the conditions ($p = n.s.$) in the task results.

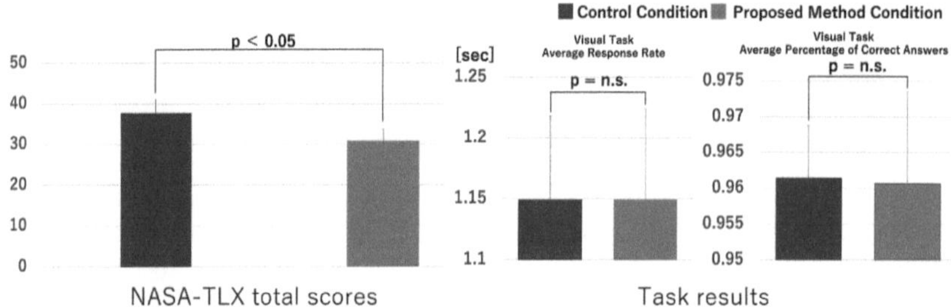

Fig. 3. The NASA-TLX total scores and task results

Discussion. The results of this experiment confirmed that using the proposed method significantly reduces subjective workload compared to the control condition. This is thought to be because separating the visual information of the distracting sound source from the direction of the task and virtually locating it to the rear made it easier for the user to psychologically ignore the distracting stimulus, thus facilitating concentration on the main task. The downward trend in items such as "mental demand" and "effort" on the questionnaire subscales supports this interpretation. On the other hand, there was no significant difference in task results between the conditions. The fact that the proposed method did not negatively affect task results can be interpreted as a positive outcome.

4   Conclusion

We proposed a method to improve the ease of performing the task by virtually moving only the visual information of the distracting sound source to a rearward direction, different from the forward-facing task the user is concentrating on. The evaluation confirmed that this method significantly reduces workload when both the task and the distractor are forward-facing, even though the actual sound source remains in front.

Acknowledgments. This research was supported by JSPS (Japan Society for the Promotion of Science) KAKENHI Grant Number 24K20824.

References

1. Stafford, T., Webb, M.: Mind Hacks: Tips & Tricks for Using Your Brain. O'Reilly Media, Inc. (2005)
2. Spence, C., Read, L.: Speech shadowing while driving: on the difficulty of splitting attention between eye and ear. Psychol. Sci. **14**(3), 251–256 (2003)

AR Superimposed Display System with Video Synchronization

Yusuke Gotoh[1]($\boxtimes$)(iD) and Yuichiro Ikeda[2]

[1] Faculty of Environmental, Life, Natural Science and Technology, Institute of
Academic and Research, Okayama University, Okayama, Japan
`y-gotoh@okayama-u.ac.jp`
[2] Graduate School of Environmental, Life, Natural Science and Technology,
Okayama University, Okayama, Japan

Abstract. Recently, with the improvement of computing power in mobile devices and the development of augmented reality (AR) technology, there has been growing interest in using image recognition for information retrieval and navigation. By using AR technology, systems that merge the real world and virtual space based on camera images and sensor data can provide users with intuitive information. However, many conventional systems require the installation of AR markers or beacons for their implementation and operation. It is important to design a highly versatile system with that does not require additional hardware or the preparation of special environments. In this paper, we propose an AR overlay display system with video synchronization. The proposed system compares camera images from Android devices with images registered in advance on a server created with FastAPI in real-time. In addition, this system can be easily operated within a server environment using devices in the same network, without the need for dedicated equipment or special environments. An evaluation of the proposed method showed that as the number of registered images increased, the amount of matching processing also increased and the execution time became longer. Furthermore, the system's recognition rate was 100% for images taken by a mobile device at angles between 0° and 30°, and images could be recognized by the system's terminal at an average occlusion rate of 65% of the entire image.

Keywords: Augmented reality · Image recognition · Superimposed display system

1 Introduction

In recent years, with the improvement of computing power in mobile devices and the development of augmented reality (AR) technology, there has been growing interest in using image recognition for displaying data and providing navigation. In particular, the latest mobile devices using iOS and Android operating systems

P. Delir Haghighi et al. (Eds.): MoMM 2025, LNCS 16329, pp. 159–174, 2026.
https://doi.org/10.1007/978-3-032-11768-7_13

can recognize images in real-time and construct AR spaces by improving the accuracy of cameras and built-in sensors.

AR technology is expected to be introduced not only in entertainment systems but also in various fields such as education and tourism. Zainal et al. [1] investigated the application of AR and VR in medical procedures and dental education. Conventional face-to-face education or online education cannot effectively convey visual and spatial images to users, but the introduction of AR and VR technologies can overcome such limitations. Bazargani et al. [2] discussed the usefulness of geographic information systems (GIS) and AR in geography education, and they analyzed an Android application using location-based AR. Amirian et al. [3] developed a support tool for sightseeing using AR technology. They applied AR technology to landmarks such as distinctive buildings to guide tourists to their destinations while displaying local data for tourists at specific locations. In addition, by adding tourist data to landmarks, they could support location guidance for both tourists and local residents.

Systems that apply AR technology can provide users with intuitively perceived information by integrating the real world and virtual space based on camera images and sensor data. On the other hand, many conventional systems require the installation of AR markers or beacons. Consequently, there is demand for highly versatile systems that do not require additional hardware or the preparation of a special environment.

In this paper, we propose an AR overlay display system with video synchronization. The proposed system mainly uses Unity's AR Foundation [4] and OpenCV [5]. The proposed system compares, in real-time, composed images from Android devices with images registered in advance on a server created with FastAPI. In this process, the text data corresponding to the content that matches both images is overlaid in the AR space.

The following major contributions are made by the proposed system:

- It efficiently manages large-scale image data and presents intuitive information in the real world.
- It can be easily operated within a server environment using devices in the same network, without the need for dedicated equipment or preparation of a special environment.

The remainder of this paper is organized as follows. We explain the AR technology in Sect. 2 and image recognition in Sect. 3. Related work is presented in Sect. 4. In Sect. 5, we explain our proposed system. We evaluate the effectiveness of the proposed system in Sect. 6. Finally, we conclude the paper in Sect. 7.

2 Augmented Reality (AR)

2.1 AR Applications

In recent years, AR applications have become widely available. For example, Pokémon Go [6] applies AR technology in the screens of mobile devices where users capture displayed monsters.

AR technology superimposes additional text and images onto images from the real world. With the spread of smartphones, AR applications are leveraged by users not only for real-time games but also in the fields of education and tourism. In addition, by utilizing the fifth-generation mobile communication system (5G), AR applications can provide users with large-capacity content such as video and 3D CG images via high-speed communication.

2.2   Features of AR Applications

Location-based AR overlays content onto the screen of a mobile device using location data obtained by GPS. This technology determines the position to display content, based on the direction and angle of view, using location data and the magnetic and acceleration sensors installed on mobile devices. In recent years, technologies for acquiring such data as user location, orientation, and tilt have become widely available on mobile devices and platforms. The accuracy of measuring user location in location-based AR largely depends on GPS, but current GPS technology cannot accurately determine a user's position because it has an error margin of several meters.

Vision-based AR using markers determines the location where content is presented by recognizing specific markers such as shapes and patterns. In such systems, libraries or engines are generally used to recognize the markers. However, markers must be physically installed. Therefore, it is difficult to set markers in places where they would spoil the scenery or where there are restrictions on their installation.

Markerless vision-based AR presents content by recognizing objects and spaces in the real environment rather than using physically installed markers. This technology specifies the position of content based on existing features and objects in the environment. On the other hand, because spatial or object recognition depends on advanced computing, the hardware requirements become severe. In addition, the operation of markerless vision-based AR applications requires specialized knowledge of spatial recognition and image processing.

3   Image Recognition

3.1   Mechanism of Image Recognition

Image recognition analyzes objects and features identified from digital images and videos. This technology is closely related to fields such as artificial intelligence (AI), machine learning (ML), and computer vision (CV), and it has evolved with the recent development of deep learning technology. As a basic mechanism in image recognition, features are first extracted from the input image. Next, by inputting the extracted features into a classifier, the recognition target is classified into one of several categories. Here, the algorithms and methods used in the feature-extraction phase and the matching phase are crucial.

In augmented reality (AR), image recognition is an important technology that connects the real world and the virtual world. By recognizing images captured with a camera and displaying virtual content, we can achieve a fusion of the real and virtual worlds.

3.2 Feature Point Extraction

Feature point extraction is the process in image recognition that detects and describes important areas within an image. Feature points are patterns that can be clearly distinguished within areas of an image that are rich in edges, corners, and textures. In the following, we explain the heuristic algorithms for feature point extraction. These algorithms are invariant to specific scales and rotations, and they can extract feature points stably in different environments.

Fig. 1. Feature point extraction: SIFT

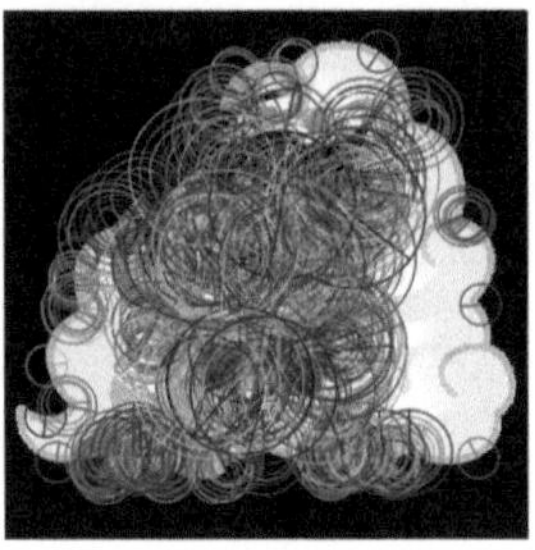

Fig. 2. Feature point extraction: ORB

Fig. 3. Feature point extraction: KAZE

Fig. 4. Feature point extraction: AKAZE

Scale-Invariant Feature Transform (SIFT) [7] can detect feature points that are invariant to scale and rotation, and it is widely used for image matching and object recognition. SIFT consists of three stages: feature point detection, feature description, and matching. It is robust to scale and rotation changes, and its feature point detection accuracy is very high. On the other hand, SIFT is not suitable for large datasets or real-time processing due to the high computational cost.

The Oriented FAST and Rotated BRIEF (ORB) [8] algorithm was proposed in 2011 to overcome SIFT's limitations in handling high computational cost.

ORB uses the Features from Accelerated Segment Test (FAST) algorithm to detect scale-invariant features. Furthermore, ORB is combined with the normalized Binary Robust Independent Elementary Features (BRIEF) description method, which is used to describe rotation-invariant features.

KAZE [9] is an algorithm proposed in 2012. KAZE utilizes a nonlinear scale space to detect feature points, and it improves matching accuracy compared to conventional linear scale-space approaches. KAZE effectively manages the influence of edge and contrast characteristics on feature point extraction. By employing nonlinear diffusion filtering, it locally adapts image blur to feature points to reduce noise. In addition, it preserves the boundaries of the subject image.

The AKAZE [10] algorithm was proposed in 2013 as an improved version of KAZE. By streamlining the calculation of the nonlinear scale space used in KAZE, it became possible to significantly reduce the computational cost of AKAZE. AKAZE maintains feature point detection performance while significantly improving computational speed over that of KAZE. In addition, AKAZE uses binary descriptors, and its feature point matching is fast. On the other hand, its invariance to scale and rotation is lower than that of other algorithms, so its accuracy may decrease in certain scenarios.

The results of extracting feature points using each algorithm are shown in Figs. 1, 2, 3, and 4. Scale information is added to the detected feature points. This scale reflects the size of the area considered in the detection of feature points, and it is visually represented as the radius of a circle when the feature points are drawn. Feature points with a small scale are detected based on image details such as edges and corners. On the other hand, feature points with a large scale depend on the image structure over a wide area.

Compared to other algorithms, SIFT extracts fewer feature points, but these are on a relatively large scale. ORB extracts feature points on the largest scale among the four algorithms. On the other hand, KAZE and AKAZE extract more feature points than SIFT and ORB. In this regard, AKAZE extracts features at a greater level of detail than possible with KAZE.

3.3   Feature Point Matching

Feature point matching is a technique that compares feature points detected in different images and determines whether they match. This process is particularly important in object tracking in AR and image recognition. Feature point matching extracts feature points from input images and reference images while calculating descriptors. Next, these descriptors are compared to identify pairs of feature points. In this comparison, the k-Nearest Neighbor (kNN) matching algorithm is used to search for neighboring points based on the descriptors of each feature point and to detect corresponding feature points. kNN matching is an algorithm that searches for the k nearest feature points specified from the search space. OpenCV provides the following two methods to perform this search.

Brute-force matching searches for the highest similarity by comparing all pairs of descriptors. Although it requires a large amount of computation and takes a long time to process, brute-force matching can reliably find the nearest feature points. Fast Library for Approximate Nearest Neighbors (FLANN) performs approximate searches to achieve greater speed and thus identifies nearby feature points without performing a full search. It is particularly effective for large datasets of feature points. On the other hand, since FLANN is an approximate method, it may not find the exact nearest neighbors.

In the proposed system, we use AKAZE for feature point extraction and brute-force matching for feature point matching. In addition, to improve matching accuracy, we combine techniques such as cross-checking and ratio testing. In cross-checking, we compare the matching results for two images from two directions and then match the images only if these results match. In ratio tests, images are matched only if the similarity ratio between the most similar feature points and the second-most similar feature points is below a certain threshold. These filtering techniques reduce false detections and improve matching accuracy.

The combination of AKAZE and brute-force matching in feature point matching offers high accuracy and versatility, but it also increases computational costs. However, with the recent improvement in mobile device performance, real-time processing has become possible. Therefore, feature point matching can be considered practical for mobile AR applications.

3.4   Image Recognition Libraries

Open Source Computer Vision Library (Open CV) is an open source library specialized for computer vision and image processing. It provides many functions such as feature extraction, image classification, and object detection. When extracting features with OpenCV, algorithms such as SIFT and ORB are generally used. These algorithms efficiently describe local features and permit a fast comparison with other images.

AR Foundation is an AR development framework for Unity that provides tools for integrating major AR platforms, such as ARKit [11] for iOS devices and ARCore [12] for Android devices. In AR Foundation, feature point extraction and matching optimize the process of recognizing and tracking objects and markers in the real world using extracted feature points. Accordingly, AR Foundation can adapt to changes in scale and perspective.

4   Related Work

4.1   Image Recognition with Deep Learning Models

Deep Learning Important Features (DeepLIFT) [13] decomposes the output prediction of a neural network for a specific input by backpropagating the influence of all neurons on each feature of the input. DeepLIFT reveals dependencies that can be missed with other approaches by considering the contribution of each neuron based on its activation. Evaluation results show that DeepLIFT significantly outperforms gradient-based methods when applied to models trained on MNIST and on simulated genome data, respectively.

SmoothGrad [14] is a method that visually clarifies gradient-based sensitivity maps to visualize which parts of an image a convolutional neural network (CNN) focuses on. By using two types of smoothing, SmoothGrad can clarify sensitivity maps that represent the gradient of the class score function for the input image. In addition, SmoothGrad reduces noise, which was an issue in previous research. The evaluation results confirm that a high smoothing effect is achieved by averaging maps created on the basis of many small changes within the image.

4.2 Overlay Display of Video Data in AR Space

Visual SyncAR [15] is an AR technology that displays video data superimposed on other video in synchronization with that video. By quickly detecting electronic watermarks embedded in images and rapidly detecting image areas in captured images to estimate camera posture, Visual SyncAR enables AR display that supports fast forward and rewinding of images. Janina et al. [16] detected ear tags from video captured by a smartphone camera to recognize the locations of cows and then present to the user video data corresponding to markers.

4.3 Template Matching

Template matching [17] is widely used as an image recognition method. This technique compares the pixel values of entire images to evaluate the degree of similarity, and it is mainly used to detect specific patterns or shapes within an image. Although template matching is a simple algorithm with low computational cost, it is not robust to changes in scale, rotation, and lighting conditions. The evaluation environment in this paper involves a diverse range of images with varying lighting, angles, and scales, so template matching is unsuitable.

5 Proposed System

5.1 Design

In this paper, we propose an AR system that superimposes content onto an AR space synchronized with camera images. The proposed method uses Unity's AR Foundation and OpenCV to recognize camera images on Android devices and then superimpose content related to the recognized images onto the AR space. Specifically, the proposed method compares camera images with images on a server in real-time and displays content related to matching images. In addition, we implement a feature for image recognition that communicates with Unity using FastAPI, a web framework necessary for web application development and API development.

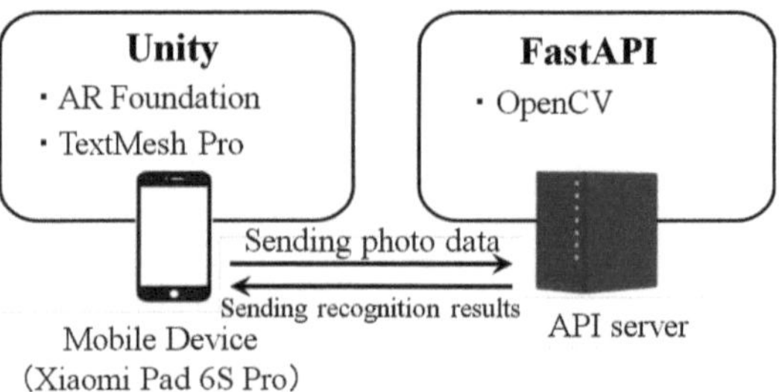

Fig. 5. Overview of proposed system

Figure 5 illustrates the configuration of the proposed system, which consists of mobile devices and an API server. The mobile device was constructed using AR Foundation and TextMesh Pro on Unity. The API server was constructed using OpenCV on FastAPI.

In the following, we explain the processing flow of the proposed system. First, the service provider in the suggestion system registers the recognized images are registered in both FastAPI and Unity. The data of these recognized images are stored in FastAPI but not in Unity. Next, the service provider executes FastAPI after building the application in Unity. Finally, users can use the proposed system.

When the system is running, the mobile device uses AR Foundation to save camera images at regular intervals and to send them to the API server. The API server compares the images it receives with the reference images stored in FastAPI using feature point extraction and feature point matching with OpenCV. This process checks whether the reference image contains the same feature points as the transmitted image.

If there are feature points in the transmitted image that match those in the reference image, the API server performs clustering on the matched feature points to determine the display location of content such as text data in the transmitted image. After determining valid coordinates based on the results of the clustering process, the name and center coordinates of the target image are stored in a JSON file. By sending this JSON file to Unity, mobile devices can display the content at the appropriate position on Unity.

5.2   AR Foundation

The proposed system implements basic functions for managing the display location of content by constructing an AR space using AR Foundation. AR Foundation integrates all key features of ARKit and ARCore. Therefore, AR Foundation provides unified access to advanced AR features such as image recognition, plane detection, feature detection, anchor placement, and self-localization. These key features enable intuitive content presentation by seamlessly integrating the real world with the virtual world in AR applications.

The proposal system uses AR Foundation to send image data of screenshots captured by mobile device cameras to the API server. Consequently, AR Foundation greatly improves development efficiency as a platform for easily implementing AR functions.

5.3   OpenCV

OpenCV is an open-source library specializing in computer vision and image processing. It provides many functions such as feature point extraction, image classification, and object detection. The proposed system uses this library to extract feature points and match them. Objects are identified by extracting feature points in images from camera footage in real-time and then comparing them with image data on the server. This system uses the following algorithms to perform image recognition.

Feature point extraction uses AKAZE to detect feature points that are invariant to scale and rotation. Feature point matching integrates kNN and BFMatcher to improve matching accuracy by combining techniques such as cross-checking and ratio testing.

5.4   Text Mesh Pro

Text Mesh Pro is a tool that permits high-quality text rendering in Unity, offering greater flexibility and visibility than the conventional Text component. The proposed system mainly uses Text Mesh Pro for the superimposed display of text information on AR screens.

Text Mesh Pro enables the clear rendering of detailed fonts and allows advanced customization of text styles and layouts. In addition, Text Mesh Pro provides features such as dynamic text generation and adjustment of color, size, and spacing. Therefore, Text Mesh Pro is useful for AR applications that require high visibility.

5.5   FastAPI

FastAPI [18] is a lightweight, high-performance web framework developed in Python that is particularly well suited for design and implementation of APIs. In this paper, we adopt FastAPI to construct a backend API using Python code within the Unity environment. In addition, FastAPI is highly compatible with Python's major libraries, so it can be easily integrated with OpenCV, the image recognition library used in this paper.

5.6   Implementation

The computing environment of the proposed system is shown in Table 1. The proposed system first registers images to be recognized in both FastAPI and Unity. Image data are stored only in FastAPI, not in Unity. Image data registered

Table 1. Computing environment

Computer	OS	macOS Sonoma Version 14.4.1
	IDE	Unity 2022.3.10f1
		Visual Studio Code Version 1.80.1
		Xcode Version 15.4
	Package	AR Foundation Version 5.0.7
		Text Mesh Pro Version 3.0.6
Mobile Device	Xiaomi Pad 6S Pro	Xiaomi Hyper OS 2.0.7.0

on the API server are managed via the API and used for feature point extraction and image recognition processing. In Unity, prefabs containing text data for each image are created in advance to display the corresponding text data. These prefabs are registered in XR Origin, which is a camera-based object used by AR Foundation.

Function for Acquiring Registered Data. The function used for acquiring registered information sends images saved at regular intervals to the API server while displaying camera images using AR Foundation. In this process of saving images, screenshots of the camera images are captured at regular intervals. The API server performs feature point extraction in advance using OpenCV for images on the server at startup, and then it stores these feature values. Next, feature point extraction and feature point matching are performed using the image data sent from Unity and the reference images stored on the API server. When feature points appearing in the transmitted image are the same as those in the reference image, the API server executes clustering based on the feature point data contained in the image to be matched. The valid coordinate data obtained from the clustering results are stored in a JSON file format with the center coordinates and name of the matching image. This JSON file is finally sent to Unity by FastAPI and used in the display processing of the AR content.

Based on the data in the JSON file, the mobile device searches for registered images. When a matching image is found, the mobile device displays the content in the AR space by inserting the corresponding prefab based on the position data. As shown in Fig. 6, a user interface that means "Learn more" is displayed at the bottom of the recognized image. This user interface is dismissed when the user taps the image. As shown in Fig. 7, registered prefabs are displayed along with detailed text data.

Fig. 6. Image recognition: Initial display

Fig. 7. Image recognition: When tapping target image

6   Evaluation

6.1   Evaluation Environment

We calculated four durations of execution time: the communication time (T_1) from sending images (from Unity to FastAPI) to receiving the JSON file (from FastAPI), the displaying time (T_2) of prefabs based on recognition results, the total processing time (T_3) for a single image recognition, and the processing time (T_4) for image recognition on Python.

We also set three evaluation items: 1) execution time according to the number of images displayed simultaneously, 2) execution time according to the number of registered images, and 3) response capability for angles and obstructions. In item 1, we measured the execution time when the number of images displayed on the screen is between 1 and 10. In item 2, we measured the execution time when the number of registered images to be matched with feature points on FastAPI is increased by 10 from 10 to 100. In item 3, as shown in Fig. 8, the angle between the normal line drawn from the center of the monitor displaying the image and the camera mounted on the mobile device held by the subject is defined as α $(0° \leq \alpha < 90°)$. The subject uses the mobile device to recognize images on the monitor as the angle α changes in increments of $15°$, and then the average number of images recognized out of the four images displayed on the monitor is calculated from all α angles. Regarding the ability to handle occlusions, as shown in Fig. 9, the range of the left side of the image that is obscured is increased in 10% increments from 10% to 100%, and the recognition success rate is verified according to the degree of image occlusion.

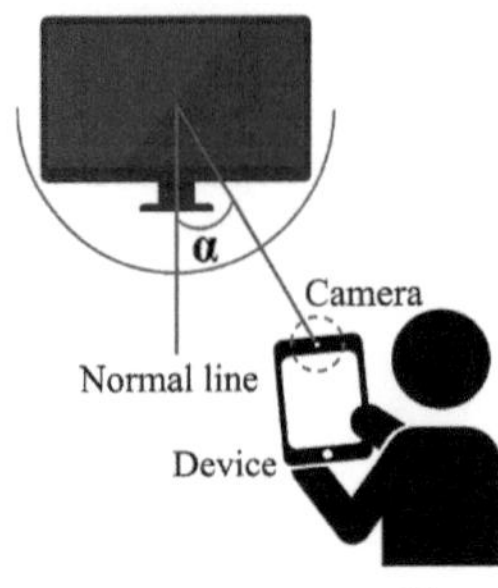

Fig. 8.   Measurement method for changes in angle

Fig. 9.   Measurement method for changes in occlusion rate

6.2   Execution Time According to Number of Displayed Images

We show the changes in execution time according to the number of images displayed simultaneously in Table 2 and Figs. 10, 11, 12, and 13. The horizontal axis of these figures represents the number of photos, while the vertical axis represents the execution time. The results in the table and figures confirm that T_1 and T_3 increased as the number of images displayed simultaneously increased. This occurred because the number of matching results described in the JSON file increased.

Table 2. Execution time for number of simultaneously displayed images

Num. of displays	T_1 (msec.)	T_2 (msec.)	T_3 (msec.)	T_4 (msec.)
1	1,070.916	0.091	1,355.445	0.413
2	1073.806	0.156	1360.296	0.434
3	1075.308	0.116	1360.289	0.434
4	1075.018	0.141	1361.167	0.443
5	1075.751	0.121	1356.807	0.433
6	1082.465	0.164	1357.451	0.413
7	1086.428	0.046	1357.672	0.434
8	1088.757	0.039	1357.635	0.453
9	1092.248	0.220	1360.754	0.432
10	1093.405	0.155	1361.554	0.457

Table 3. Execution time for number of registered images

Num. of	T_1 (msec.)	T_2 (msec.)	T_3 (msec.)	T_4 (msec.)
10	1,076.018	0.141	1,361.167	0.443
20	1,154.574	0.131	1,421.414	0.485
30	1,372.173	0.223	1,632.490	0.596
40	1,750.641	0.125	2,028.803	0.612
50	2,215,494	0.156	2,490.904	0.981
60	2,527.481	0.130	2,815.470	1.151
70	2,954.235	0.135	3,232.244	1.374
80	3,279.268	0.142	3,557.901	1.384
90	3,774.894	0.163	4,048.278	1.720
100	4,341.035	0.130	4,638.360	1.925

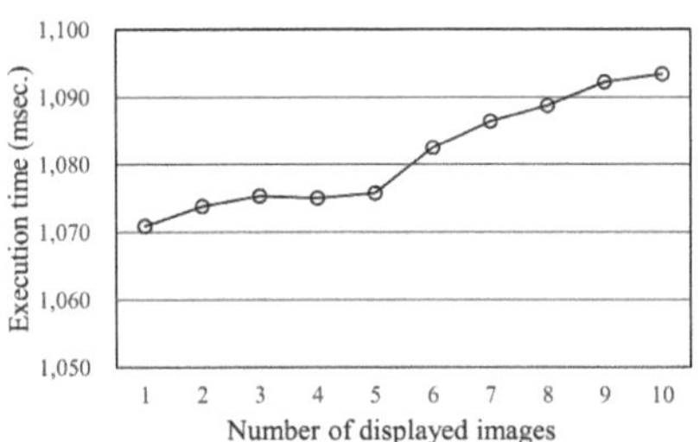

Fig. 10. Execution time according to number of displayed images (T_1)

Fig. 11. Execution time according to number of displayed images (T_2)

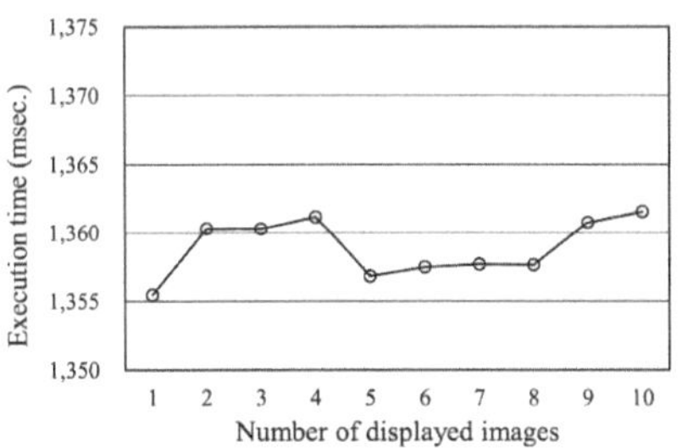

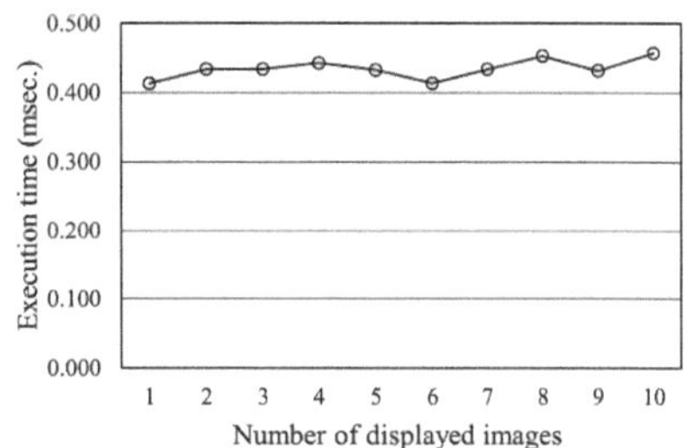

Fig. 12. Execution time according to number of displayed images (T_3)

Fig. 13. Execution time according to number of displayed images (T_4)

6.3 Execution Time According to Number of Registered Images

We show the changes in execution time according to the number of registered images in Table 3, Fig. 14, Fig. 15, Fig. 16, and Fig. 17. The table and figures show that increasing the number of registered images also increases the amount of matching processing. Therefore, the execution times of T_1, T_3, and T_4 increased proportionally. In addition, the percentage of increase in T_1 and T_3 is larger than that in T_4. In the proposed system, the execution time increases because the overall system load increases, and the processing speed decreases due to the continuous transmission of images. The execution time for T_2 was not affected by either the number of videos displayed simultaneously or the number of registered images. Therefore, the results confirm that the display time on Unity does not depend on the number of photos.

6.4 Recognition Rate According to Angle and Obstructions

In the proposed system, we evaluated the recognition rate according to angle and obstructions. First, in the evaluation of recognition rate according to angle, as shown in Fig. 8, we rotated a mobile device (angle α) while simultaneously displaying four images on an external monitor's screen, and the average number of images recognized using the mobile device's camera was calculated as angle α

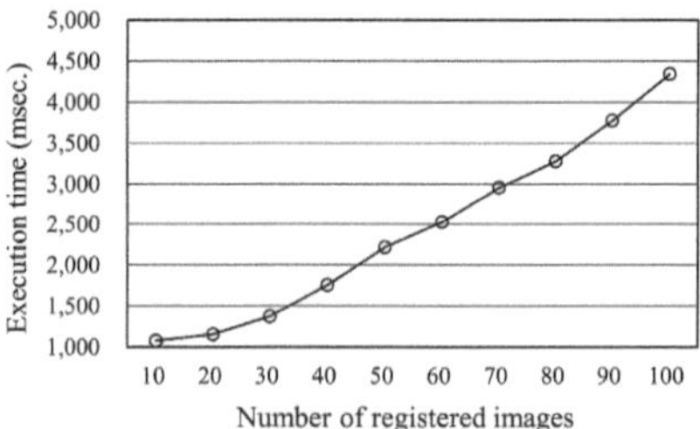

Fig. 14. Execution time according to number of registered images (T_1)

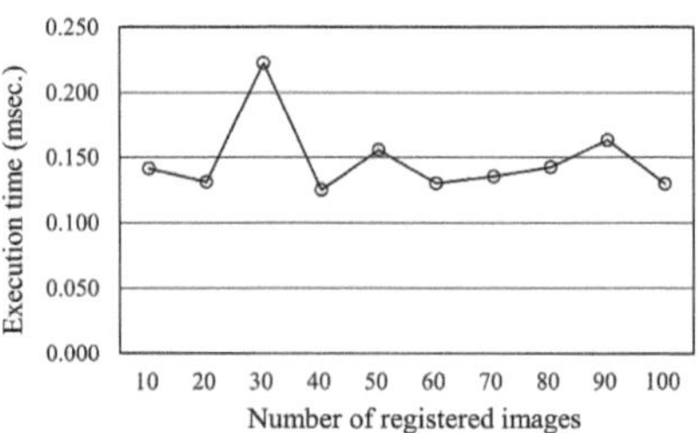

Fig. 15. Execution time according to number of registered images (T_2)

was changed in increments of 15°. The evaluation results show that the recognition rate was 100% for angles between 0° and 30°. On the other hand, the recognition rate was 80% at an angle of 45° and 50% at an angle of 60°, while none of the images were recognized at angles of 75° or greater. Therefore, we found that the proposed system could ensure sufficient recognition rates when the angle of the mobile device was ±30°.

Next, as shown in Fig. 9, we evaluated the recognition rate according to the degree of occlusion by increasing the occlusion rate from the left side of the image in increments of 10% of the entire image. The results show that the maximum occlusion rate of images that could be recognized by the device was 65% on average. In addition, we confirmed that images could be recognized if approximately 10% of the distinctive parts remained.

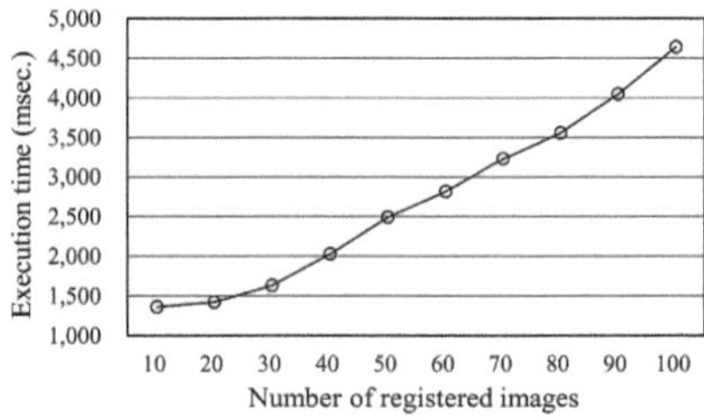

Fig. 16. Execution time according to number of registered images (T_3)

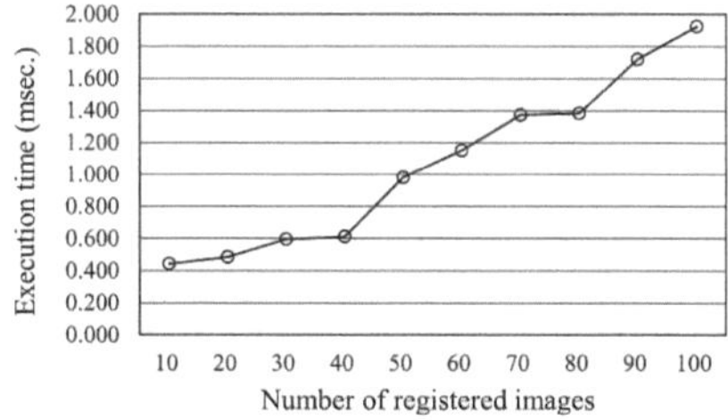

Fig. 17. Execution time according to number of registered images (T_4)

7   Conclusion

In this paper, we proposed an AR system that superimposes content on an AR space in synchronization with camera images. The proposed system matches images obtained from an Android device's camera in real-time with reference images registered in advance on a server built using FastAPI. The text data corresponding to the matched content is superimposed on the AR space. In addition, the proposed system efficiently manages hundreds of large image data on the API server and instantly displays relevant information on the device. Consequently, users can access image data intuitively and smoothly.

In its design and implementation, the proposed system uses AR Foundation to manage spatial recognition and object positions, and it implements image recognition and feature point matching using OpenCV. Accordingly, it is possible to recognize specific objects from camera images and superimpose related text data onto the AR space.

The evaluation results show that the proposed system can provide intuitive information using only general-purpose Android devices without the need for dedicated markers or special hardware. In particular, the proposed system was designed with a focus on its performance of real-time image recognition, and it is expected to be useful in various fields such as education and tourism.

Future challenges include optimizing algorithms to improve processing speed, streamlining image management methods, and improving the usability of display functions. In addition, we will consider user feedback to find ways of expanding the system's functionality and thus improving its usability. In our evaluation, we will demonstrate the usefulness of the proposed system by comparing it with conventional AR recognition systems. Furthermore, we need to evaluate the proposed system in actual environments where 2D and 3D objects are placed, such as art museums.

Acknowledgment. This work was supported by JSPS KAKENHI Grant Number 23K24843.

References

1. Zainal, N.H.M., Ramli, R., Omar, N., Mahmud, M., Salim, N.H.A.: Augmented reality (AR) and virtual reality (VR) applications during covid-19 pandemic among preclinical medical and dentistry students: a mini-review. Malays. J. Med. Health Sci. **18**(s14), 131–143 (2022)
2. Bazargani, J.S., Zafari, M., Sadeghi-Niaraki, A., Choi, S.-M.: A survey of GIS and AR integration: applications, sustainability. Sustainability **14**(16), 10134 (2022)
3. Amirian, P., Basiri, A.: Landmark-based pedestrian navigation using augmented reality and machine learning. In: Gartner, G., Jobst, M., Huang, H. (eds.) Progress in Cartography. LNGC, pp. 451–465. Springer, Cham (2016). https://doi.org/10.1007/978-3-319-19602-2_27
4. About AR Foundation: Unity (online). https://docs.unity3d.com/Packages/com.unity.xr.arfoundation@5.0/manual/. Accessed 24 Sept 2025
5. OpenCV: OpenCV team (online). https://opencv.org/. Accessed 24 Sept 2025
6. Pokémon GO: Niantic, Inc. (online). https://pokemongo.com/. Accessed 24 Sept 2025
7. Lowe, D.: Distinctive image features from scale-invariant keypoints. Int. J. Comput. Vision **60**(2), 91–110 (2004)
8. Rublee, E., Rabaud, V., Konolige, K., Bradski, G.R.: ORB: an efficient alternative to SIFT or SURF. In: Proceedings of IEEE International Conference on Computer Vision (ICCV 2011), pp. 2564–2571 (2011)
9. Alcantarilla, P.F., Bartoli, A., Davison, A.J.: KAZE features. In: Fitzgibbon, A., Lazebnik, S., Perona, P., Sato, Y., Schmid, C. (eds.) ECCV 2012. LNCS, vol. 7577, pp. 214–227. Springer, Heidelberg (2012). https://doi.org/10.1007/978-3-642-33783-3_16
10. Alcantarilla, P.F., Nuevo, J., Bartoli, A.: Fast explicit diffusion for accelerated features in nonlinear scale spaces. In: Proceedings of British Machine Vision Conference (BMVC 2013), pp. 13.1–13.11 (2013)
11. ARkit: Apple (online). https://developer.apple.com/augmented-reality/arkit/. Accessed 24 Sept 2025
12. ARCore: Google (online). https://developers.google.com/ar/. Accessed 24 Sept 2025
13. Shrikumar, A., Greenside, P., Kundaje, A.: Learning important features through propagating activation differences. In: Proceedings of 34th International Conference on Machine Learning (PMLR 2017), vol. 70, pp. 3145–3153 (2017)
14. Smilkov, D., Thorat, N., Kim, B., Viégas, F.B., Wattenberg, M.: SmoothGrad: removing noise by adding noise (online). https://doi.org/10.48550/arXiv.1706.03825. Accessed 24 Sept 2025
15. Ando, S., Yamamoto, S., Tanaka, H., Tsutsuguchi, K., Katayama, A., Taniguchi, Y.: Visual SyncAR: video synchronized AR based on mobile video watermark. IIEEJ Trans. Image Electron. Vis. Comput. **4**(2), 114–123 (2016)
16. Janina, R.-N., Kornelia, K., Gniewko, N., Magdalena, P.: Application of augmented reality in dairy cattle monitoring, journal of research and applications in agricultural. Engineering **63**, 181–183 (2018)
17. Okada, K., Saitoh, F.: High-speed image matching using partial template consisting of multiple rectangular areas extracted by genetic algorithm. Electron. Commun. Japan **94**(10), 1–9 (2011)
18. FastAPI: FastAPI features (online). https://fastapi.tiangolo.com/features/. Accessed 24 Sept 2025

Grounded in the Fields: Participatory Foundations for Human-Centered Agricultural Software in Central Borneo

Devi Karolita[1]([✉])[iD], Ariesta Lestari[1][iD], Misita Anwar[2,3][iD], Betrixia Barbara[4][iD], Fengky F. Adji[4][iD], Ferry Saputra[1], and Rafael Aryapati Soebagijo[1]

[1] Informatics Engineering Department, Palangka Raya University, Palangkaraya, Indonesia
{devikarolita,ariesta}@it.upr.ac.id,
{ferrysaputra999,rafael.aryapati224}@mhs.eng.upr.ac.id
[2] Swinburne University of Technology, Melbourne, Australia
misitaanwar@swin.edu.au
[3] Makassar State University, Makassar, Indonesia
[4] Faculty of Agriculture, Palangka Raya University, Palangkaraya, Indonesia
betrixia_barbara@agb.upr.ac.id, fengky@agr.upr.ac.id

Abstract. This paper presents human-centered design recommendations for agricultural software grounded in the practices of smallholder farmers in Central Borneo. Using a mixed-methods approach, which are survey (n = 286), interviews (n = 20), and co-design sessions (n = 20). From this study, we identified patterns of device use, connectivity, and information behavior, alongside themes of digital access, trust, and peer validation. Co-design activities further contextualized these findings, producing functional and non-functional requirements for agricultural applications. The resulting recommendations emphasize mobile-first, low-complexity interfaces, offline and data-efficient features, peer-driven knowledge exchange, localized content, and mechanisms for building trust. While exploratory and limited to one region, the study demonstrates how participatory methods can address socio-technical constraints and generate actionable requirements. It contributes to human-centered computing by showing how inclusive design processes inform the development of trustworthy and context-aware agricultural platforms for low-resource environments.

Keywords: digital agriculture · participatory design · human-centered · ICT4D

1 Introduction

Digital technologies are increasingly promoted as enablers of agricultural transformation, offering tools across the farming process from planning to post-harvest marketing [10,20]. However, adoption in rural areas remains uneven due to geographic disparities in infrastructure (e.g., unreliable internet, limited electricity) [16] and human factors such as low digital literacy and lack of culturally relevant tools [14]. These challenges often exclude smallholder farmers from fully benefiting, and many existing systems follow a one-size-fits-all design with limited user input, raising concerns about usability, trust, and long-term adoption [17].

Therefore, this paper aims to develop human-centered design recommendations for agricultural applications for farmers in Central Borneo by accounting for technical constraints (device limitations, network reliability) and local social practices, trust dynamics, and information-sharing norms. Using a mixed-methods approach, we capture broad usage patterns and in-depth insights into farmers' everyday experiences with digital tools. This study is guided by **three research questions (RQs)**: (RQ1) What are the current patterns of access and interaction with digital technologies among smallholder farmers in Central Borneo?; (RQ2) How do farmers seek, evaluate, and share agricultural information in their daily practices?; and (RQ3) What design recommendations can support trustworthy and locally relevant agricultural software in low-resource farming contexts? The main **contributions** of this study are: (1) an empirical profile of farmers' digital access and agricultural information behaviors in Central Borneo; (2) insights into the socio-technical and trust-based factors shaping technology adoption; and (3) actionable, human-centered design recommendations for locally relevant and trustworthy agricultural software. Together, these contributions provide concrete design requirements for agricultural software development while also advancing human-centered computing knowledge through participatory methods.

2 Related Work

In many low- and middle-income countries (LMICs), digital agriculture is promoted as a pathway for transformation, yet adoption remains uneven. Barriers such as poor infrastructure, low digital literacy, affordability issues, and social inequalities, particularly for women and older farmers which limit the effectiveness of these tools [8,9]. These patterns highlight the need for inclusive, context-sensitive interventions that go beyond technology provision to address local capacities and constraints.

The field of Information and Communication Technology for Agriculture (ICT4AG) illustrates this tension. Digital farming tools such as IoT devices, mobile apps, and data-driven services can enhance knowledge sharing, market access, and collaboration [14]. However, their success is frequently undermined by limited skills, weak infrastructure, and institutional gaps, underscoring the importance of training, connectivity, and supportive organisations for sustainable adoption.

Beyond technical challenges, social dynamics and trust strongly influence adoption. Farmers increasingly use online platforms such as WhatsApp and Facebook alongside traditional channels [6,13], but they continue to rely heavily on trusted peers and agricultural advisors, often valuing their input above that of technology providers [3,11]. This interplay between digital networks and interpersonal exchanges demonstrates the trust-based nature of rural information practices, where peer validation is key.

In Indonesia, these global trends manifest with added local challenges. Many rural areas face infrastructure deficits and uneven ICT skills, leaving communities underserved by government programs [17]. Farmers' skepticism toward digital information further limits uptake. To address these issues, Purnomo and Kusnandar [12] highlight the need for farmer and extension officer training, stronger institutional support, and improved rural connectivity. Similarly, research on rural digitalisation emphasizes that sustainable progress requires building on local knowledge, social capital, and adequate infrastructure [4,5].

3   Methodology

To achieve the aims of this study, we used a mixed-methods approach informed by Design Thinking principles, consisting of a survey, semi-structured interviews, and co-design sessions in Central Borneo, which are Bukit Batu and Sabangau. All participants provided verbal consent to participate in the study.

We surveyed 286 farmers[1] (155 from Bukit Batu and 131 from Sabangau) to capture farmers' technology usage and information seeking behaviours. Thirty-nine survey questions[2] are grouped into demographics (Q1-Q14), technological device usage (Q15-Q19, Q21), internet usage (Q20, Q22-Q25), general information seeking (Q26-Q28), and agricultural-related information seeking (Q29-Q39). We conducted a pilot survey was conducted with Agricultural Extension Officers (**AEOs**) at the respective Agricultural Extension Centers (*Balai Penyuluhan Pertanian*, **BPP**). Subsequently, we printed questionnaires and distributed them via farmer group leaders and then returned to each BPP. Responses were entered into Google Forms for ease of analysis.

To triangulate the survey data and provide deeper contextual insights, we conducted greyconsemi-structured interviews with 20 farmers[3], including both survey participants and non-participants. The interviews lasted approximately 30 min each and followed a guide[4].

Subsequently, two co-design workshops[5] (10 farmers each[6]) were held to collaboratively envision solution ideas, using activities like group discussions, reviewing existing apps, and sketching ideal features. These workshops were informed by social practice theory [18] to understand farmers' social routines, shared experiences, and cultural meanings within their agricultural activities.

---

[1] https://doi.org/10.5281/zenodo.15914079.
[2] https://doi.org/10.5281/zenodo.15486186.
[3] https://doi.org/10.5281/zenodo.15486176.
[4] https://doi.org/10.5281/zenodo.15486181.
[5] https://doi.org/10.5281/zenodo.15913763.
[0] https://doi.org/10.5281/zenodo.15913567.

For the data analysis, we performed *descriptive statistical analysis* towards survey responses and interview transcripts underwent inductive *thematic analysis* (following Braun and Clarke's six-phase framework [1]) yielding six emergent themes. Co-design outputs were qualitatively synthesized to extract user requirements and validate the other findings, following Sanders and Stappers' framework for co-creation [15].

4   Results and Discussions

4.1   Digital Technology Use (RQ1) and Information Practices (RQ2)

Farmers in Palangka Raya overwhelmingly rely on mobile phones—primarily basic Android smartphones—as their main digital tool for agriculture, while computer use remains very limited [7]. Nearly all respondents owned a personal mobile phone, with shared use being rare. Connectivity constraints also shape digital engagement: the majority depend on mobile data (with few having Wi-Fi access), and about half report poor signal coverage, while many others cite mobile data cost as a barrier. As a result, farmers tend to use their phones mostly for essential communication (voice calls, SMS) and social media apps like WhatsApp and Facebook [3,13], with relatively little use of more data-intensive or specialized applications.

When seeking agricultural information, farmers blend online and offline sources. Many turn to digital channels such as YouTube tutorials, Google searches, and Facebook or WhatsApp groups for quick advice or ideas. However, they seldom trust online information unless it has been validated through their personal networks. Consistent with other rural farming communities [2,11], respondents expressed greater confidence in advice from known peers, local Agricultural Extension Officers (AEOs), or seeing techniques proven by neighbors' successes, rather than anonymous internet content. Indeed, WhatsApp group chats have become a popular forum for exchanging tips and firsthand experiences—if one farmer tries a new pest control method or crop variety and it works, they share that outcome in the group, providing a form of community-based verification.

In summary, while smartphones and social media are now common tools for accessing agricultural information, farmers still place more trust in interpersonal communication and local experience. This dual reliance suggests that any successful e-agriculture solution must integrate digital information delivery with mechanisms that leverage community trust and peer validation [19].

4.2   Design Implications for ICT4AG (RQ3)

In addition to survey and interview findings in 4.1, the design recommendations were validated and refined through two co-design sessions (one in each subdistrict) with 10 farmers per session. These sessions involved group discussions, a gallery walk reviewing existing agricultural apps, and a sketching activity using mobile phone templates, which together yielded concrete insights into farmer needs. Farmers expressed strong preferences for short, practical video tutorials tailored to local soil, weather, and crop conditions, and frequently requested features such as real-time market price panels, fertiliser calculators, and peer discussion forums. Participants favored smaller, trusted groups for sharing information and were skeptical of passive features like suggestion boxes, instead preferring feedback mechanisms with visible outcomes. They also emphasized the importance of offline access, support for local language and voice-based content, and compatibility with low-end smartphones. Concern about cost led them to call for free apps, ideally supported by agricultural agencies to ensure sustainability. These co-design sessions informed the derivation of both functional and non-functional requirements grounded in local farming practices.

Based on our findings, the software should be greyconmobile-first and lightweight, meaning it runs well on low-end Android phones with a small install size and built-in offline capability to handle intermittent connectivity. It should also feature greycona familiar low-complexity UI (for example, an interface similar to WhatsApp or Facebook) with intuitive navigation, clear icons, and simple workflows; audio/video guides in local languages can support farmers with basic literacy. In addition, ensuring offline access and low data usage is critical: the app should minimise bandwidth by enabling asynchronous content downloads and offline viewing, and models like data sponsorship or free access can keep usage affordable given poor signal coverage and high costs.

The software should further encourage a peer-driven community exchange by including in-app discussion groups (Q&A forums, storytelling threads, etc.) where farmers can consult trusted peers just as they do in person; enabling features like content upvoting supports social learning and information validation. It should also offer integrated local marketplace tools, such as local price listings, crop catalogs, and buyer–seller contact information, reflecting how farmers already use social media to trade. By providing real-time, location-specific pricing data (ideally verified by the community), the app can help farmers negotiate better deals and bypass intermediaries. greyconContent must be localised and visual: advice should be tailored to local crops and practices and presented as short videos or infographics in the local dialect, since farmers prefer concise visual tutorials over long text manuals. Finally, the platform should build trust through transparency by establishing clear feedback loops and accountability (e.g., involving local extension officers or moderators and visibly showing how farmer feedback leads to improvements) so that users see that their input is acted upon rather than lost in an anonymous suggestion box.

5   Conclusion and Future Work

This study investigated digital technology use and agricultural information practices among farmers in Central Borneo using surveys, interviews, and co-design sessions. The participatory approach revealed socio-technical factors (e.g., cultural norms, trust, and everyday practices) that shape technology adoption and informed design recommendations and requirements, refined through co-design.

While limited to one region and subject to potential sampling bias, triangulation across methods strengthens confidence in the findings. Future work will extend this process through additional co-design workshops with farmers and focus group discussions with stakeholders (e.g., agricultural departments, AEOs, and academics) to capture preferences, refine requirements, and align institutional roles. Insights from these activities will inform the development of a prototype application, which will be field-tested to validate its effectiveness and provide feedback for further iteration. This work contributes both to practical system development and to HCI/ICT4D research by emphasizing trust, local context, and co-creation in rural technology design.

Acknowledgments. This study was funded by the Indonesia Ministry of Higher Education, Science, and Technology and the Indonesia Endowment Fund for Education (LPDP) through the Sustainable Development Research Funding (PRPB) program, Inclusivity scheme (contract number 069/E5/PG.02.00/PRPB.INKLUSIVITAS/2024).

Disclosure of Interests. The authors have no competing interests to declare that are relevant to the content of this article.

References

1. Braun, V., Clarke, V.: Using thematic analysis in psychology. Qual. Res. Psychol. **3**(2), 77–101 (2006). https://doi.org/10.1191/1478088706qp063oa
2. Chowdhury, A., Kabir, K.H., Asafo-Agyei, E.K., Abdulai, A.R.: Participatory and community-based approach in combating Agri-food misinformation: a scoping review. Advancements Agric. Dev. **5**(2), 81–104 (2024)
3. Dilleen, G., Claffey, E., Foley, A., Doolin, K.: Investigating knowledge dissemination and social media use in the farming network to build trust in smart farming technology adoption. J. Bus. Ind. Market. **38**(8), 1754–1765 (2023)
4. Fahmi, F., Arifianto, A.: Digitalization and social innovation in rural areas: a case study from indonesia. Rural Sociol. **87**, 339–369 (2021). https://doi.org/10.1111/ruso.12418
5. Fahmi, F.Z., Mendrofa, M.J.S.: Rural transformation and the development of information and communication technologies: evidence from Indonesia. Technol. Soc. **75**, 102349 (2023)
6. Kiraly, G., et al.: Information behaviour of farmers, foresters, and advisors in the context of digitalisation in the EU. Stud. Agric. Econ. (2023)
7. Ma, W., Qiu, H., Rahut, D.B.: Rural development in the digital age: does information and communication technology adoption contribute to credit access and income growth in rural china? Rev. Dev. Econ. **27**(3), 1421–1444 (2023). https://doi.org/10.1111/rode.12943
8. Mhlanga, D., Ndhlovu, E.: Digital technology adoption in the agriculture sector: Challenges and complexities in Africa. Human Behav. Emerg. Technol. **2023**(1), 6951879 (2023)
9. Montesclaros, J.M.L., Teng, P.S.: Digital technology adoption and potential in southeast Asian agriculture. Asian J. Agric. Dev. **20**(2), 7–30 (2023)
10. Morchid, A., El Alami, R., Raezah, A.A., Sabbar, Y.: Applications of Internet of Things (IoT) and sensors technology to increase food security and agricultural sustainability: benefits and challenges. Ain Shams Eng. J. **15**(3), 102509 (2024)

11. Paulus, M., Herrera, B., Knierim, A.: Who do German farmers trust when making decisions about digital technologies? An analysis of the trustworthiness of innovation actors. Stud. Agric. Econ. **126**(3) (2024)
12. Purnomo, S.H., Kusnandar.: Barriers to acceptance of information and communication technology in agricultural extension in indonesia. Inf. Dev. **35**(4), 512–523 (2019)
13. Rust, N.A., et al.: Have farmers had enough of experts? Environ. Manag. 1–14 (2022)
14. Saidu, A., et al.: Application of ICT in agriculture: opportunities and challenges in developing countries. Int. J. Comput. Sci. Math. Theory **3**(1), 8–18 (2017)
15. Sanders, E.B.N., Stappers, P.J.: Co-creation and the new landscapes of design. CoDesign **4**(1), 5–18 (2008). https://doi.org/10.1080/15710880701875068
16. Santoso, A.B., et al.: Assessing the challenges and opportunities of agricultural information systems to enhance farmers' capacity and target rice production in Indonesia. Sustainability **15**(2), 1114 (2023)
17. Seminar, A., Sarwoprasodjo, S.: ICTS for small scale farmers in Indonesia: how to make it possible? In: IOP Conference Series: Earth and Environmental Science. vol. 335, p. 012028. IOP Publishing (2019)
18. Shove, E.: The dynamics of social practice: everyday life and how it changes. SAGE, Los Angeles, Philippines (2012)
19. Sullivan, C.S., Gemtou, M., Anastasiou, E., Fountas, S.: Building trust: a systematic review of the drivers and barriers of agricultural data sharing. Smart Agricultural Technology, p. 100477 (2024)
20. Wei, C.: Agroecology, information and communications technology, and smallholders' food security in Sub-Saharan Africa. J. Asian Afr. Stud. **55**(8), 1194–1208 (2020)

Human-in-the-Loop Generative AI for Explainable Insurance Decision Support

Arianna Anniciello[ID], Simona Fioretto[ID], Elio Masciari[ID],
and Enea Vincenzo Napolitano[(✉)][ID]

DIETI, University of Naples Federico II, Naples, Italy
`eneavincenzo.napolitano@unina.it`

Abstract. The use of Artificial Intelligence (AI) in the insurance industry covers a wide spectrum, including risk analysis, fraud detection, personalized policies, and customer support through chatbots. However, there is still room for improvement, as many techniques still rely heavily on manual processes. In this paper, we discuss both current solutions and a new system aimed at improving decision-making in the insurance field. We introduce a modular decision support system that weaves a Large Language Model (LLM) into crucial stages of the insurance decision-making process. Unlike fully automated systems, our approach embraces a Human-in-the-Loop (HITL) model, prioritizing transparency, user control, and explainability. This prototype allows insurance professionals to interact with data and AI tools using natural language, making it easier to handle tasks like portfolio analysis, customer segmentation, drafting personalized proposals, and querying structured data, without need for technical know-how.

Keywords: Generative AI · Human-in-the-Loop · Insurance

1 Introduction

The insurance sector requires fast, data-driven decisions in a regulated and risk-averse environment. Despite access to large volumes of structured and unstructured data, adoption of AI remains limited compared to other industries, with decision-making still relying heavily on manual procedures and rule-based systems. Concerns over opacity, compliance, and usability have slowed the integration of advanced methods such as Deep Learning and generative AI. Recent advances in large language models (LLMs) offer new opportunities, enabling natural language interfaces for portfolio analysis, client segmentation, policy drafting, and querying structured data. However, their adoption requires careful strategies to ensure trust, explainability, and human oversight, especially given the legal and financial implications of insurance decisions. To address these challenges, we propose a Human-in-the-Loop (HITL) decision support prototype that integrates a generative LLM into a modular web application. The system

P. Delir Haghighi et al. (Eds.): MoMM 2025, LNCS 16329, pp. 182–188, 2026.
https://doi.org/10.1007/978-3-032-11768-7_15

supports core insurance tasks while prioritizing transparency, user agency, and responsible interaction between human expertise and AI assistance. This work contributes by (i) demonstrating a feasible path for applying LLMs in real-world insurance workflows, and (ii) providing a replicable model for responsible AI adoption in regulated domains.

2   Related Work

Human-in-the-Loop (HITL) approaches represent collaborative methods, weaving human contribution and specialist knowledge into the entire operational timeline of ML and AI systems. These HITL techniques are designed to refine the precision, dependability, and flexibility of ML systems, capitalizing on the distinct strengths possessed by both human agents and automated tools [12]. The utility of HITL has been widely investigated, specifically to advance both model accuracy and the ethical dimensions within ML practices.

Mosqueira-Rey et al. [6] provide a comprehensive review, categorizing HITL techniques into active learning, interactive machine learning, and machine teaching, emphasizing their relevance in domains requiring high reliability, such as insurance. Vicente and Matute [11] demonstrate that presenting AI suggestions after human judgment reduces automation bias and improves decision accuracy, highlighting the importance of designing HITL systems that support, rather than override, human expertise. Zanzotto [14] advocates for a fairer AI paradigm, proposing that HITL systems should recognize and compensate human knowledge contributors, aligning with ethical considerations in AI deployment within industries like insurance. Monarch [5] discusses practical strategies for integrating human feedback into machine learning workflows, emphasizing the importance of human oversight in high-stakes domains.

The heavy dependence of insurers on openness and adherence to regulations highlights the crucial need for Explainable AI (XAI) within the sector. This is also highlighted by a number of studies focusing on it. In fact, Owens et al. [8] conducted a systematic review of XAI applications in insurance, identifying that methods such as knowledge distillation and rule extraction are prevalent in underwriting and claims management. Krùpovà et al. [3] introduced an Explainable Boosting Machine for predicting claim severity and frequency in car insurance, combining high predictive performance with interpretability. Saarela and Podgorelec [9] conducted a systematic literature review, highlighting recent applications of XAI in various domains, including insurance, and emphasizing the importance of transparent models for stakeholder trust.

Among the applications of AI in insurance domain, recent advancements focused on enhancing underwriting processes through AI. Gummadi [1] presents a framework that integrates various XAI techniques to provide personalized insurance policy recommendations. Orji and Ukwandu [7] explore the use of ensemble machine learning models for predicting medical insurance costs, employing XAI methods to elucidate the influence of different factors on premium pricing. Kuo and Lupton [4] propose a framework for explaining machine learning models in insurance pricing, addressing the challenges posed by black-box models.

3   System Overview

This project introduces a web-based, modular prototype developed to investigate how generative AI can assist insurance professionals in data-heavy decision-making. The system adheres to the HITL approach, prioritizing transparency, user agency, and clear explanations throughout its operation.

3.1   System Architecture

The architectural design of the prototype is structured around three principal components: the user interface layer, the data management layer, and the AI service layer. These components are designed to function autonomously from a logical point of view, allowing independent development, testing, and maintenance, and providing a foundation for future extensibility.

The user interface is developed using Streamlit, a Python framework that enables the creation of interactive and responsive web applications with minimal overhead [2]. The interface is structured into multiple functional tabs, each corresponding to a distinct operation within the insurance decision-making process. This layout mirrors the typical analytical workflow followed by insurance professionals, from exploratory data analysis to the formulation of customized proposals.

The back-end of the system is managed using MongoDB Atlas, a cloud-based, document-oriented database that offers the flexibility needed to store heterogeneous insurance data. Unlike relational databases, which require predefined schemas, MongoDB allows for dynamic and nested data structures [13], making it well suited to represent insurance policies that vary across clients and products. Through the use of the `pymongo` library, the application is able to interact with the database efficiently, executing read and write operations, validating queries, and managing exceptions.

The AI component is powered by Gemini 1.5 Flash [10], a proprietary generative LLM offered via Google Generative AI APIs. This model is utilized in two contexts: first, to generate natural language drafts of insurance proposals based on user-defined parameters, and second, to respond to user queries formulated in free-text form. Before submission, structured data such as client profiles and asset information are serialized into a textual format suitable for prompt construction. This pre-processing step includes the conversion of MongoDB-specific data types, such as `ObjectId` and timestamps, into plain text to ensure compatibility with the LLM. The responses generated by the model are post-processed to improve readability and are presented to the user alongside the original input context, supporting traceability and validation.

3.2   Functional Modules

The system is organized into four main functional modules, each corresponding to a specific class of tasks within the insurance decision pipeline. These modules are not merely technical interfaces, but operationally meaningful components that map onto real-world activities carried out by insurance professionals.

The *Portfolio Overview* module offers users a synthetic and interactive view of the insurance portfolio.

The second module, *Customer Segmentation*, applies unsupervised learning techniques to classify policyholders into distinct groups based on economic indicators, such as premium amounts or insured asset values.

The third module, *Proposal Generator*, enables the semi-automated creation of personalized insurance proposals.

The final module, *Natural Language Query*, is designed to lower the barrier to data access by allowing users to interrogate the dataset using free-form questions.

An overview of the four functional modules is summarized in Table 1.

Table 1. Overview of implemented modules

Module	Input	Output	Technologies
Portfolio Overview	None (reads full dataset)	Aggregate statistics, contract status, payment method distributions	`pandas`, `matplotlib`
Customer Segmentation	Economic variables (e.g. premiums)	3 customer clusters visualized via scatter plot	`scikit-learn` (`KMeans`), `StandardScaler`
Proposal Generator	Client name, asset type, coverage options, asset value	Natural-language insurance proposal, risk score, estimated premium	Google Gemini 1.5 Flash API
Natural Language Query	Free-text query from the user	Model-generated answer based on structured data subset	Google Gemini 1.5 Flash API, JSON serialization

3.3   Data Management and Interface Design

Effective data management ensures system reliability through error handling for disconnections, invalid queries, and timeouts. A document-oriented database supports heterogeneous records and future integration of external sources, such as actuarial tables or claim histories. Non-serializable objects are converted into plain text for compatibility with the LLM, ensuring semantic consistency. Model inputs and outputs are logged to enhance explainability and support retrospective analysis. The interface minimizes cognitive load with a tab-based workflow, clear instructions, and visual feedback. Users progress naturally from portfolio overview to proposal generation, with opportunities to refine inputs iteratively. Combining robust engineering and user-centered design, the system offers a modular and transparent decision-support prototype for responsible AI adoption in insurance.

4   Human-in-the-Loop Design

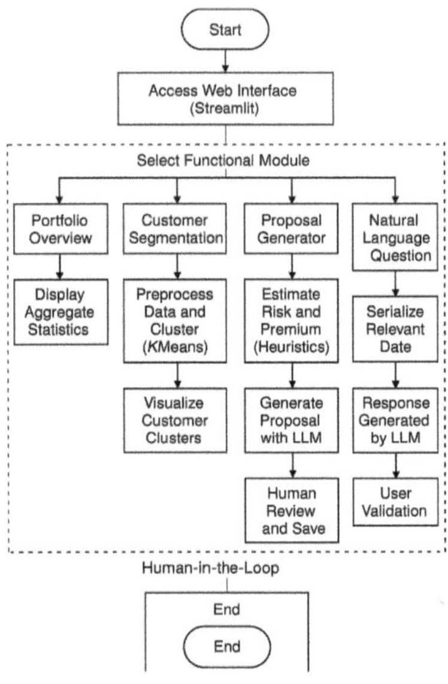

Fig. 1. Overview of the modular architecture and Human-in-the-Loop interaction flow.

The Human-in-the-Loop (HITL) paradigm is central to the philosophy and implementation of the system presented in this work. As illustrated in Fig. 1, each module is designed to preserve user control while leveraging generative AI support in a transparent and modular style. Unlike fully automated AI solutions, which may operate as opaque black boxes, a HITL approach ensures that human decision-makers remain integral to each stage of the interaction with artificial intelligence. This is particularly important in domains such as insurance, where decisions often carry financial, legal, and ethical implications. The system is thus designed to empower the user, not to replace them, by offering transparent, controllable AI functionality that supports, rather than substitutes, professional judgment.

Within each module, the design emphasizes traceability. In the segmentation tab, clustering results are visualized directly alongside the data used to generate them. In the proposal tab, the estimated risk score and premium are displayed with the proposal draft, anchoring the generated text in quantitative metrics. In the natural language query tab, the data context used to generate the answer is shown explicitly, allowing the user to verify the source of the information. These design choices ensure that the model's output is never presented in isolation, but always in relation to interpretable input features.

5 Conclusion and Future Work

In this paper, we presented a flexible and extensible prototype that integrates Large Language Models (LLMs) into the insurance decision-making process through a Human-in-the-Loop (HITL) approach. In a sector marked by regulatory scrutiny, risk sensitivity, and the need for accountability, our system demonstrates that generative AI can be responsibly deployed to support human expertise. The design emphasizes usability, transparency, and explainability, offering professionals intuitive interaction modes and tailored automation.

In conclusion, this work shows that integrating generative AI into regulated decision-making processes is not only feasible but can provide tangible value when centered around human control and transparency. The framework we propose offers a practical path for deploying LLMs in sensitive domains such as insurance, where responsible, user-centric AI can make a meaningful impact.

References

1. Gummadi, H.S.B.: Explainable AI-enhanced underwriting automation for personalized insurance policy recommendations. Eur. J. Comput. Sci. Inf. Technol. **13**(19), 24–40 (2025)
2. Khorasani, M., Abdou, M., Fernández, J.H.: Web application development with streamlit. Softw. Dev. 498–507 (2022)
3. Krùpovà, M., Rachdi, N., Guibert, Q.: Explainable boosting machine for predicting claim severity and frequency in car insurance. arXiv preprint arXiv:2503.21321 (2025)
4. Kuo, K., Lupton, D.: Towards explainability of machine learning models in insurance pricing. arXiv preprint arXiv:2003.10674 (2020)
5. Monarch, R.: Human-in-the-loop machine learning. Manning Publications (2021)
6. Mosqueira-Rey, E., Hernández-Pereira, E., Alonso-Ríos, D., Bobes-Bascarán, J., Fernández-Leal.: Human-in-the-loop machine learning: a state of the art. Artif. Intell. Rev. **56**, 3005–3054 (2023)
7. Orji, U., Ukwandu, E.: Machine learning for an explainable cost prediction of medical insurance. arXiv preprint arXiv:2311.14139 (2023)
8. Owens, E., et al.: Explainable artificial intelligence (XAI) in insurance. Risks **10**(12), 230 (2022)
9. Saarela, M., Podgorclec, V.: Recent applications of explainable AI (XAI): a systematic literature review. Appl. Sci. **14**(19), 8884 (2024)
10. Team, G., et al.: Gemini 1.5: Unlocking multimodal understanding across millions of tokens of context. arXiv preprint arXiv:2403.05530 (2024)
11. Vicente, S., Matute, H.: The impact of AI errors in a human-in-the-loop process. Cogn. Res. Principles Implications **8**(1), 1–15 (2023)

12. Wu, X., et al.: A survey of human-in-the-loop for machine learning. Futur. Gener. Comput. Syst. **135**, 364–381 (2022)
13. Yange, S., Gambo, I., Ikono, R., Onyekwere, O., Soriyan, H.: An implementation of a repository for healthcare insurance using MongoDB. J. Comput. Sci. Appl. **27**(1) (2020)
14. Zanzotto, F.M.: ViewPoint: human-in-the-loop artificial intelligence. J. Artif. Intell. Res. **64**, 243–252 (2019)

Lyric-Aware DJ Track Recommendation Based on Semantic Relationships

Wakana Kuwata[(✉)] and Hiroaki Ohshima

University of Hyogo, Hyogo, Japan
`af25x004@guh.u-hyogo.ac.jp, ohshima@ai.u-hyogo.ac.jp`

Abstract. In this paper, we propose a song recommendation method for DJs that focuses on song lyrics. A DJ plays and connects a variety of songs. There are two ways to connect songs in DJ: based on musical similarities and based on semantic similarities. DJs of J-POP and anime songs tend to use connecting methods based on semantic similarity. In this paper, we focus on the lyrics of songs to support DJs of J-POP and anime songs. The task is to recommend the next song for the currently selected song. To train our model, we create a dataset from actual set lists played at DJ events. We fine-tune the Japanese pre-trained BERT in two ways: a Bi-Encoding model and a Cross-Encoding model. We experiment with Japanese pre-trained BERT as a baseline. In MRR, the Cross-Encoding model showed superior scores. In user tests, the Bi-Encoding model showed superior scores.

Keywords: Song recommendation · Lyric recognition · DJ

1 Introduction

A disc jockey (DJ) plays and connects a variety of music in places such as clubs. As DJ culture spreads around the world, there is a style of DJ that has developed uniquely in Japan, which is DJs of J-POP and anime songs. In contrast to dance music, J-POP and anime songs are not typically composed for DJs.

There are two main ways for a DJ to connect songs. The first is (A) connection based on musical similarities. Two or more songs are mixed together using a mixer based on acoustic information such as tempo (BPM) and key. The second is (B) connection based on semantic similarity. Semantic similarities include lyrics, singers, and context (tie-up information, original author, production company, etc.). DJs of J-POP and anime songs tend to place emphasis on (B) semantic similarity. In this way of connection, it is more important to find connections between song titles or lyrics than to match the BPM.

Previous research in DJ has proposed methods for automating music selection and mixing [1–4,8]. Most of these are aimed at dance music, where audio information dominates. They do not target songs whose semantic similarity is important, such as DJs of J-POP and anime songs. Previous research on song recommendation has proposed many methods that utilize user preference data

P. Delir Haghighi et al. (Eds.): MoMM 2025, LNCS 16329, pp. 189–195, 2026.
https://doi.org/10.1007/978-3-032-11768-7_16

in addition to audio and text features [5–7]. However, DJs must choose tracks that excite the entire audience rather than individual listeners.

In this paper, we propose a method for recommending songs for DJs of J-POP and anime songs that focuses on lyrical similarity, one type of (B) semantic similarity. Our contributions can be summarized as follows:

1. We create a dataset that focuses on the connections between lyrics of songs played consecutively in DJ events.
2. We show that training a model using a dataset including lyrics connection is effective.
3. We analyze the differences in the trends of recommendation results using two learning methods, Bi-Encoding model and Cross-Encoding model.

2 Problem Definition and Dataset

In this paper, we address the task of song recommendation for DJs focusing on lyrics. Let a song collection denote as $X = \{x_1, x_2, \cdots, x_n\}$. As described later, we collected $n = 38{,}781$ songs. The currently selected song $x_{\mathrm{in}} \in X$ is input. Given an input song $x_{\mathrm{in}} \in X$, the objective is to recommend a next-song candidate $x_{\mathrm{out}} \in X \setminus \{x_{\mathrm{in}}\}$. We summarize the notations used in this paper as follows: X is the song collection, n is the number of songs, $x_i \in X$ is a song, x_{in} is the input song, x_{out} is the next song, f_{x_i} is the first lyric, and l_{x_i} is the last lyric.

We create a dataset from set lists played at DJ events of J-POP and anime song. From each set list, we extracted every pair of consecutively played tracks, labeling the preceding track as x_{in} and the following track as x_{out}. We create a DJ pair dataset by aggregating these pairs across all set lists. DJ setlist data were collected from set lists that DJs personally shared on social media. A set list consists of the selected songs and their playback order. We extracted the title and artist name of each song, and created 305 lists of songs that preserve the original order. Lyric data were obtained from Uta-Net[1], a popular lyrics search service. We obtained 38,781 unique songs from the view-count ranking page and the anime-song feature page. The resulting set of songs with available lyrics constitutes our song collection X. For $n = 38{,}781$ songs in X, we obtained first lyric f_i and last lyric l_i of each song $x_i \in X$ ($i = 1, 2, \cdots, 38781$).

We split the 305 DJ set lists into training, validation, and test subsets using an $8 : 1 : 1$ ratio. For each set list, each song is annotated with lyrics drawn from the 38,781 songs in the collection X. From each set list, we form a data pair x_{in} and x_{out} from every pair of consecutively played songs that have lyrics. We annotate the input song x_{in} with its last lyric l_{in}, and the next song x_{out} with its first lyric f_{out}. An example of the paired data is shown in Table 1. Since each pair corresponds to two tracks played consecutively in a DJ set, all samples constitute positive pairs.

---

[1] https://www.uta-net.com.

Table 1. DJ pair dataset created from the set list played at a DJ event. The input song x_{in} and its next song x_{out} are paired. Each song is annotated with lyrics.

Input song: x_{in}			Next song: x_{out}		
Title	Singer	Last lyric: l_{in}	Title	Singer	First lyric: f_{out}
Beyond the BLADE	風鳴翼 (水樹奈々)	剣は剣としか呼べぬのか? 違う、友は翼と呼ぶ ...我が名は「夢を羽擊く者」也	黄昏のスタアライト	南條愛乃	傷ついた想い出は 時に愛しい 幼い僕らは目を閉じた "真実が大事"だと 誰が決めたの? 遠く星が消える

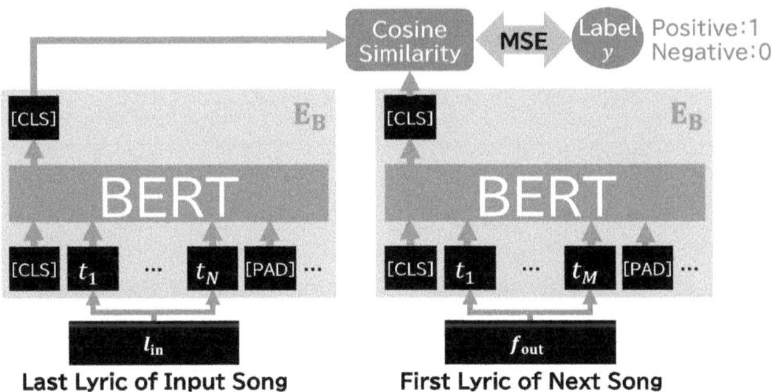

Fig. 1. The architecture of the Bi-Encoding model. A pair of texts is input to two BERTs with shared weights.

3 Lyric-Aware Song Recommendation for DJ

To output the ranking, we create a model that outputs a score indicating whether the two songs are played consecutively for the pair of input song x_{in} and the next candidate song x_{out}. The task to train this model is to classify whether the two songs were played consecutively or not for the pair of input song x_{in} and the next candidate song x_{out}. In this paper, we fine-tune the Japanese pre-trained BERT for this task. The trained model outputs the scores of all songs $\forall x_i \in X \setminus \{x_{in}\}$ for input song x_{in}. By sorting these songs in descending order of score, we output a ranking of candidates for the next song x_{out}.

To train a model to classify whether two songs are played consecutively, negative examples are also necessary. Therefore, we augment the negative pair data based on the positive pair data created in Sect. 2. We create a negative pair using the input song x_{in} and the next song x_{out} from the positive pair as input song. One song is randomly selected from 38,780 songs excluding the input song in song collection X and used as the next song. The positive pairs are oversampled by a factor of two to match the negative data. The training data and validation data are 7,188 and 680 items, respectively.

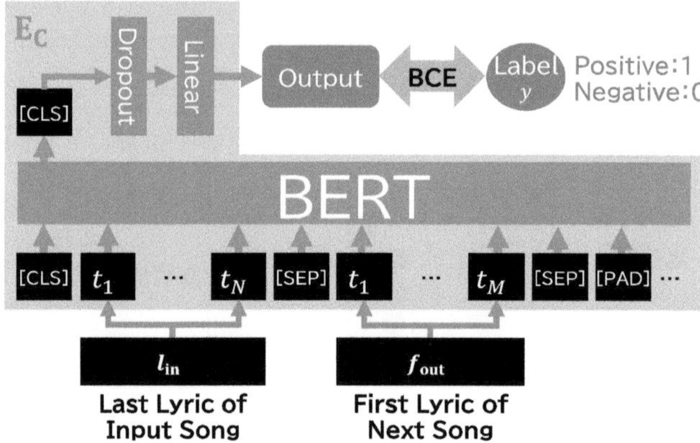

Fig. 2. The architecture of the Cross-Encoding model. A pair of texts are joined with [SEP] to form a single text. The joined text is then input BERT.

We fine-tune the Japanese pre-trained BERT on the DJ pair dataset. We use the Tohoku University model[2] as the Japanese pre-trained BERT. The models are trained using Bi-Encoding and Cross-Encoding, respectively.

The Bi-Encoding model is a learning method as shown in Fig. 1. A pair of texts is input to two BERTs E_B with shared weights. Cosine similarity is calculated between the [CLS] vectors output from each BERT. The model is trained so that the loss between this cosine similarity and the label y of the paired data becomes smaller. The mean square error (MSE) loss is used to calculate the loss. In song recommendation, the first lyric f_i of each song $\forall x_i \in X \setminus \{x_\text{in}\}$ is encoded separately. The last lyric l_in of song x_in is encoded. The cosine similarity is calculated using the score from the first lyric f_i of each song $\forall x_i \in X \setminus \{x_\text{in}\}$ and the last lyric l_in of the input song x_in. The cosine similarity is calculated as many times as $\forall x_i \in X \setminus \{x_\text{in}\}$. The ranking of songs in $X \setminus \{x_\text{in}\}$ is output in descending order of cosine similarity.

The Cross-Encoding model is a learning method as shown in Fig. 2. A pair of texts are joined with [SEP] to form a single text. The joined text is then input BERT. The [CLS] vector output from BERT passes through a dropout layer and a linear layer. The output from the linear layer is used to classify whether two songs are selected consecutively or not. Let the output from the linear layer denote $E_C(l_\text{in}, f_\text{out})$. Let y denote the label indicating whether the pair of songs were played consecutively. The binary cross-entropy loss is calculated using $E_C(l_\text{in}, f_\text{out})$ and y. In song recommendation, The last lyric l_in of song x_in is paired with the first lyric f_i of each songs $\forall x_i \in X \setminus \{x_\text{in}\}$. Pair of texts are joined with [SEP] to form a single text. The joined text is input BERT, which outputs a score. The score is calculated as many times as $\forall x_i \in X \setminus \{x_\text{in}\}$. The ranking of songs in $X \setminus \{x_\text{in}\}$ is output in descending order of score.

---

[2] https://huggingface.co/tohoku-nlp/bert-base-japanese-v3.

4   Experiment

Three methods are compared: Japanese pre-trained model (**Baseline** model), BERT fine-tuned on the DJ pair dataset (**Bi-Encoding** model), and BERT fine-tuned on the DJ pair dataset (**Cross-Encoding** model). As a baseline, we use the Japanese pre-trained BERT model from Tohoku University. The baseline outputs songs ranking in the same way as the Bi-Encoding model. In the experiments, the learning rate was 5e-7 for Bi-Encoding and 2e-7 for Cross-Encoding, with a constant scheduler. Training ran for up to 50 epochs with early stopping (patience = 3), stopping at epoch 24 for Bi-Encoding and 22 for Cross-Encoding. Of the 193 test data created in Sect. 2, data containing duplicates of the input song x_{in} are excluded. The test data results then in 188 unique items.

Table 2. Mean Reciprocal Rank (MRR) and User evaluation (Hit@1 and Weighted score) for the baseline, Bi-Encoder, and Cross-Encoder models.

model	MRR↑	Hit@1↑	Wighted Score↑
Baseline	0.000332	0.45	0.29
Bi-Encoding	0.000569	**0.53**	**0.36**
Cross-Encoding	**0.000768**	0.33	0.20
Real	–	0.22	0.13

We compare the models by calculating the MRR for each model. In test data, each input song has a real next song, which is ground truth. We determine whether this real next song is ranked Nth in the output ranking and calculate the reciprocal rank $RR = \frac{1}{N}$. We calculate the MRR by averaging the RRs for each model. The MRR for each model is shown in Table 2. The Cross-Encoding model performed best, and the Bi-Encoding model outperformed the Baseline, indicating the effectiveness of training on the DJ pair dataset. Comparing top recommendations, the Cross-Encoding model often suggested certain songs repeatedly, unlike the Bi-Encoding model.

We conduct a user evaluation comparing each model's top-ranked recommendation with the real next song. For each input, four songs are evaluated: three model recommendations and the ground-truth next song. For each input song, the four next songs are shuffled and shown to users. Users read the input song's last lyric and the next song's first lyric, then rate each song on a three-point scale: 0 (no), 1 (weak), 2 (strong semantic similarity). We compute Hit@1 and Weighted Score from user ratings. In Hit@1, Weak or Strong similarity is correct (1.0), No similarity is incorrect (0.0). In Weighted Score, No, Weak, and Strong similarity are scored 0.0, 0.5, and 1.0, respectively. In this paper, three users performed the evaluation. For each input song, four next songs are recommended: the three model's recommended songs and the real song. We average each score across the three users and four models. The Hit@1 and Weighted

Score are shown in Table 2. The Bi-Encoding model scored highest, while the real next song scored lowest. This indicates that the songs are selected based on something other than the lyric connections. DJs of J-POP and anime songs often select songs based on information other than the lyrics, such as information about the singer or tie-ups. However, real's Hit@1 of 0.22 suggests DJs select songs by lyric relevance about 22% of the time. Since the training data likely shares this distribution, the Bi-Encoding model's better performance indicates it captured lyric-based selection patterns from these cases.

5   Conclusion

We propose a lyric-aware song recommendation method for DJs of J-POP and anime songs, aiming to predict the next song in a set list. Using a DJ pair dataset from lyrics and DJ setlist data, we fine-tuned Japanese BERT with Bi-Encoding and Cross-Encoding approaches. The Cross-Encoding model achieved the highest MRR, but tended to repeat certain songs. A user test showed that the Bi-Encoding model recommends the most connected songs.

Future work includes incorporating text information beyond lyrics. DJs of J-POP and anime songs often select songs based on artist, composer, or anime information, as reflected in our dataset. We aim to combine lyrics with such text information for DJ song recommendations.

Acknowledgments. This work was supported by JSPS KAKENHI Grant Numbers JP25K03229, JP24K03228, and JP25K03228.

References

1. Chen, B.Y., Hsu, W.H., Liao, W.H., Ramírez, M.A.M., Mitsufuji, Y., Yang, Y.H.: Automatic DJ transitions with differentiable audio effects and generative adversarial networks. In: Proceedings of ICASSP'22, pp. 466–470 (2022)
2. Hirai, T., Doi, H., Morishima, S.: MusicMixer: automatic DJ system considering beat and latent topic similarity. In: Proceedings of MMM'16, pp. 698–709 (2016)
3. Kim, T., Yang, Y.H., Nam, J.: Reverse-engineering the transition regions of real-world DJ mixes using sub-band analysis with convex optimization. In: Proceedings of NIME'21, pp. 1–13 (2021)
4. Kim, T., Yang, Y.H., Nam, J.: Joint estimation of fader and equalizer gains of DJ mixers using convex optimization. In: Proceedings of DAFx20in22, pp. 312–319 (2022)
5. Nakata, H., Nakanishi, T.: Music recommendation method for time-series emotions from lyrics using valence-arousal-dominance model. In: Proceedings of IIAI-AAI'22, pp. 443–448 (2022)
6. Tsukuda, K., Ishida, K., Goto, M.: Lyric jumper: a lyrics-based music exploratory web service by modeling lyrics generative process. In: Proceedings of ISMIR'17, pp. 544–551 (2017)

7. Tsukuda, K., Nakano, T., Hamasaki, M., Goto, M.: Unveiling the impact of musical factors in judging a song on first listen: insights from a user survey. In: Proceedings of ISMIR'23, pp. 561–570 (2023)
8. Vande Veire, L., De Bie, T.: From raw audio to a seamless mix: creating an automated DJ system for drum and bass. EURASIP J. Audio Speech Music Process. **2018**(13), 1–21 (2018)

Author Index